From John Paul to Saint Jack

Public Relations in Ireland

Edited by
Francis Xavier Carty
President, Public Relations Institute of Ireland

Able Press

Other books by Francis Xavier Carty from Able Press

In Bloody Protest - The Tragedy of Patrick Pearse; 1978
Why I Said No To God; 1986
Farewell to Hype - The Emergence of Real Public Relations; 1992

First published in 1995 by
Able Press
35 Sandymount Avenue
Dublin 4
Ireland

Typeset 10/13 pt Garamond Book

British Library Cataloguing-in-Publication Data
A catalogue record for this book is available from the British Library.

ISBN 0 906281 14 8

Printed by Brunswick Press Limited
17 Gilford Road, Sandymount, Dublin 4

To Pope John Paul 11
and
to Jack Charlton
who
by coming to Ireland
made it possible
for this
special book
not to have
a boring old title

CONTENTS

ACKNOWLEDGEMENTS ix

PUBLIC RELATIONS PRACTICE xi

FOREWORD xii

SPECIAL EVENTS

1 "I Have Come to You as Bishop of Rome" Niamh Lyons 1
 —Pope John Paul 11 in Ireland

2 A Good Excuse for a Party Rachel Dowling 11
 —The Dublin Millennium

3 What's Another Song Sinéad Whooley 17
 —The 38th Eurovision Song Contest,
 Millstreet, 1993

4 Chief Executive Drives Tractor
 Around Ireland—Twice Claire Donnelly 24
 —The 1990 Gorta Tractor Drive

LAUNCHES

5 Behind the Arches—A Céad Míle McFáilte Dara Cosgrave 29
 —The Launch of McDonald's in Ireland, 1977

6 Millions of Pounds in Prizes Alma K. Feeley 35
 —The Launch of Ireland's National Lottery

7 Hot, Hot, Hot, Hot 2FM - The Birth of a Sound Lisa Ryan 41
 —The Relaunch of RTE's Second Radio Station

8 The Course That Jack Built John Collins 46
 —The Opening of Mount Juliet Hotel
 and Leisure Estate

PUBLIC INFORMATION

9 Leading the Race into Europe Sinéad O'Toole 51
 —Ireland's Entry into the EEC

10 The Taste of the Mediterranean   Francis Xavier Carty   59
    —The Olive Oil Information Campaign

11 Maximising Health and Safety at Work   Michèle Aboud   66
    —The Extension to the European Year of Safety,
    Health and Hygiene at Work

12 Cider Fights to Clear its Name   Barry Kenny   74
    —The Role of the Cider Industry Council

POLITICAL CAMPAIGNS

13 Do Brilliant Campaigns Win Elections ?   Barry Roche   79
    —Fianna Fáil and the General Election of 1987

14 A Triumph of Style and Substance   Ian O'Doherty   87
    —The Election of Mary Robinson,
    President of Ireland, 1990

COMMUNITY RELATIONS

15 The Future Comes to Tallaght   Nicola Whelan   95
    —The Opening of The Square,
    Ireland's Largest Shopping Centre

16 Wooing and Winning the People of Cork   Jonathan Grey   103
    —Sandoz comes to Ireland

POLITICAL LOBBYING

17 No VAT—A Great Idea for a Book   Amber Kehoe   109
    —The Removal of VAT on Books

18 If Theatre is to be—VAT is the Question   Amber Kehoe   114
    —The Removal of VAT on Theatre Tickets

19 No Irish Served Here   Antoinette Harbourne   118
    —The Lobby to Allow Restaurants Serve
    Beer and Spirits

FINANCIAL & CORPORATE

20 Bank Reflects Irish Heritage and
    Global Commitment   Morgan Walsh   126
    —AIB's New Corporate Identity

21 How Irish Life Went Private   Fiona O'Riordan   131
   —The Privatisation and Flotation of
   Irish Life Assurance plc

22 A Battle for Milk and Money   Harriett Ryan   137
   —The Formation of Lakeland Dairies
   Co-operative Society Ltd

CRISIS MANAGEMENT

23 "God Gave Us Bantry, We Gave it to Gulf Oil"   Paul O'Shea   143
   —The *Betelgeuse* Explosion at Whiddy Island

24 Last Exit from Baghdad   Frances Keegan   150
   —PARC and the Gulf War

25 An Eventful Day for the 9.25 Train from Tralee Brian Harmon   155
   —Irish Rail's Crisis Plan in Action

SPONSORSHIP

26 The Human Airport with a Warm
   and Friendly Face   Miriam O'Callaghan   162
   —The Aer Rianta Arts Festival

27 37 Years On— Still Rewarding
   Ireland's Tidiest Town   Melanie O'Sullivan   170
   —The Bord Fáilte Tidy Towns Competition

28 Giving a Light to the Community   Jill Börnemann   176
   —The John Player Tops

29 Horse Classic Gives Bud Long Reach   Catherine Dolan   181
   —The Budweiser Irish Derby

30 Olé, Olé, Opel— Driving Irish Football
   into a New Era   Joseph Hanley   186
   —The Opel Sponsorship of the
   Football Association of Ireland

SOME FURTHER READING   192

INDEX   195

ACKNOWLEDGEMENTS

The following are some of the many people who have assisted in the publication of this book. I thank them all for their time, their expertise and their generosity:

Barry Ahern, Fleishman-Hillard Saunders
Ray Bates, National Lottery
Dervla Brophy
John Brown, MPRII, Bord Failte
Victoria Brown
Donie Butler, Football Association of Ireland
John Butterly, MPRII, Pembroke Communications
Jim Cantwell, MPRII, Catholic Press and Information Office
Yvonne Clarke, The Communications Partnership
Flan Clune, MPRII, Aer Rianta
Michael Colley, FPRII
Tom Connolly, AIPPA
Jack Craig, Brunswick Press
Patrick Crane, MPRII, Grayling
Gabrielle Croke, MPRII, AIB plc
Yvonne Cullen, Gilmore Communications
Michael Dennehy, MPRII, Dennehy Associates
Orla Diffily, Kerry Group plc
Anne Dowling, Gilmore Communications
Brian Duncan, Irish Life plc
Gillian Fanning, Grayling
Patrick Farrell, Fianna Fail
Cyril Ferris, MPRII, Iarnród Eireann
Mary Finan, MPRII, Wilson Hartnell Public Relations
Fergus Finlay, Department of the Tánaiste
Sally-Anne Fisher, DIT
Sharon Fitzgerald, AIB plc
Ann Fox, MPRII, Ann Fox Public Relations
John P. Gallagher, MPRII, Aer Rianta
Michael Gill, Gill & Macmillan
Noel Gilmore, MPRII, Gilmore Communications
Sinéad Gorby
Gerry Grogan, John Player & Sons
John Grumley, Brunswick Press
Deirdre Henchy, MPRII, RTE
Jim Hickey, DIT
Pat Keating, MPRII, Keating and Associates
Mike Keely, Quinn McDonnell Pattison
Andrew Kelly, Bill O'Herlihy Communications
Paul Kelly, MPRII, Bain Communications (Dubai)
Ruairi Keogh, Slattery Public Relations
Aisling Kilroy, Curzon Communications

Brenda King, Bord Fáilte
David Kingston, Irish Life plc
Frank Lane, DIT
Nora Lucey, MPRII, Irish Life plc
P.J.Mara
Winifred McCourt, McMahonSheedy
John McMahon, MPRII, McMahonSheedy
Bill McMunn, The Square, Tallaght
Mike Mehigan, Pantry Franchise Ireland Ltd
Michael Moloney, MPRII, Setanta Communications
Arnold O'Byrne, General Motors Distribution Ireland Ltd
Aideen O'Carroll, MPRII, AIB plc
Con O'Donovan, DIT
Niall O'Flynn, MPRII, Niall O'Flynn Consultants
Bill O'Herlihy, MPRII, Bill O'Herlihy Communications
Aidan O'Hanlon, FPRII
Fionnuala O'Kelly, MPRII, RTE
Robin O'Sullivan, MPRII, O'Sullivan Public Relations
Eilish MacCurtain Pearce, MPRII, Pearce Public Relations
Colin Preston, Sandoz Pharma
Vincent Quinn, Setanta Communications
Philip Reilly, Monarch Properties Ltd
Dick Roche
Jim Rowe, MPRII, Grayling
John Saunders, MPRII, Fleishman-Hillard Saunders
Padraig Slattery, MPRII, Slattery Public Relations
Ronny Smiley
Leonie Stevenson, Greencore plc
Brenda Tierney, Myles Tierney & Associates
Myles Tierney, MPRII, Myles Tierney & Associates
Teresa Ward, DIT
Amanda Whelan, Aer Rianta

PUBLIC RELATIONS PRACTICE

The function of public relations is to create a climate of mutual understanding between an organisation, the publics which it serves and the community as a whole.

The 'community' or the 'general public' can be divided into a number of segments— government, civil service, local government representatives and officials, consumers, potential investors, financial institutions, employees, trade associations, local community groups.

Public relations professionals create lines of communication between the organisation and its publics; communicate policy decisions to the relevant 'publics' using the most effective media for the task; and interpret reaction to this communication process.

This involves anticipating reaction to policies or programmes and providing an input into policy formation in order to help gain acceptance by the groups affected.

Public relations is a management function which is responsible for an organisation's reputation; for determining what that reputation is, what it should be, how to promote it and how to protect it. Public relations professionals deal in reality, not in trying to create false or misleading images.

While every individual in every organisation helps to shape the reputation of the organisation, it is essential that someone takes overall responsibility for the public relations function. Ideally the public relations professional should report directly to the chief executive of the organisation.

—Public Relations Institute of Ireland.

Public relations is about reputation: the result of what you do, what you say and what others say about you.

Public relations practice is the discipline which looks after reputation— with the aim of earning understanding and support, and influencing opinion and behaviour.

It is the planned and sustained effort to establish and maintain goodwill and mutual understanding between an organisation and its publics.

—Institute of Public Relations (UK)

FOREWORD

From John Paul to Saint Jack: Public Relations in Ireland, covers 30 experiences in Irish public relations. The researchers and writers are the 1994 graduates of the Diploma in Public Relations at Dublin Institute of Technology (DIT). I have been initiator, co-ordinator and editor. The long list of acknowledgements show how much of a team effort it has been.

While students will benefit from this book, it is intended also for all who practise public relations or have an interest in it. Public relations practice involves a lot and these experiences do not pretend to give the complete Irish story, but just a taster.

These experiences happened in Ireland, but they also have relevance abroad because many of the issues raised and strategies adopted are international.

Public relations has a long and proud tradition in DIT. The College of Commerce in Rathmines, now relocated in Aungier Street, had a public relations course as far back as the 1950s. The present course was born in 1978 and has been held every year since then. For some years it was the only course in public relations in Ireland, but such has been the demand for education in public relations, despite the shortage of jobs, that other courses have started. At first the DIT course was a certificate, open to schoolleavers, but as years went on it became apparent that the industry needed people who already had a third level education. That is why it was redesigned as a diploma in 1990.

DIT, with more than 25,000 students enrolled, is an autonomous university-level institution with the authority to confer its own awards. It comprises the six third level colleges that were formerly within the City of Dublin Vocational Education Committee. The single identity of DIT is one which, I am sure, will continue in the new millennium to represent excellence and relevance in education.

As President of the Public Relations Institute of Ireland, I welcome and support the efforts made by PRII to develop and encourage public relations education, to promote high standards and professionalism. As course director for the DIT course since 1982, I am proud of the pioneering role that DIT has played and I thank successive presidents, national councils, members and staff of PRII for their support.

I am pleased to have devoted the past twenty-one years of my life to public relations. I am honoured to have been elected President of the Public Relations Institute of Ireland for 1995 and see it as my duty to bring the message of public relations to wherever it needs to be brought.

I am not one who wants to get rid of the term "public relations" because it has become "user-unfriendly". There are no better words to describe what public relations is all about and to explain its important contribution to society. However, I abhor the nickname "PR" which is so commonly used, and I reach for my gun when people violate English grammar by describing public relations people as "PRs".

Public relations is an honourable and an honest profession, an essential component in the management structure of any organisation. If public relations did not exist it would have to be invented. Organisations, both commercial and non-profit-making, can— if they are foolish—opt not to advertise, not to market themselves, not to get oil for the central heating, but they have no choice with public relations. They have a moral duty to engage in it.

Public relations is the conscience of the organisation and it must ensure that the final objective is the public good. Organisations must serve the public good and explain themselves to their publics, or audiences, and take into account the good of these audiences in all that they say or do. Public relations ensures that organisations serve the public good and that they engage in dialogue.

When we sum up public relations as reputation, it seems too simple for some people, but it is true. Public relations deals with reputation, something that has to be earned, and not with images that can be fabricated overnight and are often false.

To survive today, organisations must behave in the public interest. Power, in a democracy, lies with the people and public relations, real public relations, ensures that power remains with the people.

Francis Xavier Carty
Sandymount
Dublin
February 1995

"I HAVE COME TO YOU AS BISHOP OF ROME"

Pope John Paul 11 in Ireland
by Niamb Lyons

BACKGROUND

On 21 July, 1979, it was announced that Pope John Paul 11 would visit Ireland. He would arrive in Dublin on 29 September and would leave for Boston via Shannon on 2 October. There was nine weeks to plan the visit.

Peter Sweetman, president, Public Relations Institute of Ireland (PRII), volunteered the services of almost one hundred Institute members. PRII realised that the Catholic Hierarchy might not have the facilities, nor the professional resources, to plan in such a short time for the huge media interest that the event would generate. The PRII offer was immediately accepted by Bishop Edward Daly of Derry, on behalf of the Hierarchy's national organising committee, and by Jim Cantwell, director of the Catholic Press and Information Office (CAPO).

Pat Heneghan, past president, PRII, represented the Institute on the organising committee which included representatives from such bodies as Bord Fáilte (The Irish Tourist Board) and the Department of Posts & Telegraphs. Other senior PRII members—Eilish MacCurtain Pearce, Aidan O'Hanlon, Joe Jennings and James Larkin—were asked to serve on a media advisory committee which was established by CAPO. Michael Dennehy was the liaison between the two committees. Bishop Daly asked Michael's father, Tim Dennehy (a former president of PRII), to set up a special organising committee. The remaining PRII members were to direct and staff the nine press centres at the places that the Pope would visit.

THE CHALLENGE

The papal visit would be the largest media relations programme ever handled in Ireland. John Paul 11 was the first Pope ever to visit Ireland and he was a new Pope who wanted to travel the world and meet his people. Ireland was only his third overseas visit, following Mexico and his native Poland; it was his first to an English-speaking country.

To ensure that the over-riding objective of providing the best ever media relations programme was achieved, it was imperative that the world media be given every facility to cover the event efficiently and that the Pope's message be spread. It was important, through the achievement of both of these aims, that Ireland and its people be portrayed in the best possible light.

For the event to run smoothly, planning and organisation had to be meticulous, personal contact had to be made with all who wished to attend, access and coverage had to be facilitated and the credibility of the organisers had to be established. The planning was helped by the fact that Jim Cantwell and Paul Gleeson, who was RTE's executive director of the radio and television coverage, had visited Poland.

Bishop Daly summarised the media relations challenge:"The Holy Father is making a pastoral visit to Ireland, but when he speaks he will, in a sense, be speaking not solely to the people of Ireland, but of the whole world. Our concern will be to provide the best possible facilities to enable the Irish and the world media to report the visit in words and pictures".

PLANNING

All of the organising committees became effective as soon as they were set up.The entire basis of the programme was laid by Captain Jack Millar, the former Army officer who was chief press officer at Aer Lingus.The most difficult problem, which he immediately iden-tified, was the sheer size of the project. It was estimated that close to 2,000 journalists from all over the world would attend.The actual number came to more than 3,000.

Jack Millar decided that there would have to be a press centre in every place that the Pope visited, and that each centre would be fully staffed and equipped to deal with the needs of the individual journalists.This would involve having televisions to relay cover-age to journalists not intending to travel to the other sites. They would have to have access to pictures, scripts etc and the machinery by which they would readily relay this news back to their respective countries. It would involve installing telephones, telex machines, wire photo terminals, Xerox machines and also having translators available. There were no faxes then.

One of the Michael Dennehy's biggest contributions to the event was his success in obtaining the loan of this expensive equipment, free of charge. Rank Xerox, for instance, flew photocopying machines from the USA and Spain. Irish TV Rentals donated televi-sions and video recorders.

The second part of the plan provided for the telecommunications system and for the personnel and their tasks .

The Department of Posts & Telegraphs rose to the occasion, without any fuss, and provided an extensive telephone network.They provided 1,000 telephones, 300 telex machines, 20 telecopiers and 100 wire photo machines for the press centres.They also switched all international lines to the press centres, resulting in Dublin phone numbers operating everywhere, as at that time there was no international direct dial anywhere else in the country. It also meant that nobody else could dial abroad while the Pope was in Ireland because all lines were being used !

Dublin Castle
Dublin Castle was selected as the overall centre for the operation because much of the equipment was already there. It had been used previously by the Department of Foreign Affairs for EC conferences.

The plan provided for an internal system, an old plug-in style switch board, by which Michael Dennehy could communicate directly with the director of each press centre.

There were to be press centres at each location that the Pope would visit—Phoenix Park, Knock, Maynooth, Drogheda, Cabra, Limerick and Galway (see figure 1). A mobile unit which would cover Clonmacnoise (it was a late option to include this ancient monastic site, in Bishop Cahal Daly's diocese, if time permitted) and act as a back-up if needed elsewhere. Michael Dennehy, Bishop Daly and Jim Cantwell vetted each centre and decided on its exact positioning, where the photographers' stands would be, etc. Directors were appointed for each centre, some of whom had previous connections with the area and knew the local media. They nominated their own staff and kept regular contact with Tim Dennehy. They had to negotiate with architects, security authorities, the post office and local committees and draw up their own operations plans.

It was important that there be a system of accreditation for those intending to cover the event. It would involve getting the name, address, date of birth and authorisation

Figure 1: MEDIA LIAISON COMMUNICATIONS PLAN

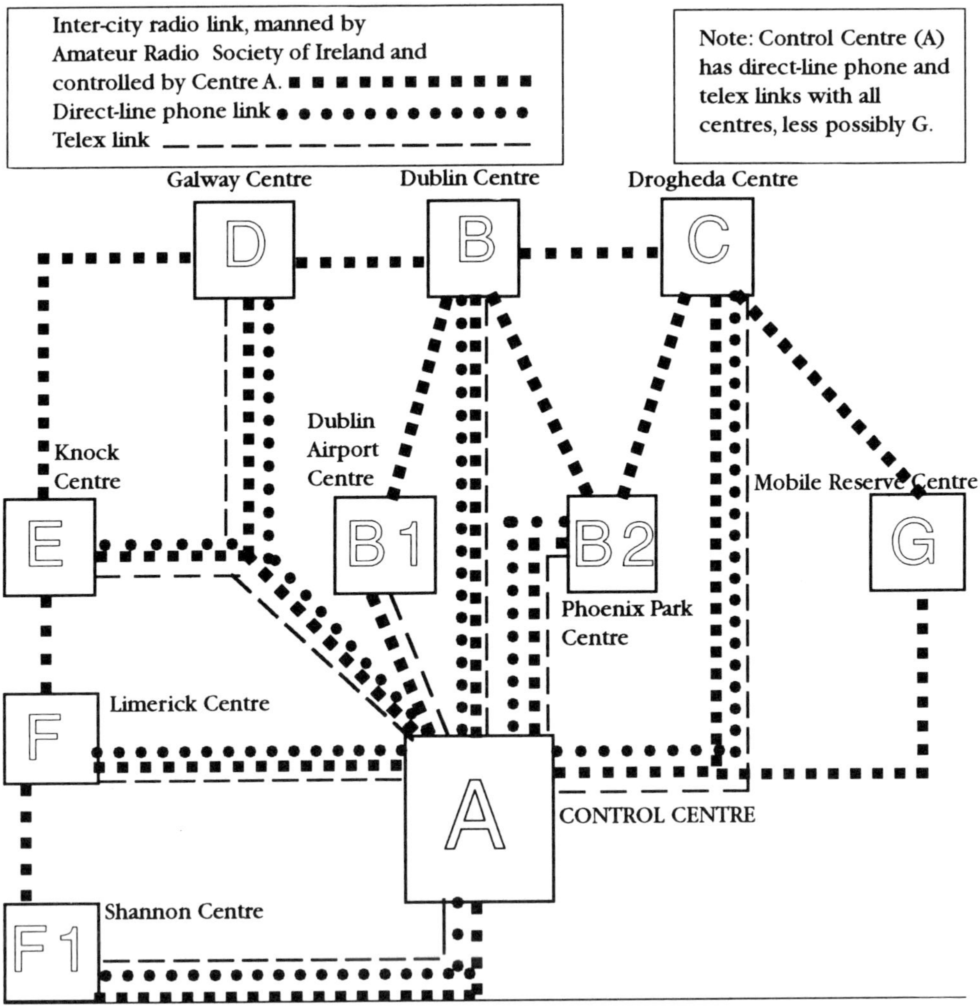

Inter-city radio link, manned by Amateur Radio Society of Ireland and controlled by Centre A. ■ ■ ■ ■ ■ ■ ■ ■ ■ ■
Direct-line phone link ● ● ● ● ● ● ● ● ● ● ● ●
Telex link _ _ _ _ _ _ _ _ _ _ _ _

Note: Control Centre (A) has direct-line phone and telex links with all centres, less possibly G.

Galway Centre — D
Dublin Centre — B
Drogheda Centre — C

Knock Centre — E
Dublin Airport Centre — B1
Phoenix Park Centre — B2
Mobile Reserve Centre — G

Limerick Centre — F
CONTROL CENTRE — A

Shannon Centre — F1

"I HAVE COME TO YOU AS BISHOP OF ROME"

3

from editors. Jim Cantwell sent a telex to all international news agencies, informing them of the accreditation procedure. It was a sophisticated operation, set up with the Garda Síochána who had close contact with the FBI and Interpol. The accreditation cards were to be issued to individual journalists from Tuesday, 25 September, four days before the Pope's arrival.

Michael Dennehy, with Aidan O'Hanlon as his assistant, had now taken over as director-in-chief of the entire media operation because Jim Cantwell had fallen ill. He had also been co-opted to the Hierarchy's national organising committee.

Pooling

Pooling is a major headache at all international events as not all journalists, especially photographers, can be facilitated equally. Only a small number of photographers can be fitted into the vantage points at any venue. Arrangements therefore have to be made for a small number, selected or nominated on a rotating basis, to make their pictures available to the others.

The organising committee decided that priority in pooling be given to Irish media, North and South, and also to international news agencies. Michael Dennehy telexed the British and international papers asking for their co-operation. The plan was then formulated and sent back to Peter Smith of *The Sun*, who had been nominated co-ordinator in Britain. There were two major press briefings a fortnight before the Pope arrived to try and sort out the pooling and other matters. It was still a sensitive issue and the system was not finalised until a week before the event. If it had not been agreed beforehand, the credibility of the organising committee would have been undermined.

Initially the foreign journalists were distrustful of the arrangements being made. In the event, the system worked "reasonably well", to quote the official PRII report, and the centre directors "dealt flexibly with momentary problems as they occurred". The significance of the pooling system was not simply its ingenuity or detail but the involvement of the journalists themselves in preparing it.

Problems from the Polish visit were anticipated and prevented through planning. For instance, transport to the different locations was going to cause problems. The Pope would fly everywhere by helicopter but the journalists and public would have to use rail or road. An elaborate plan for transporting journalists was formulated in Dublin Castle by Joe Jennings, public relations manager of CIE (the public transport authority), assisted by his colleagues, Cyril McIntyre and Cyril Ferris. The plan allowed for the journalists to be brought everywhere free, unlike Poland where they had been charged for a very inadequate service and there had been many complaints.

In Poland, scripts of the Pope's speeches were not made available to the media until approximately six hours after they were made. The committee was determined that this would not happen in Ireland and they saw it as a major challenge to obtain the scripts before the Pope began to speak. To a great extent, the success of the whole media operation depended on the press getting the scripts in time. Pressure was put on the hierarchy, especially through Cardinal Tomás Ó Fiaich, who in turn pressurised the Vatican. The result was that two days before the Pope's arrival, the speeches for the first day were delivered to Dublin Castle by Fr. Michael Glynn of the Vatican Press Office, a former member of PRII. The remaining scripts were brought on the Papal flight by Fr. Romeo Panciroli, Vatican press officer.

Plans had to take into account the violence in Northern Ireland and the security issue. This was one reason why each press centre had to co-ordinate under the head centre at Dublin Castle while also being able to act autonomously should the need arise. The possibility of the Pope being assassinated, or an attempt being made, had to be considered. Each centre had to have a crisis plan which would be easily operational.

The real danger to the Pope's life was shown a few years later when he was shot and wounded in St. Peter's Square. It was realised that during the Irish visit he would be addressing the men of violence and pleading with them to stop it.

On 27 August, the day the plan was being finalised, the IRA killed 79-year-old Lord Louis Mountbatten, cousin of Queen Elizabeth, along with his 14-year-old grandson and a 17-year-old boatman. They were fishing, as they did every summer, in Mullaghmore, Co. Sligo, when an IRA bomb blew up their boat. On the same day, another IRA bomb killed 18 British soldiers in Co. Down. This was one reason why Armagh, the ancient ecclesiastical capital of Ireland, was taken off the Pope's itinerary.

IMPLEMENTATION

On Tuesday, 25 September, accreditation began. Volunteers worked quickly to issue the cards. So much red tape was cut to get the job done with speed and efficiency, that some journalists began to question the system rather than praise it. They were soon to find out, however, that the card granted the access it promised.

Dublin Castle, the fulcrum of the media relations operation, opened its doors on Thursday, 27 September. One room was set aside as a typing area. It contained long tables with 50 typewriters in all. Some had French keyboards. During the visit more typewriters and tables were fitted into the room.

In another room were the banks of telex machines which would, when a script was released from the control centre in the room above, almost simultaneously relay it to each press centre. The director of the press centre would then make copies of the script and distribute it to journalists.

As already noted, the advance delivery of the scripts was a major achievement. On the morning of Saturday, 29 September, as soon as the Papal plane landed, Joe O'Brien of Bord Fáilte, by arrangement, took them from Fr. Panciroli before the Pope disembarked. He was rushed into a limousine, and escorted by four Garda outriders, got back to Michael Dennehy at Dublin Castle within 15 minutes from touchdown. There were 29 scripts in all, starting with the speech at the airport and finishing not with his landing in Boston, but his speech to the United Nations General Assembly in New York. All were locked in a safe in Dublin Castle and Michael Dennehy was made to swear "on a stack of bibles" that he would release them one by one. As he said: "It had taken weeks. It was vital. Everything else we had done would all fall to nought if, when the Pope stood up to make his speech, we could not hand out the script". Their plan worked and each script was distributed a half hour before the Pope spoke.

Another important element in the plan came into operation on the Saturday evening.

It was thought that after the Pope's Mass in the Phoenix Park, and his visit to Drogheda, he might make an unscheduled stop at the shrine in Dublin's Sean McDermott Street to Matt Talbot, the venerated Dublin labourer who is a candidate for canonisation. The mobile unit, under Jack Mooney, was ready. In the event the Pope's cavalcade did not stop, to great disappointment for the people of the area. Jack Mooney's staff also looked after Clonmacnoise. The helicopter did touch down and this was one of the less crowded and more informal moments of the weekend, including a hug and a kiss for the Pope from a young girl in a Discover Ireland tee-shirt. On Sunday and Monday, the mobile unit helped at the Maynooth Centre.

Audience for journalists

There could have been a major media crisis on Saturday evening. The problem was due to time. Traditionally the Pope, on the last evening of his visit to a country, gives an audience for journalists and other accredited personnel. However, because of the way the itinerary was running (see appendix), it was fixed for Saturday evening in the assembly hall of the Dominican Convent girls school in Cabra. It was in the same grounds as the Papal Nunciature where the Pope was staying for the night. Buses were provided free for all the journalists from Dublin Castle to Cabra. Tim and Michael Dennehy, who had been stuck to their desks, took this single opportunity to meet the Pope. On arrival, Michael found a thousand people packed into a room which could hold 400. He had to tell them that the Pope was delayed and would not be there for an hour.

Eventually the Pope arrived but Bishop Daly said the audience was being cancelled. The journalists had been waiting for two and a half hours, packed like sardines into the small hall. Michael Dennehy went to Archbishop Paul Marcinkus, who acted as the Pope's effective bodyguard and right-hand man on all visits. Marcinkus said: "His Holiness is extremely tired and there is no way we are going to do the audience with the journalists". Dennehy, fearing a riot, said: "There is no way you cannot do it". So, Marcinkus went back to the Pope who agreed to the audience.

The Dennehys then hastened back to Dublin Castle ahead of the fatigued journalists and Michael ordered his biggest ever round of drinks: "I went into the bar and I said 700 pints of Guinness, 300 pints of Smithwicks and 100 pints of Carlsberg and 700 sandwiches. Start pulling now, the buses are on their way".

The following day the Pope went to Galway for the Youth Mass, then to Knock and back to Dublin for his formal meetings with the Irish bishops. The communications between these centres and Dublin Castle worked excellently. It was a credit to the Department of Posts & Telegraphs.

Archbishop Marcinkus was so impressed that he asked to be plugged into the system himself. His foresight was rewarded when on Monday morning, because of fog, the Pope was delayed leaving Dublin and Maynooth. Marcinkus rang Michael Dennehy on the internal line and told him to ring Limerick and get the Mass started before the Pope arrived. Dennehy rang Cathal O'Shannon and told him to get the Mass started. There was a pause and Marcinkus himself repeated the instruction. The Bishop of Limerick, Jeremiah Newman, agreed.

The planning had also provided for a radio system, as a back-up in case the telephone

Pope John Paul 11 meets the Irish people, September 1979

network might be unable to take the pressure. It was set up with the help of the Amateur Radio Society of Ireland and one of these radios was placed in each press centre. There were no mobile phones in 1979 !

The Aer Lingus Boeing 747 took off from Shannon with the Pope and his party at 13.30 on Monday. Irish organisations, which beforehand had been worried about the glossy professionalism that the Americans might produce at the next stage in the Papal tour, realised that they had succeeded beyond many expectations.

EVALUATION

When the plan for the Papal visit was formulated in July 1979 it had three aims:
*   Facilitate the world media in covering the event
*   Spread the Pope's message
*   Portray Ireland and its people in the best possible light

All of these objectives, and the over-riding objective of carrying out the best ever media relations programme, were achieved. The sheer volume and content of the correspondence which followed indicated the success. Many letters of thanks were received from media people around the world in praise of the facilities. *Reuters* published a special feature article commending the Irish effort.

"I HAVE COME TO YOU AS BISHOP OF ROME"

Some typical comments were:

- "Superb press arrangements" — John Smith, feature writer, *Sunday People*
- "The sheer organisation in looking after so many journalists from all over the world was a staggering task and I heard many appreciative comments from my colleagues about the smooth organisation" — Tony Black, Independent Broadcasting Authority
- "First-class press arrangements.....for once the media were given every facility to transmit the Pope's message to the world quickly and accurately...." — chief news editor, *Reuters*.
- "......truly remarkable facilities.....the arrangements were the most comprehensive I have ever experienced....." — churches correspondent, *The Guardian*
- "....a masterpiece of planning and operation, faultlessly executed...— Stephen Creston, Southern Correspondent, *Sunday News*, Belfast.

The issuing of the scripts a half-hour before delivery was a particularly fine achievement, given what had been previous Vatican policy. It involved much hard talking between the committees, the bishops and the Vatican.

The free loan of so much communications equipment was impressive as was the telecommunications system. The co-operation and the wish to make the event work was a credit to such bodies as the Board of Works (now the Office of Public Works), the Department of Foreign Affairs and many more.

Michael Dennehy, when asked if he would do anything differently today, said he would not:"...where we succeeded and why we succeeded was because a group of very senior public relations practitioners in Ireland, all of whom had been involved in large scale events for one person or another, who knew each other, immediately sat down together, decided what should be done and got Jack Millar to write the plan in detail and then that was just followed."

He said the second reason for succeeding was "whatever we asked of Posts & Telegraphs (and others) they delivered. It was remarkable".

The enthusiasm of the Vatican was perhaps the greatest triumph, as they were not known for their love of media relations. This enthusiasm was tangibly expressed in the US speeches being given to Michael Dennehy in Dublin Castle for distribution prior to the Pope's departure from Shannon. Also, the subsequent Vatican referral of people to the Irish for advice in planning later papal visits was a tribute. Michael Dennehy was visited by, for instance, the British, the Canadians, the French and the Swiss when the Pope was planning to visit their countries.

Apart from the extensive help from public and commercial bodies in lending personnel and equipment and providing services, often free of charge, there were other considerable expenses. These were borne by the Catholic Hierarchy who subsequently raised £4 million through a national collection.

The final word is best left to the official PRII report:"The entire operation was a triumph for all those who participated, for the profession of public relations in Ireland, and for the Institute which demonstrated that it could, at short notice, mount the most comprehensive news media relations operation ever carried out in this, or perhaps, any other country".

APPENDIX

Itinerary of Pope John Paul 11 during pastoral visit to Ireland
Saturday, September 29
10.00 Arrival of the Pope at Dublin Airport. Official reception.

10.40 The Pope leaves Airport by helicopter for the Nunciature at Navan Road, Cabra.

11.30 Pope leaves Nunciature by helicopter for Phoenix Park.

12.00 Phoenix Park Mass begins.

14.00 Papal drive through crowd begins.

15.30 Papal helicopter leaves Phoenix Park for Drogheda

16.00 Pope presides at Liturgy of the Word (Scripture readings and prayers).
Delivers homily. Drives through crowds.

17.30 Pope returns by helicopter to Dublin Airport.

18.00 Motorcade from Airport through Central Dublin to Aras an Uachtaráin.
Meeting with President Hillery.

19.00 Pope returns to Nunciature by private car.

19.20 Pope meets Taoiseach, Government, Diplomatic Corps.

21.00 (approx) Pope meets representatives of other Christian churches in Dominican
Convent, Cabra.

21.15 (approx) Pope meets journalists and other personnel accredited to the Papal Visit
in St. Patrick's Hall, Dominican Convent. All media personnel who can be there
are admitted.

Sunday, September 30
08.00 Pope meets group of mentally handicapped people at Dominican Convent, Cabra..
Immediately after (about 8.25) meets Irish-Polish community on the lawn at the
Nunciature.

09.00 Pope leaves Nunciature by helicopter for Galway.

10.00 Pope arrives in Galway

10.30 Mass for Youth begins.

12.30 Papal drive through crowds.

13.15 Pope lunches in Galway

14.10 Pope leaves Galway by helicopter.

14.30 Helicopter arrives at Knock helicopter pad. Pope taken up ramp to the walkway
which forms the roof of the covered passageway around the basilica.
Enters Basilica sacristy to vest, then goes to meet invalids in the Basilica.

15.00 Open-air Mass begins.

17.00 Pope visits Gable-Wall Shrine to pray.

17.10 Pope drives around crowd. Irish bishops leave by helicopter for Dublin.

18.00 Papal helicopter leaves for Dublin. Private transport to Nunciature.

Evening: Pope has formal meeting with Irish bishops, Dominican Convent, Cabra.

"I HAVE COME TO YOU AS BISHOP OF ROME"

Monday, October 1

07.30 Pope leaves Nunciature by helicopter for St. Patrick's College, Maynooth, to meet priests, sisters, brothers, university students and local residents.

08.00 Pope visits college Chapel at Maynooth and delivers short address to seminarians, then goes to podium in high field at rear of College to address crowd.

09.00 Pope leaves Maynooth by helicopter for Limerick.

10.00 Papal helicopter arrives at Limerick racecourse.

10.15 Mass begins at Limerick racecourse.

12.00 Pope drives through crowd at Limerick racecourse.

12.30 Papal helicopter departs for Shannon.

12.50 Papal helicopter arrives at Shannon. Official farewell.

13.20 Aer Lingus Boeing 747 taxies for take-off.

13.30 Papal plane takes off for Boston.

This was the original itinerary. There were some changes, as described, most notably the brief call to Clonmacnoise on the way to Galway.

Niamh Lyons has a BA Degree in French & History from University College, Cork and the DIT Diploma in Public Relations

A GOOD EXCUSE FOR A PARTY !

The Dublin Millennium
by Rachel Dowling

BACKGROUND

In October 1986, Dublin Corporation and Dublin & Eastern Regional Tourism set up Dublin Promotions Organisation Ltd (DPOL) to organise, co-ordinate and promote a major programme of events for 1988 in celebration of one thousand years of Dublin's history.

Anniversary celebrations were seen as a fitting way to generate confidence and highlight the positive attributes of a city. They had been successful in Galway and Cork and in other European cities like Amsterdam, Berlin and Brussels.

It was felt that such an event would boost Dublin's self-confidence and promote a positive picture of the city abroad. Many areas of the city had been designated for improvement and upgrading but the pace was sluggish and centred around the efforts of the public sector.

A small start-up group developed into a team of ten with Matt McNulty, managing director, Pat Seager projects director, Aisling Kilroy public relations executive, David Rusk information officer, Paul O'Toole finance officer (on secondment from Dublin Corporation), plus administrative support personnel. At times this group was augmented by people working on the Social Employment Scheme of FÁS—The Training and Employment Authority. The management team was headed by a board of directors, chaired by the Lord Mayor.

OBJECTIVES

DPOL realised that it had to say something different. The Millennium could not just be a bigger St. Patrick's Day or a better Dublin Street Carnival (which had been running since 1985). To be taken seriously it had to provide:
- a programme of events in which people could participate, and
- a new emphasis on improvement of physical amenities.

THE CHALLENGE

- To develop a significant relationship between the public and private sectors involving financial support and long-term maintenance.
- To promote public morale and business. It was very much a civic exercise. The wit and talent of the people of Dublin had never been in doubt but the task of motivating

them could be extremely difficult.

- To lift the image of "dirty auld Dublin". The Millennium, based on Dublin's heritage, was also looking towards its future. For example, Dublin was the only city in the world that boasted three Nobel prizes for literature. It was the home of U2, at that time the hottest rock band in the world. It had many sports achievements behind it, the most recent being Stephen Roche's victory in the Tour de France in 1987.

Said the Lord Mayor, Carmencita Hederman: "My wish is that the Millennium can be a motivating force in throwing off the shackles of non-cooperation, negativeness and inaction. Non-cooperation frustrates, negativeness depresses and inactivity paralyses".

STRATEGY

Initially DPOL had great difficulties. Its offices were one large room in Dublin Corporation's Capel Buildings, Great Strand Street, with limited equipment and neither a photocopier nor a telephone system of its own. The telephones were linked through the Corporation system which operated only from nine to five, so if meetings continued later, nobody could be contacted.

Forward planning, for many organisations, was not part of their culture which meant that DPOL had problems devising and planning a programme for 1988. For instance, when asked in May 1987 what they were doing for the Millennium companies often said: "It's only May, come back to us in October".

There was also some cynicism which had to be overcome. Cork had had its 800th and Galway its 500th. Now Dublin wanted its 1000th. What was it celebrating? There had been a Viking settlement from as early as 841. One significance of 988 was that the Viking rulers of the city levied taxes on the citizens for the first time!

From the outset, there was no system to collate and cross reference all incoming information. Nor were there any computers. ICL Computers then devised a comprehensive package and system which enabled all information to be stored in a most efficient and effective manner. It was important to have both control of and access to the information and a strategic plan to disseminate it.

DPOL compiled a list of every organisation in the city and asked what plans they had for the Millennium. Matt McNulty met as many organisations and people as he could, asking for ideas and co-operation.

The Year was to have a number of peaks :
- Formal launch on New Year's Eve 1987
- Festival around St. Patrick's Day to be called Spraoi Átha Cliath (Spirit of Dublin)
- The Dublin Street Carnival on 9 and 10 July and the city's birthday
  DPOL decided to base the implementation of its strategy on four factors:
- commercial
- tourism
- community
- entertainment

IMPLEMENTATION

There were hundreds of events in Dublin in 1988. Many of them were put on by sponsors to mark the Millennium, others happened as part of the normal life of the city and others were specially promoted by DPOL from the funds which they raised from sponsors. It is only possible to allude to a few of them here to give a flavour of how the strategy of DPOL was put into effect.

The Naval Service agreed to make a ship, the *L.E. Aisling*, available for the media launch at noon on 17 November 1987. More than a hundred journalists came to hear about the programme of events and activities planned for the Millennium. DPOL chose a ship because it wanted something typical of Dublin. The city end of the River Liffey is a part of Dublin's history, being integral to the site where the city was founded.

The Lord Mayor estimated that an extra 250,000 visitors would come to Dublin for the celebrations, raising the tourist spend in the city from £125 million to £150 million.

There were two public information offices, one in the Royal Hibernian Way, courtesy of Friends Provident Life Assurance and the other at the General Post Office (GPO) where Millennium Radio broadcast from March 1988. A monthly calendar of events was published with contacts for further information. DPOL had by now moved to offices in Lower O'Connell Street above Kentucky Fried Chicken, courtesy of that company.

Bord Fáilte and the Department of Foreign Affairs facilitated the spread of information abroad resulting in extensive media coverage for both the Millennium and Dublin. Aisling Kilroy gave approximately 250 briefings for overseas journalists between May 1987 and the end of 1988.

The Dublin Millennium Logo

Graphic designers were invited to submit ideas for the logo. The winner, chosen in association with the Society of Designers in Ireland, from hundreds of submissions, was Jim O'Connor, a 24-year-old graduate of Dun Laoghaire School of Art, with his re-interpretation of the Three Castles of Dublin. The striking yellow, blue and red adaptation was adopted for the year and franchised to producers of merchandise. It was used in the most unlikely places and went on all Aer Lingus planes and B & I ships as well as company fleets of trucks and vans.

Substantial funds were generated from merchandising and franchising of the logo.

Commercial

The commercial factor was a vital component in the success of the Millennium. Without commerce, ancient Dublin would have remained merely a settlement.

DPOL established a system of patronage (sponsorship) to support its central administration and enable patrons to pursue their own programmes of events. Public and private sectors came together, resulting in 30 separate projects, all of which were completed by the end of 1988.

Premier Dairies did a special milk bottle which went on to become a collector's item. It had the Millennium logo and was delivered to about 150,000 customers and celebrities on New Year's Day.

A GOOD EXCUSE FOR A PARTY !

The following were the foundation sponsors:Aer Lingus,Aer Rianta,Allied Irish Banks, Bank of Ireland, Bord Fáilte, Dublin Corporation, Dublin and Eastern Regional Tourism Organisation, Guinness Ireland, ICL Computers (Ireland), Irish Distillers, Irish Life Assurance, Jefferson Smurfit Group, Philips Electronics Ireland and Stokes Kennedy Crowley.

Tourism

Ireland has always had a good position in the holiday market, but in the years preceding the Millennium Dublin had failed to capitalise on its opportunities, both in terms of the product on offer and how it was marketed overseas.

In promoting Dublin abroad, it became evident that the city's identity was indistinguishable from that of the whole island. There is no doubt that Dublin, like any other capital city, offers many social and cultural activities, but at that time it was often seen merely as a transit point to the green fields, rivers and lakes beyond.

Promotional campaigns were undertaken jointly by the tourism industry and DPOL to improve the profile of Dublin in its main tourist markets. The Lord Mayor travelled extensively in late 1987 and the early part of 1988 bringing the millennium message in person and launching the special programme of events.

Community

One of the main reasons for the Millennium was to remove apathy and restore a sense of pride for Dubliners in their city. Frustrated by economic difficulties, the community had low morale and many groups were cynical at the idea of a civic celebration.

In June 1987, 200 community leaders assembled in the Mansion House to consider the proposal. Dialogue continued for five months and people gradually came to recognise that a great deal could be achieved if they grouped together and shared their resources at a local level. By November 1987, there were 80 Millennium community committees around the city and suburbs.

The Millennium was celebrated through more than 800 separate events.The people of Dublin far exceeded expectations and demonstrated a degree of resourcefulness and resolve that they could take pride in.This active participation by the people of Dublin was a major key to the success of the Millennium.

Several companies organised award schemes to highlight the work of individuals and groups which, in the normal course of events, might go unnoticed. For example, Superquinn, the supermarket chain, and *The Sunday Independent* gave awards for special service to the community. People nominated local, often unsung heroes, such as the barman who made the special effort to welcome handicapped people to his premises, or the school porter who gave up his spare nights and weekends to run events for the old, the sick and the poor.

Entertainment

Some say it's the weather, other claim the whiskey but whatever potion is involved, the creative resources of Dublin are manifold. Names like Joyce and Beckett spring to mind at once, but the city's reputation for culture is born of a much wider base of talent.The Millennium provided stimulating and adventurous projects in a three-tiered approach:

- It looked to professional bodies and encouraged them to gear their programmes towards a Dublin theme
- Proposals were invited from independent producers for projects they wished to pursue
- Several projects were specially created by DPOL.

There was a succession of open-air spectacles, all free to the public. They included the Literary Festival, the Carnival, the Gulliver Spectacle and the Viking Festival. These events drew large crowds into the streets and parks.

The Carnival weekend and the Gulliver Spectacle attracted some of the largest crowds ever. DPOL themselves put more than £70,000 into the Gulliver Spectacle through the Galway group, Macnas, one of the best in creative street theatre. They created a giant model of Jonathan Swift's character, Gulliver, who visited the tiny people of Lilliput on his travels. At one stage he was "washed ashore" on Dollymount Strand, on the north side of the city. Crowds came out to see him and climb on his giant arms and legs. Then Gulliver, or his replicas, was used in Dublin parades and converted into a raft which sailed down the River Liffey. Gulliver was appropriate to Dublin because Swift was Dean of St. Patrick's Cathedral and spent most of his life in the city.

Ships came from seven countries for the Viking Festival. The people of the Ringsend docks, long famous for their boat-building, built their own authentic Viking longboat which took pride of place in the Viking Festival.

Other events included the Literary Pub Crawl, the appearance of TV puppet favourites, Zig and Zag, in St. Stephen's Green and the outdoor production of Sean O'Casey's *The Plough and The Stars* in Gardiner Street, the area of the city where it is set. Dublin Bay, in July, saw the city's most spectacular ever fireworks display. The roads around Sandymount Strand were blocked for hours as an estimated 350,000 to 400,000 people came to watch.

A legacy to the city

The Millennium was not just to be a series of celebrations; it was to leave a permanent legacy to the city. An example was ten new site-specific pieces of sculpture, commissioned in association with the Sculptors' Society of Ireland. They include *The Shoppers* at the Dublin Woollen Mills and *The Footsteps* on O'Connell Bridge. *The Joycean Trail*, also a legacy from 1988, is significant to visitors and Dubliners alike because *Ulysses*, probably the greatest work of 20th century literature, encapsulates for all time the story of Dublin, the city built beside Anna Livia Plurabelle.

The Smurfit family erected the *Anna Livia* fountain in O'Connell Street in memory of Jefferson Smurfit, founder of one of Ireland's largest international companies. It became a landmark from its official opening in June 1988, receiving a myriad of affectionate nicknames from witty Dubliners.

Irish Life Assurance set up the Viking Adventure in the ancient St. Audeon's Church. In a continuous pageant, it recreated life in Dublin at the time of the Vikings, including costumes, food, household items and authentic smells. It ran for a couple of years after 1988 and was a popular tourist attraction.

EVALUATION

The media coverage of the Millennium was colossal, and generally favourable, both at home and abroad. It was mentioned in some way or another every day of the year. DPOL could not take direct credit for all of this but facilitated it. Journalists, by and large, were supportive. They usually gave the organisers a chance and a fair hearing, but if an event was rubbish they did not hesitate to say so.

The Millennium regenerated city pride and made people realise that Dublin was a nice place to live in. It facilitated a change of attitude. Today, the most casual observer would see that Dublin has improved. Most significant has been the regeneration of the city centre with a new cultural area in Temple Bar and people moving to new city centre apartments. The International Financial Services Centre has grown rapidly in the formerly neglected docks area. If the Millennium had just been a tourist exercise it would have failed. It needed the co-operation of the citizens, and despite the jokes and the cynicism, which are part of Dublin humour anyway, it got that co-operation.

DISCUSSION

DPOL was conscious of the pitfalls in planning a celebration for a city with seemingly little to celebrate. A great part of what was proposed would undoubtedly be celebratory, but it was planned so as to re-awaken the city to its own potential and revive the spirit and interest of the citizens. When the Lord Mayor, at the press launch, distilled the aspirations for the Millennium into a single sentence that "the hope is that by the end of 1988 Dublin city would be a better place", there were many who doubted and saw it at best as a celebratory party. From the beginning there was a clear idea of what was being attempted, but the means of achieving it were less clear. Economically, times were difficult, but that was not going to be a reason for spending the year apologising. Instead, DPOL concentrated on getting good sponsors and creating genuine projects.

There was great sadness as the DPOL team broke up. They felt that Dublin needed a special body to promote itself and there was so much more they could do particularly in terms of developing the huge momentum which was generated throughout 1988. Says Aisling Kilroy: "We began to shed staff in October. Myself and Pat Seager were the last two to leave. We packed away the files. I have the cuttings on microfiche in four large boxes. It was awful. Everyone came back for our Christmas party at Slane Castle which was great fun but sad. We came back again in January, just Pat and myself and Paul O'Toole from Dublin Corporation who was doing the books. He was in for one day a week. It was really quiet. I finished at the end of January. Everybody had hoped it would go on. We did joke about organising a second millennium for the year 2001 !"

Aisling Kilroy and David Rusk are now the senior partners in Curzon Communications which offers communications and marketing services. Matt McNulty is director general of Bord Fáilte—The Irish Tourist Board.

Rachel Dowling has a BA degree in French and Spanish from University College, Dublin and the DIT Diploma in Public Relations.

WHAT'S ANOTHER SONG ?

The 38th Eurovision Song Contest, Millstreet, 1993
by Sinéad Whooley

BACKGROUND

On 15 May 1993, the 38th Eurovision Song Contest was held in Millstreet, a small town in west Cork. Seen live by 200 million people and relayed later to another 100 million, the contest featured singers from a record number of 25 countries. This was the fourth time that Ireland, as the previous year's winner, had hosted Eurovision. It was the most extensive live broadcast that Radio Telefis Eireann (RTE) had ever mounted outside Dublin.

THE CHALLENGE

Eurovision '93 presented several challenges to RTE
* geographical
* communications and technological
* social
* structural

Geographical
* to take the Eurovision Song Contest, and all that was connected with it, outside a major city for the first time. The contests of 1971, 1981 and 1988 had been held in Dublin.

Communications and technological
* to create the necessary communications links with the participating countries as well as with other countries around the world from the USA to the Far East
* to extend the frontiers of Irish design technology by creating in effect a new studio and mounting the biggest single Outside Broadcast Unit outside Dublin
* to maintain a steady flow of detailed and up-to-the-minute information to national and international media.

Social
* to create the Eurovillage in Millstreet, providing all the facilities and services required
* to co-ordinate the social aspects at every level, including accommodation, delegate arrival and departure, tourism, transport, social events - concerts, receptions, accreditation.

Structural
* to transform the Green Glens Showjumping arena, owned by local entrepreneur

Noel C. Duggan, into the massive Eurovision stage set and reveal an expected spectacular stage design;

- to provide all the auxiliary structures needed to support the Green Glens complex and Eurovillage.

Deirdre Henchy, RTE's head of press and public relations for the event, says that "while superficially Millstreet was newsworthy, vast advances in technology and production techniques, with which RTE had kept pace, meant that the venue was, in reality, the least extraordinary facet. International news crews had, after all, reported live from the Falkland Islands".

Given RTE's extensive experience of mounting outside broadcasts, from the complexities of a papal visit, to general elections, to telethons and showjumping from Millstreet itself, the station was already in the top league. Beaming signals from Millstreet to Morocco, Australia, Korea and the US was all in a day's work. Transporting and being responsible for 600 delegates from 25 countries and an international media corps 400 strong was a different sort of challenge.

However, in terms of getting people from A to B, looking after accommodation and transport, RTE had this down to a fine art with its experience of hosting three previous contests. Working closely with the tourism interests in Cork and Kerry, who fully appreciated the commercial advantages for the region, the delegate services aspect of the operation went very smoothly.

STRATEGY

Despite RTE's own confidence, from the point of view of public relations strategy, Millstreet had to be sold strongly as a venue and RTE's own brand of Eurovision for 1993 had to be marketed to the media at home and internationally.

From the start, RTE's Eurovision was different: it was a "green" Eurovision. A small nation, a modest-sized television station operating in one of the most competitive environments in Europe, was taking the world's biggest light entertainment show to a rural venue. Millstreet and RTE were well-matched partners.

Another key issue was the selling of the Eurovision Song Contest itself. RTE sought to improve the perception of the Contest, which had attracted some negative comments over the years. RTE aimed to give the event cult status and to this end developed an excellent working relationship with the international Eurovision fan club.

To develop the profile of the international fan club, RTE provided it with a display and video facilities in a central location in the foyer of the complex. Eurovision "trivia" in the media packs were also much used by journalists and featured in competitions, in the print media and on local radio stations in addition to interviews with self-confessed fans, some of whom were going to host Euro-parties on the night of the contest. Eurovision interest had a practical pay-off: merchandise from mugs and pens to cute teddy bears were sold like hot cakes by RTE Commercial Enterprises. Capitalising on the cult of the "trekkies" of *Startrek* fame and the 60s nostalgia boom, it proved possible for RTE to revitalise interest in the contest.

IMPLEMENTATION

Geographical

In his introductory greeting, executive producer, Liam Miller, said that by bringing the 38th Eurovision song contest to Millstreet, RTE had "on that occasion, changed the mould of Eurovision activity by bringing the contest outside the major cities of Europe for the first time". For that very reason Eurovision '93 became unique.

The decision to go to Millstreet had been taken after detailed appraisal of potential venues in the south and west of Ireland as an alternative to Dublin. RTE director general, Joe Barry, said that "the prime criterion in selecting the venue was to originate a production that would at least match the standards achieved in 1988".

Millstreet helped to provide RTE with the unique and separate identity it sought for the song contest. It was newsworthy because people were curious to see how a small Irish town would cope with the enormity of Eurovision.

The venue was well-equipped and RTE never had any worries about it. The Green Glens arena is one of the most adaptable and accommodating complexes in the country, while the hotels and other facilities in nearby Killarney are top grade.

Millstreet was a novelty for the regular Eurovision travellers who wanted something different. RTE was determined to make it different from start to finish, from the moment delegations arrived until the closing credits went up. Not only in production terms but also in the overall experience this Irish Eurovision was very different.

Eurovision Song Contest Information Desk, Millstreet 1993

Communications and technology

On Eurovision night the pictures and sound from RTE's eleven cameras and over one hundred microphones came via fibre-optic link cables supplied by Telecom Eireann. A 140 mega-bit vision circuit then linked Millstreet with Dublin, from where RTE beamed up the images from the Dublin Earth Station Satellite (SBNI), a nine-metre diameter dish, located at RTE headquarters. A satellite stationed at 7 degrees east over the African Equator called "Eutelsat 2 Flight 4" then picked up the images and linked them to the 29 European receiver satellite dishes. The programme was shown as far afield as Morocco and Russia, Australia, Korea and the USA.

The shell of the Green Glens arena was converted into a full television studio—probably the largest of its kind in the world. 200 RTE personnel worked on the installation.

The technical requirements included:
* 102 kilometres of cabling and circuits;
* 11 operational cameras, including a remote-controlled super sky mote and, inside the roof, a cam trak mounted on 50 metres of rail;
* an operational crew of 128;
* 100 microphones;
* 800 luminaires including 60 computer-controlled intelligent light heads;
* 1.6 megawatts of electrical power;
* 225 sound and visual circuits;
* 5,000 circuit and cable connections;
* 40 commentary boxes.

The £1.5 million outside broadcast unit was a massive logistical operation. The 128-strong operational crew were drawn from sound, lighting, cameras, technical operation, electrical, wardrobe, make-up, construction, staging, rigging, vision mixing, floor management and engineering design and development

The Electricity Supply Board (ESB) installed extensive additional infrastructure to accommodate the 1.6 mega watt peak demand required to service the complex for the contest.

Social

The social programme comprised a state reception in Cork city, civic receptions in Killarney and Millstreet and another hosted by the music industry. Rehearsal breaks were the opportunity for trips to show the beauties of the scenery and local manufacture. For Deirdre Henchy and her staff each event has its guest list, its speeches, its protocol, its running order and publicity opportunities.

Each delegation was taken to a suitable tourist attraction for the filming of "postcard videos". Sponsored by Bord Fáilte, these postcards were used to introduce the songs and the singers and represented enormous value for the Irish tourist industry. For RTE, it was further mileage in the local media for Eurovision 1993.

Everyone concerned with the hotel and transport industries in the region including Cork Kerry Tourism, members of the Irish Hotels Federation, CIE Tours, Irish Rail, and the Gardai assisted cheerfully and the people of Millstreet gave a magnificent welcome to everybody.

As is traditional in the Eurovision Song contest, there was interest and speculation about how the presenter would be dressed on the night. It remained a tight secret until she came on stage in a style that was modern and rich with luxurious detail, fitting in exactly with the overall look of the show.

Structural

Eurovision was also an opportunity to profile the skilled work behind the scenes in RTE. And who said that the nuts and bolts and behind-the-scenes couldn't be made interesting? After months of construction work in Dublin the massive Eurovision set was ready on Easter Tuesday for transportation to Millstreet in carefully-packed sections. Lighting and sound operators, engineers, painters, carpenters, electricians and other skilled staff transformed Millstreet's famous showjumping arena into a dazzling international auditorium. Over six months, RTE's Eurovision production designer, Alan Farquharson, saw his elaborate stage design turn into a reality, from plans on paper, to a maze of polycarbonate girders and piping and almost 7,000 light bulbs.

The stage blended traditional design with a number of mechanical effects, an elaborate lighting system and a hydraulically controlled walkway for the winner's entry at the grand finale and a 10 feet tall slope at the rear of the stage. The floor was mirrored in the ceiling which featured a corresponding display of lights and lamps weighing three and a half tons.

The peripheral areas of the arena were transformed, softening the image of the complex and creating front-of-house delegate foyers, restaurants and an international press centre and backstage facilities such as green room and dressing rooms.

This was the first time that RTE used its computer-aided design system (CAD) for Eurovision. Ideal for such a large show, it enabled the design team to develop and redraught the set on-screen rather than undertake tedious revised drawings. It was also used to exchange information with engineering, lighting and other contractors.

As soon as the show started, the imagination was captured by the opening graphics in a sequence that pushed the boundaries of television graphics further than had been seen before, employing a theme based on Celtic mythology that was both beautiful and thought-provoking.

MEDIA INTEREST

While the media side of Eurovision '93 started officially in the RDS, Dublin, in 1992, as soon as the Irish song was declared the winner, the RTE press office got into full swing in mid-February when it was possible to assign three public relations staff full-time to it. From then on, there was a non-stop ten week schedule of positive stories and pictures.

The Eurovision Song Contest made news many times during the year as the build-up continued through the National Song Contest to pick the Irish entrant. When Ireland are hosting there is interest in the choice of venue, song, singer and presenter and lots of speculation about the design of the set and the presenter's clothes.

At first some were sceptical about the suitability of Millstreet. The Point Theatre in Dublin was the first choice of many, with the RDS also in the running. When the Millstreet contract was official the journalists were brought down the following day to a press conference. Although the story was of national significance and the announcement could more easily have been made in RTE, the selling of Millstreet as venue began immediately. The reaction to the complex and town was favourable, although one reporter from the *Sunday World* was negative, suggesting that the delegates and other visitors would miss the night life of Dublin's Leeson Street. Events were to prove that an Irish Eurovision was an experience for seasoned and at times jaded Eurovision delegates. There was a further visit by journalists to see the completed set one week before the event.

Fionnuala Sweeney was chosen to be the sole presenter. She was a journalist from the newsroom. "She represented a youthful Ireland, a well-trained professional Ireland, and also, represented a sophisticated RTE", says Deirdre Henchy. "She was accustomed to live television and she had a cool head.

Noel C. Duggan, owner of Millstreet Green Glens complex, spoke for the Cork community. But RTE had its own identity, personified at popular level by Fionnuala Sweeney who fronted photocalls and, in policy matters by executive producer Liam Miller.

A fully-equipped press centre was located in the Eurovillage. Fax machines, photo transmission facilities, phones and computers were provided for the 400 journalists and 38 commentators who covered the week's events.

In total there were over 30 press conferences—more than an average EU summit—and a myriad of photocalls as sections of the world focused on Millstreet. Press releases were issued daily. *Eurovision News* broadsheets provided all the facts and details and RTE's experienced staff dealt with all levels of press enquiries.

As at all international events, there was an accreditation system for the media. About 50 were from Ireland, with around 400 from Europe where Eurovision is always "a huge story", according to Deirdre Henchy. "It is like turning the clock back to the 60s. It still has a huge following".

The Bosnian entry was targeted as a news story for papers like *The Irish Times* and *The Sunday Times*, *Observer* and the BBC in the UK. The singers would not have been of great interest to them but Bosnia, with the war, was newsworthy. Some wondered why people should risk their lives going through battle-torn Sarajevo to sing pop music.

RTE regarded it as a human story and did not let it get too politicised. The papers asked lots of questions about what religion the singers were, was it true that one of them was a former soldier, were they going to make a political statement on television, and were they going to exploit the song contest for political ends.

RTE decided to answer honestly and get all of these questions out of the way immediately. With the help of interpreters there was a press conference as soon as the Bosnian delegation, the first to arrive, landed at the airport. After that it was down to the singing for the Bosnians as for everybody else.

Conscious of the importance of good staff relations and the value of the Contest in terms of internal public relations, some of the announcements were first published in the RTE staff journal from where they were picked up by the newspapers.

EVALUATION AND REFLECTION

The 1993 Eurovision Song Contest was a triumph for RTE and for Ireland. The concept of the event as major television and radio entertainment reaching around the world was well-served by every department within RTE. The decision to go to Millstreet was imaginative and successful.

It cost £2.2 million but a cost-benefit analysis spoke of the benefits, including tourism. A subvention from the European Broadcasting Union, in addition to sponsorship, meant that it finally cost RTE £750,000 for three hours live programming. However, there were other hidden costs, especially in personnel. The contest, being a huge undertaking involving a lot of people, puts a strain on the already busy programmes area. Unlike other programmes, RTE cannot sell the song contest to other stations; it is done as part of Eurovision and all countries get it free.

There were benefits for RTE in staff morale and prestige. It was a huge challenge for all who were involved and showed once more how in quality and organisational skills they were able to compete with much larger and wealthier organisations like the BBC. Eurovision '93 gave the station a much-needed psychological boost at a time of shrinking revenues and changes in broadcasting legislation.

While RTE needed to stress its own identity, the benefits in other areas of the economy were considerable, especially in tourism. RTE co-operated closely with Bord Failte, a special interest being the postcard shots that introduced the songs and the singers. It was an exposure that normal advertising could not buy for all that was best in Ireland.

The relatively remote and small location was not the problem that many had imagined. It was necessary, however, to reassure some people, especially overseas media, about the technical and back-up facilities. There was considerable attention and bemusement when a BBC man said the contest was being held in a cowshed. All now admit that he said it tongue-in-cheek, but RTE turned it to its advantage, encouraging others to say how marvellous, hi-tech and professional everything was. RTE recall it as an opportunity rather than an embarrassment.

And, by the way, the Irish song won at Millstreet. For RTE, the whole operation started all over again. As the closing credits rolled, the RTE press team was organising the next morning's press conference and went onwards to a hectic three days comprising a photocall with the Taoiseach, a civic reception with the Lord Mayor of Dublin and a state reception in Dublin Castle. It was the Point Theatre in 1994 and, yes, Ireland scored a hat-trick. Now someone must be wondering will it ever stop! "Maybe we'll set up an international consultancy service after all this", concludes Deirdre Henchy.

Sinéad Whooley has a BA Degree in English & Celtic Civilisation from University College, Cork and the DIT Diploma in Public Relations.

CHIEF EXECUTIVE DRIVES TRACTOR AROUND IRELAND—TWICE

The 1990 Gorta Tractor Drive
by Claire Donnelly

BACKGROUND

Gorta— The Freedom from Hunger Council of Ireland, was the first Third World development organisation to be set up in Ireland. It was established by the Department of Agriculture in 1965 in response to an international campaign initiated by the Food and Agricultural Organisation of the United Nations. Gorta is the Irish word for hunger.

Gorta believes that helping people to provide for themselves is the most effective form of aid. It concentrates on *Farming against Famine* projects which contribute to long-term development. At present it has over 140 self-help projects in 27 countries. Its patron is the President of Ireland, Mary Robinson. Its revenue in 1992 was £1.07 million. Gorta does not provide emergency relief in response to disaster appeals.

The foundations for the 1990 tractor drive were laid in 1988 when Gorta staged one as a fund-raising venture following cutbacks in Government funding. This first tractor drive raised £18,000.

The novel idea of a tractor drive emerged during a brainstorming session in the offices of Ann Fox Public Relations. It utilised the hobby of driving enjoyed by Ronny Smiley, Gorta's 55-year-old chief executive, and the tractor, a symbol of Gorta's agricultural role.

THE CHALLENGE

In 1990, Gorta's Silver Jubilee year, the focus of the tractor drive had changed. The challenge now was to raise public awareness by getting into *The Guinness Book of Records*. In a time limit of 19 days, Ronny Smiley planned to drive 3,350 miles around Ireland on a tractor. The only comparable Guinness record was a lawn mower which had covered 3,000 miles.

While fund-raising was a secondary aim in 1990, Gorta hoped to raise enough funds to purchase and install two grinding mills in Tanzania.

OBJECTIVES

The four objectives of the tractor drive were to:
* raise awareness of Gorta through inclusion in *The Guinness Book of Records*

FROM JOHN PAUL TO SAINT JACK.....

- increase Gorta's publicity profile on a national scale
- raise funds for a grinding mill in Tanzania, the target of £20,000 to be achieved through sponsorship and collections at each town through which Ronny Smiley would pass.
- raise public awareness of the sponsors Massey Ferguson, Irish Shell, Superphone and Ballygowan Spring Water.

PLANNING

The pursuit of the record provided a platform to attract media publicity and increase public awareness of Gorta.

Planning and implementation covered three areas:
- meticulous organisation prior to the event
- ensuring the smooth running of the event
- generating and maintaining media coverage

- **Mapping the route**

The Automobile Association (AA) provided assistance in drawing up an itinerary. The tractor had to pass through the major country towns, use primary routes and achieve the 3,350 miles necessary to set the record.

The AA developed a 10-day itinerary which had to be covered twice. It consisted of daily journeys: Dublin—Cork, Cork—Ennis, Ennis—Limerick, Limerick—Mullingar, Mullingar—Sligo, Sligo—Cavan, Cavan—Ballaghaderreen, Ballaghaderreen—Drogheda, Drogheda—Carlow, Carlow—Dublin.

The Mansion House in Dublin's Dawson Street, residence of The Lord Mayor, was the starting and finishing point.

- **Finding sponsors and cash donations**

To minimise costs it was necessary to find sponsors. Massey Ferguson donated a tractor which had to be specially fitted with a milometer. Irish Shell supplied diesel, Ballygowan donated bottled water and Superphone offered a mobile phone which was fitted in the tractor cab. The phone accommodated live interviews with local radio stations.

The sponsors gained two benefits:
- Their actions conveyed social responsibility and community spirit
- Their company logos were carried on the tractor.

The only costs incurred by Gorta were lunches and evening meals as in many places members of the local Gorta committee provided overnight accommodation.

Gorta's secondary objective was to raise £20,000 for the Tanzania grinding mill. Three methods were used:
- mailshots requesting donations were targeted at the top 500 companies
- sponsorship cards were sent to the 20 Gorta county committees and they rallied local people.
- street collections were made in all the towns through which the tractor passed.

- Informing *The Guinness Book of Records*

The Guinness Book of Records were first contacted more than six months before the record-breaking attempt.

The *Records* officials stated that a record would be acknowledged for "the greatest distance travelled by a standard farm tractor in one continuous journey, including overnight stops". The same vehicle and driver had to be used throughout. A log-book which recorded mileage, rest breaks and meal-times had to be signed and dated every morning and evening in the local Garda station. The *Records* officials also required additional evidence in the form of local and national newspaper cuttings and photographs.

There was no guarantee that even if a record was made, it would be included in the book. It was possible that Gorta would simply receive a certificate stating a record had been established.

IMPLEMENTATION

- **The Farewell**

After weeks of planning, the tractor chugged into action on 4 July 1990, at 10 am, outside the Mansion House. The Lord Mayor of Dublin, Councillor Michael Donnelly, provided the official send-off. A fanfare was supplied by the Artane Boys Band. The Gardai escorted the tractor in and out of the city on both the departure and the return to the Mansion House.

The Dublin offices of Ann Fox Public Relations were the nerve centre for co-ordinating the tractor drive. From here, radio and press interviews were set up, photocalls arranged and even the fitting of a new milometer was organised on a Sunday morning when the first one failed. Working with Ann Fox were Yvonne Clarke and Leonie Stevenson. The only Gorta official on the road with Ronny Smiley was Melanie Boast, the development officer. She travelled behind to collect donations in the towns.

The farewell generated strong media interest and was an excellent photo opportunity. Invitations had been issued to press photographers, news editors, columnists, religious correspondents and editors of religious publications. An RTE television crew and correspondents from the Dublin radio stations also attended.

On the evening of the farewell a follow-up press release was circulated to the national and provincial press and local radio stations.

- **Life on the Road**

Ronny's daily routine, at a maximum speed of 20 mph, started at 8.30 am, stopped for a short break at lunch and finished at 8 pm. The log-book, recording mileage and rest breaks, was signed every morning and evening in the local garda station.

An additional publicity opportunity was provided by the newly-established local radio stations. They were kept informed about Gorta's record-breaking attempt. As a result, Ronny's daily routine included radio interviews via mobile phone.

He also had daily press interviews and photocalls with provincial press. In areas with no press photocalls, it was arranged that photographers would provide photos for the local papers. The journey was reported in the local paper of every town that Ronny passed through.

On Day 10, an update was issued to the media. It provided information about the journey and progress towards the fund-raising target.

The effect of the widespread coverage over the 19 days was to personalise Gorta. The public became familiar with Ronny Smiley and his fund-raising campaign.

Apart from the cavernous potholes and Ronny's aching muscles, the only major setback was caused by the milometer on Day 7. Due to an electrical fault, the wipers interfered with it, resulting in a "loss" of 500 miles. However, time was still on Ronny's side and a new milometer was installed immediately.

- **The Homecoming**

On 24 July 1990, Ronny Smiley was received at the Mansion House by the Lord Mayor. The challenge had been won. He had achieved a world record by covering 3,350 miles in 19 days on a tractor.

Four days before the return, invitations were issued to the journalists who had attended the farewell. A fresh news angle was provided by the presence of Donald McFarlan, editor of *The Guinness Book of Records.* His presence maximised the publicity value of the homecoming and the achievement of the record. Press photographers were able to show him presenting the certificate of the record to Ronny Smiley.

EVALUATION

The well-organised and executed public relations campaign for the 1990 Gorta tractor drive achieved its objectives:
- Ronny Smiley's entry into *The Guinness Book of Records* for 1991 raised public awareness of Gorta
- Gorta's publicity profile was increased by the national media coverage
- The fund-raising target of £20,000 was achieved and exceeded, with a final figure of £30,000.

DISCUSSION

This experience highlights the importance of approaching public relations with creativity and freshness. The tractor drive was novel and effective and it reinforced Gorta's agricultural role while increasing public awareness.

It also showed the importance of co-ordinated, credible public relations campaigns. Events must be planned and implemented with meticulous attention to detail. All contingencies must be catered for, even replacing a milometer on a Sunday morning. Ann Fox Public Relations was commended for its efficiency by the Gardai. The *Guinness Book* officials deemed the organisers to be one of the most professional groups they had encountered.

This was an excellent opportunity to gain nation-wide publicity over 19 days, avoiding the disadvantages of a single provincial base or an event occurring only for one day. The continuous, proactive media relations campaign built up a picture of the tractor drive in the media over the 19 days. Sustained communications with journalists produced quality coverage which heightened public awareness. The level of this awareness was reflected in the sum of £10,000 — half the final target — already raised after only 350 miles.

There was a danger that media interest might decline after the first week. This was prevented by advance planning and innovation. An update at the half-way mark maintained the media's attention. The presence of *The Guinness Book of Records* editor at the homecoming provided a news angle which differed from the farewell ceremony. The public relations team did not neglect the media importance of human interest and novelty.

There were many congratulatory and humorous comments in the press coverage. As Michael O'Toole wrote in the *Dubliner's Diary* column of *The Evening Press:* "Any man who is prepared to drive 3,350 miles in a tractor on the roads of Ireland is entitled to sainthood, let alone an accolade". Miriam Lord of *The Irish Independent* noted how Ronny Smiley "did his John Wayne walk across the room and eased himself gingerly onto a cushion. Gorta's chief executive looked like someone who had just undergone an intensive course at the Lester Pigott school for potential Derby winners, followed by a brave attempt to conquer the Alps on his penny farthing".

Claire Donnelly has a BSc Degree in Human Communications from the University of Ulster and the DIT Diploma in Public Relations.

BEHIND THE ARCHES—A CÉAD MÍLE McFÁILTE

The Launch of McDonald's in Ireland, 1977
by Dara Cosgrave

BACKGROUND

McDonald's arrived in Ireland in 1977. The launch of their first restaurant, in Dublin's fashionable Grafton Street, was handled by Mary Finan, Wilson Hartnell Public Relations. The client was Mike Mehigan, who had worked for the McDonald's corporation in Canada and suggested that they come to Ireland. He is still the main McDonald's franchisee in Ireland with 12 stores and more than 800 staff.

Were it done today the launch, due to McDonald's size and international visibility, would be quite simple. However, at the time, despite the company being a household name in the United States and building an enviable international reputation, it was unknown in Ireland. They opened their first European restaurant in Amsterdam in 1971 and moved to the UK in 1974.

This presented a number of problems for Wilson Hartnell:

* The benefit of McDonald's corporate reputation was not available as a springboard for the launch
* The renowned McDonald's formula of Quality, Service, Cleanliness and Value (QSC + V) was unknown to the Irish people. Some of McDonald's predecessors had given the fast-food industry a poor and undesirable reputation.

Taking account of these factors, Wilson Hartnell wanted to promote not just a new restaurant but the McDonald's ethos and all that the company stood for.

OBJECTIVES

The public relations objectives for the launch were:

* to maximise awareness of McDonald's corporate identity—and thus establish credibility for the QSC + V claims
* to set the right initial tone—by making it clear from the beginning that McDonald's was a family, fast-food restaurant and that it took this role seriously
* to project the QSC + V formula—by ensuring that aspects of it were inherent in all publicity connected with the launch
* to maximise the impact of McDonald's arrival—by using the hard news potential of the opening as a peg for as much attention-getting activity as possible
* to establish good community relations—by taking steps from the beginning to integrate McDonald's into the local community

---

PLANNING AND IMPLEMENTATION

Objective 1: Establishing corporate identity

The public relations team was convinced of the importance of communicating the size, success, rapid growth, stability, international recognition and entrepreneurial flair of the McDonald's corporation to the Irish public. They sought to portray McDonald's as a long-term investor and employer in Ireland.

This international dimension and success story of the company also helped in attracting the national press to the story but it had to back up the standards and benefits which it claimed.

When Wilson Hartnell convinced McDonald's International Department to use the backing of the whole corporation, together they produced an information package of carefully selected material about McDonald's. This included a *Time* magazine cover story, a *Sunday Times* feature article and the latest McDonald's annual report.

First press function: Official opening ceremony and VIP lunch

The information package was used in organising the press functions and shaping the attendant publicity. Its first use was to secure the attendance of a Government minister at the official opening ceremony. The package was sent to the Minister for Labour, Michael O'Leary, TD, with a letter noting that McDonald's would be purchasing considerable quantities of Irish beef and dairy produce as well as creating over 50 new jobs. The Minister could not afford to ignore these points at a time of high unemployment, especially as a General Election was known to be imminent. He accepted the invitation.

Another important figure who agreed to attend the official opening was the United States Deputy Ambassador to Ireland (President Carter had just been elected and the new Ambassador had not been appointed).

The next step in the campaign was to convince the press to attend. The official opening and VIP lunch were designed specifically for news editors and business editors.

"Initial probings among key journalists confirmed our fears that they knew little about McDonald's", recalls Mary Finan. "Moreover the business scene was quite active at the time and there were several good stories vying for publicity".

In order to ensure coverage Wilson Hartnell isolated six to eight key journalists in the national press, radio and television. They were all given individual briefings in advance, with exclusive angles, and their stories embargoed for the day after the launch. The briefings included the specially prepared package along with a press release and the showing of the *Philpott File* BBC film on McDonald's.

These briefings, although time-consuming, won the co-operation of the journalists and paid off handsomely in terms of:
* in-depth and accurate newspaper coverage
* a nine-minute report on national radio
* a 20-minute report on national television

The day itself went off perfectly. The photocall and official opening ceremony were outside the restaurant at noon. The Minister cut a tape made of pound and dollar notes at the entrance, flanked by the Deputy Ambassador and Mike Mehigan. Pictures of this cutting ceremony were used extensively and the novel idea of the pound/dollar tape has been used since for other openings.

Lunch, speeches and a press conference were then held in the nearby Royal Hibernian Hotel. The entire ceremony was over by 3 pm. The reason for the hotel rather than the restaurant was:

- the restaurant was open for business and such a function, even for a relatively small number of guests, would have meant closing down the entire upstairs section at the peak lunch-hour, and
- some silence and privacy was needed for the speeches and press conference

Wilson Hartnell realised it was slightly irregular to hold the press conference away from the restaurant, so they gave the journalists Be Our Guest cards for themselves and their families and also an invite to the evening function.

Mike Mehigan was given emphasis as the local man setting up a new business. Journalists were keen to interview him even though they already had the main story.

Objective 2: Establishing family orientation.

McDonald's identification of parents and children as its key target audience was a huge break from the norm of fast-food restaurants. It was a top priority for Wilson Hartnell to communicate this family orientation to potential customers.

For this, two evening receptions were held at the restaurant for journalists and their families, one on the day of the launch and the other the next evening. The journalists were divided into two groups—feature writers, women editors and social columnists in one and cookery editors and correspondents in the other. They were given different press releases. The family atmosphere was enhanced by the presence of the Lord Mayor of Dublin, Michael Collins, with his wife and several of their 12 children.

Present on both evenings was Ronald McDonald, the world-famous clown who is McDonald's ambassador. He represents the feeling of fun, family and community spirit that McDonald's projects, particularly to children. He performed for all the guests and then treated the children to an additional show of magic and videos.

The search for Ireland's Ronald McDonald was a story in itself. McDonald's had a very precise profile of the sort of person they wanted. It was the same in every country. For instance, a person who might already be too famous and well-known to children would have been unsuitable. Wilson Hartnell contacted Irish Actors' Equity, acting schools, theatre groups, and model agencies, giving them the required profile and requesting suitable names. Wilson Hartnell's sister advertising agency was also asked for suggestions.

From these sources, about 50 names were collected and seven people invited to a first interview—two magicians, a ventriloquist, two models, a mime artist and an actor. The final four had a second interview when McDonald's international marketing team was in Dublin. Finally, they selected a very polished performer who had an excellent children's act which was a mixture of tricks, magic and puppetry. He was tall, well-built and pleasant. He was, in fact, the personnel director of a local Dublin company, but at no stage was his identity revealed. He was given intensive training for the remaining three weeks before the official opening.

Objective 3: Projecting QSC + V formula.

These elements were stressed in the two press releases for the evening functions. Also, there was a radio feature on a weekend magazine programme.

Careful attention was given to every detail of the evening receptions. No effort was spared to ensure that the quality of food, calibre of service and cleanliness of the restaurant were impeccable. Members of the "crew", as McDonald's describe their staff, were hand-picked for the occasion.

Objective 4: To maximise awareness

The main event to maximise awareness was the Grand Opening, held the second Saturday after the official opening.

The Grand Opening centred on a parade around the Grafton Street area, followed by a Ronald McDonald magic show and concert. This was the first time an individual company had organised a parade through Dublin city centre, so there were quite elaborate preparations to be made. It was necessary to win the co-operation of the city's traffic department because it was not certain that permission would be given for such a parade during peak shopping-hours. Wilson Hartnell fixed a meeting with the traffic superintendent—a letter would have been too easy to refuse—and secured his permission with two small provisos: not to distribute balloons to children in the street nor hold the concert in an area leading directly onto a public thoroughfare.

This meant that the Ronald concert had to be held indoors. To cover themselves for large numbers and the possibility of two sessions, they booked the ballroom of the nearby Shelbourne Hotel for the day. As the event was designed to generate goodwill, it would have had the opposite effect if people had to be turned away. Everything was therefore anticipated, but in the end, one session was enough for the 650 parents and children who attended.

There were two nearby outdoor venues, a large car park which was unattractive and the public St. Stephen's Green which was not available to commercial concerns.

For the parade, they combined the Irish and American dimensions with Dublin's premier brass band and a group of young Dublin majorettes. Instead of using costly floats they had brightly decorated vintage cars. They looked for a popular personality who would be an attraction for the children and introduce Ronald McDonald to make him instantly acceptable and were lucky to get Maureen Potter. She was the most popular television and pantomime star in the country, but was willing to let Ronald McDonald be the main star of the day. The parade was from 10 am to noon, starting parallel to Grafton Street, picking up Ronald McDonald at the restaurant, going to the Shelbourne for the concert and finally leaving Ronald back again at "his house".

Objective 5: Establishing good community relations

McDonald's emphasis on good community relations was shown in several ways. For instance, Ronald McDonald was driven in his gaily-coloured vintage car to the nearby National Children's Hospital in Harcourt Street on the afternoon of the Grand Opening. Ronald McDonald performed a Magic Show and distributed happy hats, balloons and hand puppets.

A reception for families was held at the restaurant on a weekday evening from six o'clock to eight, to thank everybody who had helped in the smooth running of the launch. These included suppliers, members of the garda siochána, traffic department, customs officials, Minister's staff, Lord Mayor's staff and local shop owners.

Ronald McDonald was invited to participate two weeks later in the National Children's Day Parade. This was another success and McDonald's entertained a party of 20 orphans at the restaurant.

COST EFFECTIVENESS

The cost of implementing the public relations programme was £2,800, including fees and expenses—incredibly great value by to-day's standards. Advertising cost only £598—notices in the two Dublin evening newspapers for the Grand Opening, as well as three television slides. The publicity generated from the campaign was immense. Wilson Hartnell had been asked to run the event in the most cost-effective manner and both sides were delighted with the results. The excellent media coverage led to the cancellation of advertising features that had been planned for the following weeks. The programme for the Irish launch has since been used by McDonald's as an example for other countries.

DISCUSSION

Mary Finan believes that the strategy of stressing McDonald's international dimension, and the reputation it had built for impeccable quality, service, cleanliness and value (QSC + V) was the key to the success of the launch. Without that dimension, "it is unlikely that the official opening would have merited more than a couple of paragraphs, if that, in the national press. To attract McDonald's kind of customer into the Grafton Street restaurant we had to give him sound reasons for believing in the unique benefits we were claiming for McDonald's. The McDonald's story gave us the endorsement and authority we urgently needed to substantiate our claims".

McDonald's brand and story had to be given sufficient news value to justify its publicity as the media, quite correctly, are opposed to mere commercial plugs. Wilson Hartnell decided against the slow build-up of publicity leading to a burst surrounding the opening ceremony that had been a feature of McDonald's openings in some other countries. They opted not to issue any statements, other than in reply to specific press queries, prior to the formal proceedings on opening day. This meant that the McDonald's story was still hard news and was given a position of prominence in all of the national newspapers.

Some details of the campaign could not be repeated too often. For instance, it is very rare that anybody, and especially a commercial company, is given permission to block off one of the main city streets for a parade at peak shopping-time. Wilson Hartnell succeeded in winning over such groups as gardaí and corporation officials to make them appreciate that this was a family affair, a community celebration. They also had to react to the sensitivities of other shops in Grafton Street, a quality shopping street where some felt a fast food restaurant would lower the tone.

Anyone handling the public relations for such a public opening should remember that the client and restaurant staff have several competing demands upon their time. Wilson Hartnell admit that they did not appreciate at first the pressures under which a local McDonald's team operated. They expected that Mike Mehigan would be available for planning meetings, preparation of press statements, interviews etc. during the weeks surrounding the opening. They tended to forget that he also had to cope with more immediate problems associated with builders, architects, customs officials, staff recruitment, telephone installers. This means that the public relations team, on such occasions, need to keep the demands on the client's time to an absolute minimum—avoid ad hoc phone calls, and have a comprehensive agenda for one rather than several meetings.

FOOTNOTE

Public relations dominated the first opening in Grafton Street in 1977 and, to a lesser extent, the second opening in O'Connell Street soon after. At first there was very little advertising. In the following years the public relations activity reduced and advertising increased.

Materials for McDonald's restaurants are sourced, where possible, in Ireland but they must conform to the McDonald's specification. The beef is from Carrickmacross, Co. Monaghan, and potatoes made to McDonald's standard are imported from the UK. McDonald's have looked at local growers but it is not possible to achieve the quality and length of potato that McDonald's require.

In response to the new awareness of both environmental and health issues, McDonald's packaging is now made from recycled paper and the cups are biodegradable. They have moved from lard to vegetable fats and now sell mineral water. McDonald's are constantly looking at alternative items and recently tried Vegetable McNuggets. McDonald's believe that people should follow a healthy diet and their Big Macs, Hamburgers, Fries and Shakes, eaten in conjunction with other foods, all go to making for a healthy, balanced diet.

The increased number of suburban restaurants and the company emphasis on the family has led to more customers bringing small babies, creating a need for more changing rooms, high chairs etc. Unlike 20 years ago, there can be few people now who have not heard of McDonald's and been welcomed in strange towns and cities by the familiar arches logo.

Worldwide they have more than 10,000 restaurants and have sold more than 50 billion burgers. In the UK, where they have 32,000 employees, they have passed 500-store landmark and boast they will reach the thousand within the next ten years. McDonald's served 30,000 Russians on the opening day in Moscow in 1990, instantly making it the company's largest volume store.

In Ireland, while not quite that big, McDonald's restaurants today are a significant and profitable Irish industry, employing nearly 1500 between all franchisees, achieved without any government grants.

Dara Cosgrave has a BA Degree in Italian & Economics from University College., Dublin and the DIT Diploma in Public Relations.

MILLIONS OF POUNDS IN PRIZES

The Launch of Ireland's National Lottery
by Alma K.Feeley

INTRODUCTION

Journalist Frank Kilfeather once wrote:"The Irish gamble.....it doesn't matter whether it's on horses, dogs, raffles, bingo, lotto or buying prize bonds.We all dream of getting rich. Money makes all our dreams come true and solves all our problems. Everybody is waiting for that wonderful day when they are financially free to come into the office and tell the boss what they really think of him. One gets dizzy at the thought of it."

The National Lottery has, since it was introduced eight years ago, become a normal part of Irish life; it is now part of the Irish psyche.The ritual of buying a weekly scratch card or selecting six numbers in the twice-weekly lotto game has become part of what the people are with 60 per cent of adults taking part.

From a communication perspective, the National Lottery was perhaps the most intensive marketing, advertising and public relations campaign ever implemented for a new product launch in Ireland. It was unprecedented, not just in its scale, but also in its novelty, its character and the degree to which it embraced every adult in the country.

BACKGROUND

The idea of establishing a National Lottery was first mooted in the Fine Gael/Labour Coalition government's National Economic Plan of 1984, *Building on Reality.* A year later the franchise for operating the National Lottery was awarded to An Post, the national postal service.The legislation formally enacting the establishment of the National Lottery went through the Dail on 15 July 1986. In September the board of directors was announced by the Minister for Finance.

The company shares are divided in a ratio of 80:20 between An Post and the Minister for Finance.The sole function is to generate money, through the lottery, for distribution by the Government to selected beneficiary projects all over Ireland.The allocation of Lottery proceeds is the prerogative of the Government, with 51p of every £1 share going on prize money, and 32.7p going to the Government.The selected beneficiaries are divided into four main areas:

* Irish language
* health and welfare
* arts, culture and heritage
* youth, sport, recreation and amenities

The country became aware of the imminent arrival of the National Lottery when the company held its first press conference in October 1986; it was to start with a scratch-card game giving immediate prizes and, for some, the chance to enter a weekly televised game where they could spin a giant wheel and win up to £250,000. The projected sales target for the first year was £20 to £25 million.

PLANNING

There was a staff recruitment programme, followed by selection and appointment of an advertising agency and public relations consultancy. Wilson Hartnell Public Relations (WHPR), and its sister company Wilson Hartnell Advertising were appointed. The public relations team was headed by WHPR managing director, Mary Finan and Brenda O'Hanlon, account executive. For the National Lottery, John Fitzpatrick was the first director, Malachy Moynihan, sales & marketing manager, Tony McGinty, operations manager and Bob Lane, public relations manager. Both groups worked together in virtually every aspect of the programme: corporate identity design, monitoring evolving consumer attitudes, game design, generating interest in the key trade markets, agent recruitment and training, plus all the normal activities involved in designing a marketing campaign for a brand new product.

MARKET RESEARCH

The first market research, in August 1986, showed that two thirds of the adult population would take part in the lottery. There was tremendous goodwill towards the idea of setting up a National Lottery and everyone wanted it to work. This close monitoring of feedback from the market has been a major factor in the success of the Lottery.

Intensive research also took place into lotteries in other countries, particularly the United States, which was visited on several occasions by senior management. This research confirmed that a national lottery which began with an instant game would be successful.

AGENT RECRUITMENT

Work began in September 1986 on the agent recruitment programme. It was necessary to select and train some 3,000 agents in the six months to the launch date. From a public relations point of view, the challenge was to attract the right calibre of agent. An extensive advertising campaign in both national and trade press was launched, focusing on the benefits a lottery licence would bring to agents—increased traffic and the five per cent commission on sales. As a result, some 8,500 applications were received from almost precisely the high-calibre retail outlets desired. The selection process necessitated store visits, interviews, and a huge amount of paperwork. By Christmas, 3,000 agents had been selected and had embarked on a series of 990 training seminars in 51 locations around the country. It was important to notify all unsuccessful applicants by letter before a list was published.

The signage programme was completed well in advance of the launch date. This ensured that by the time tickets officially went on sale on the morning of Monday, 23 March, virtually everyone in the country knew where their nearest lottery agent was located. The production of pre-launch and launch issues of a special agent newsletter was another communications mechanism to enthuse the trade. The newsletters were packed with details of up-to-the-minute launch plans and also contained information already given at the training seminars.

Mary Finan, MPRII, managing director, Wilson Hartnell Public Relations

At the press conference on 7 October 1986, the Minister for Finance formally presented the statutory licence to operate the Lottery to the company's new Board. The event received saturation coverage on television, radio and press.

From that date onwards, stories were released at regular intervals to maintain a constant level of awareness. This period was also used to assess some of the negative media issues which An Post would be likely to confront when the initial euphoria subsided. Senior management were given simulated media "grilling" sessions.

By January, the main public relations programme was ready to put into action. It had to integrate with the overall advertising concept of fun and excitement for everyone, incorporating the fantasy of winning big prizes; it had to acknowledge the dignity and integrity of the National Lottery company, while at the same time generating excitement.

IMPLEMENTING THE PUBLIC RELATIONS PROGRAMME

Phase One included a calendar of activities to create and sustain media and public interest in the National Lottery in the lead-up to the launch.

The first of these was to familiarise the public and the media with the National Lottery logo and the signs erected outside the sales agents. The logo was a series of 12 blue/white cubes and one emerging blue/red cube in the middle with "National Lottery" written beneath it in red.

Press releases explained the logo and a photocall was set up for the erection of the first sign at a sales agent's premises in Dublin. RTE cameras covered it. Preparation of a 30-page media fact book also began in January with anticipated questions in an indexed question and answer format as a guide for journalists. Through January and February, a steady flow of stories was maintained.

A number of other projects were also underway, including the production of agent newsletters, design of an elaborate float for the St. Patrick's Day Parade and preparation of editorial features for the Sunday newspapers for the eve of National Lottery Day.

CRISIS

In January, however, crisis struck. The Dail was dissolved on 20 January and a general election called for 17 February. The launch date for the Lottery had been fixed provisionally, but not yet announced, for 23 February. The entire publicity plan had been designed around this date.

The election meant that detailed planning of a champagne brunch for VIPs and press could not go ahead, nor could the final details be made for a nationwide balloon launch. Advertising schedules had to be revised. The launch date was deferred to 23 March so that the distraction of the election campaign could be out of the way before the excitement of the launch.

At an early stage, the need was realised for a newsletter to keep agents abreast of the Lottery's activities. Two newsletters were mailed to agents in the pre-launch period, focusing attention on the launch date, introducing the telesales team, and reiterating some of the information already given at the training seminars. A question and answer piece on customers' most commonly-asked questions was prepared and agents were reminded to use Freefone Lottery Help Line if they needed a swift response to queries. The presentation of clear, concise information to the network of agents was a vital communications exercise, as in the first hectic days they would be handling the bulk of public enquiries.

The float for the St. Patrick's Day Parade was the next project. A giant replica of a champagne bottle was produced, complete with glasses, bubbles (i.e. balloons emerging from the bottleneck) and colourful streamers.

On 12 and 13 March, National Lottery director John Fitzpatrick made a nationwide tour by helicopter with chairman Gerry Harvey, to host eight press conferences in two days. They briefed dignitaries in each provincial centre about the National Lottery and the plans for regional launches. They explained how the Grand Prize game operated by demonstrating on a huge simulated ticket. They distributed press kits with sample tickets and the media fact book.

The nationwide tour was followed by a champagne breakfast for press and celebrities at the Royal Hospital Kilmainham, on Sunday, 15 March. The event was hosted by television and radio celebrity, Gay Byrne, and guests were given specially-produced lottery tickets with which they played a simulated game. A fundamental part of the marketing strategy was the one-in-nine chance of winning, and to emphasise this, that exact ratio of winning tickets was distributed among the 150 guests. To emphasise the fun and celebration aspects of the event, there were prizes of champagne in different sizes, equated to the prize structure. For instance, a £2 prize equated to a snipe, a £10 prize to a bottle. For the Grand Prize game, which had a much larger range of prizes, a nebuchadnezzer—a giant bottle of champagne—went to the £250,000 winner.

The idea of holding two major press events on consecutive Sundays was unusual, but wise. It would take the press some time to assimilate how the instant games were designed and operated and how the Grand Prize game event would be staged. By giving that lead-time of seven days to the launch, enormous publicity was generated in the week beginning 16 March. For instance, on Friday, 20 March, a photocall was organised for all the national newspapers as a Garda escort was arranged for a huge truck carrying the first delivery of lottery tickets to sales agents nationwide. An enormous sign emblazoned on the side of the truck carried the legend *The National Lottery—Millions of Pounds in Prizes*.

Sunday, 22 March saw the publication of full-page features in the *Sunday World, Sunday Press, Sunday Independent* and *Sunday Tribune*.

EXECUTION

The focal point of National Lottery Day, Sunday, 22 March, was the release of thousands of colourful balloons at special ceremonies around the country—Cork, Waterford, Galway, Limerick, Athlone, Dundalk and Dublin. One in nine of these balloons was tagged with special coupons for free bottles of champagne—again reminding people of the odds of winning a prize. A London-based company specialising in promotional events and launches was given the contract for release of the 50,000 balloons in the Lottery corporate colours at each of the seven launch venues. They also looked after the staging, and provided sound equipment, gas and manpower.

Following the General Election, Charles Haughey was elected Taoiseach on 10 March. The VIP launch, also at the Royal Hospital Kilmainham, was attended by numerous members of the Government and opposition parties. There were 30 journalists among the 200 guests. The balloon ceremony took place in the Royal Hospital quadrangle following the formal speeches and presentation to the Taoiseach of a specially-designed silver replica of the Lottery logo, which was commissioned from Kilkenny Design Workshops. 15,000 Dublin balloons were released in a spectacular display and many people also turned up to see the balloon releases in the other centres.

The Taoiseach participated in a photocall the following morning when he made the first official purchase of a lottery ticket from a Dublin newsagent. For this there was a full turn-out of press, radio and television. Mr. Haughey had a much-publicised £2 win. By mid-morning, there were reports of other larger winners. The first £1,000 winner made the one-thirty radio news and evening television news. Numerous other winners were interviewed and had their names published in a press release at the end of the first day, by which time more than one million tickets had been sold.

Day two was equally hectic for both sales and publicity—front-page stories in all the national newspapers, radio mention on *Morning Ireland* and *The Gay Byrne Show*. The Lottery continued to release stories and interviews with winners, and daily bulletins were issued on sales, which continued at about one million a day.

By the end of a week of saturation coverage, most of which was congratulatory, the criticism, which had been anticipated, raised its head. It ranged from the relatively low odds of winning one of the big prizes in the Grand Prize game, through "profiteering" by An Post through the sales of stamps for people entering their successful scratchcards for the Grand Prize game, to the accusation that too good a marketing job had been done thereby encouraging people to spend money they could not afford. This was when the simulated media-grilling session proved useful. However, it had not any noticeable affect on sales which had reached £13 million when the preliminary draw and the first Grand Prize game took place on the *Late Late Shows* on 3 and 10 April.

Lotto was introduced in April 1988 with a 36-number formula and a similarly spectacular nationwide launch, also in the Royal Hospital Kilmainham. In August 1992 Lotto was changed to 39 numbers and then three more were added in November 1994.

EVALUATION AND CONCLUSION

The company had aimed for £20 to £25 million sales in the first year. That figure was rapidly passed and after only twelve weeks sales had reached £37 million; £6 million was made in the first five days alone !

The success of Ireland's National Lottery is internationally recognised. James Hosker is former director of the Massachusetts State Lottery, the biggest one in the United States. He says Ireland's lottery is probably the most successful in the world, with 60 per cent of the adult population playing the games—well above the international norm.

The Annual Report of the National Lottery for 1993 showed that, since 1987, £1,062 million had been returned to the community in prizes and support for selected projects at community, regional and national level. Under the original four headings the money had gone to:

- youth, sport, recreation and amenities— £147 million
- arts, culture, national heritage— £111 million
- health and welfare—£144 million
- Irish language— £31 million

In 1994 six instant games were operating simultaneously. The introduction of a Lotto grand-prize event and the huge amounts of money being given to a winning six-number combination from a 39 number formula, had taken the Lottery's success to even greater heights. The ratio of Lotto sales to Instant Games sales stood at 65:35.

In anticipation of the British National Lottery in November 1994, the numbers in the Irish lotto game were increased to 42, ensuring a minimum jackpot of £500,000 twice a week which would roll over until it was won. There was concern at a possible loss in cross-border areas where residents of Northern Ireland accounted for 10 per cent of all sales. It was a challenge to the public relations team to strengthen and maintain player loyalty.

The British launch, televised live on BBC, was also a success beyond all expectations, starting with a lotto game of 49 numbers and a first night jackpot of nearly £7 million.

However, the success of the Irish Lottery to date and the way it has become a normal part of Irish life means that its future is guaranteed.

Alma K. Feeley has a BA Degree in History & English from University College, Dublin and the DIT Diploma in Public Relations.

HOT, HOT, HOT, HOT 2FM - THE BIRTH OF A SOUND

The Relaunch of RTE's Second Radio Station
by Lisa Ryan

BACKGROUND

R adio Telefis Eireann is the Irish national broadcasting organisation. It had a monopoly until 1988 when the Government introduced legislation to licence independent radio stations, national and local, and an independent television station. In practice, the monopoly was dented from the 1960s, and especially through the 1980s by a growing number of illegal, "pirate" radio stations. Some of these stations were highly successful enterprises with impressive listenership figures and they were having a serious effect on RTE radio, especially on its popular music and chat station, 2FM (formerly Radio 2).

The newly-licensed stations, due to come on air from mid-1989, were designed to put the pirates out of business, but were also expected to take listenership, advertising and personnel from RTE.

RTE, therefore had to ensure that:
*   it kept its traditional listeners and attracted new ones and
*   retained the key staff within the organisation.

It decided to do this by making 2FM an exciting new prospect, involving internal as well as external audiences.

RTE planned to get its retaliation in first; it would relaunch and revamp 2FM before the independents came on air. Due to the scale of the undertaking, it would use an outside public relations consultancy. It had been the practice for 2FM, in its public relations, to retain its own identity and a certain independence from the rest of RTE.

Seven consultancies were approached by Colm Molloy, RTE's newly appointed marketing director, and asked to submit proposals for the re-launch of 2FM, on the basis of a one-page briefing document. Paul Kelly, managing director, and his team in Golley Slater, which included Ray Wasserman, partner and creative director, Isabel Morton, Anne Davey and Colm Maguire, account executives, presented their proposal on 9 January 1989. Two days later they were awarded the contract.

It had been intended to launch the new look 2FM on St. Patrick's weekend, thus telescoping the entire project into four to five weeks. The launch date was later changed to 27 March.

The majority of the proposals made by Golley Slater were accepted by RTE with one major exception. The consultancy had suggested a research project by Behaviour & Attitudes Ltd to find what was the actual imagery of 2 FM, "rather than just take a seat of the pants approach". RTE, however, felt that the consultancy's own appraisal of the problem with 2FM's image was accurate and that further research, costing £17,000, would be unnecessary. There was also a critical time problem to be considered.

Golley Slater did not mince words with RTE. They told them that 2FM was perceived as "staid, slightly culchie, remote and old-fashioned". Colm Molloy reckoned that they had got it right, even if RTE did not like to hear it.

Another element in the proposal was that Zig and Zag, the two popular puppets from the planet Zog, would be involved. Much of the advertising and promotional activities would have been based around the participation of the puppets who were stars on 2FM, a phenomenal success for RTE and for the two Trinity College students who were their minders. Due to contractual difficulties this part of the proposal did not go ahead.

What could have been a disaster as far as the major competition prize element was concerned, had also to be dealt with at a later stage. A holiday for ten years was to be given away. The chosen travel company, Blueskies, a subsidiary of Aer Lingus, closed down two years later. However, Aer Lingus honoured the commitment.

One of the difficulties for Golley Slater was that RTE wanted to launch a surprise attack on the pirate stations. Secrecy was therefore essential. Correspondence with third parties had to be limited and discreet. This was difficult, particularly as there were seven consultancies going around Dublin making initial enquiries from travel agents, music companies, motor distributors, designers, printers etc for a major promotional joint venture tie-up, without naming the client !

OBJECTIVES

- **Image**

Changing the image of 2FM was the greatest challenge facing the consultants and the fundamental root of the problem for the radio station. The perception at the time was that 2FM was staid, remote and old-fashioned. It had no "street cred".

2FM reached in excess of 50 per cent of the 18-24 year old bracket, but there was still a perception that it was not a success. RTE needed to change the "sound" of 2 FM, and this was the kernel of the consultancy's proposal.

The station, essentially a young person's station, needed to present itself as such. It needed to escape from the civil service, fuddy-duddy image that surrounded it. There was a feeling at the time that the station may have become complacent and lost touch with what the young people of Ireland wanted to hear on the radio. The DJs needed to get out of their ivory towers and get back to their "roots". 2 FM needed to return to the people.

- **The star is the station**

The station had been overly dependent on its handful of "stars". This would prove a major problem with the advent of the independent stations. If their stars were lured away to greener fields what would be left ?

The consultancy had to create an atmosphere where it would be recognised that the station was the star of the show and if the listener tuned into 2FM, there would be a guarantee of high quality, exciting broadcasting.

- **The urban-rural divide**

2FM had a problem in that it was, and still is, the only "pop" station to broadcast nation-wide. Its urban audience, as a result, perceived it as "hick" and "culchie" while its rural audience saw it as Dublin-based, due very much to its geographical location. There was, in other words, a culture gap which the station had to straddle. It could ill afford to further alienate its audiences.

- **Internal**

The project could never have been carried off without the help and commitment of the 2FM staff. They were, in a way, the key to the whole endeavour. The prevailing feeling among staff at the time was uncertainty, and this was a further problem for the station. The consultancy had to sign them on to the proposal.

- **General**

The overall objective of the re-launch was to regain audience share and give the station a face-lift. The proposed way to do this was to return the station to the people, to get them involved in the promotional activities surrounding the re-launch. 2FM had to cultivate a feeling of accessibility, excitement, fun and friendship.

MECHANISMS FOR CHANGE

- **Branding**

This was the way 2FM hoped to change its image. The disjointed nature of the station made it hard for its audience to relate to it. Its ownership was therefore transferred back to the public by mass marketing the slogan: *2FM Is Mine*.

This slogan was to appear on 15 million items of promotional material distributed throughout the country, on corporate stationery, posters etc. The ownership concept was further enhanced with the slogan: *2FM Does It For You and For Me*, which was introduced at a later stage.

The over-riding success of the whole campaign was the introduction of a package of jingles created by a Dallas company, P.A.M, recognised as one of the worlds' best jingle producers. Paul Kelly, and two of the 2FM DJs spent five days in Dallas working round the clock to produce about 50 new, themed jingles. Up to this time there had been little continuity between jingles and intros on 2FM. It was the newly introduced jingles that gave the station its much sought after "sound". They gave it an upbeat, "with it", "happening" sound. They were, and still are, catchy and memorable with such messages as: *Your station 2FM* and *Nationwide 2FM*.

The up-beat, 'trendy' image was portrayed in jingles such as : *Hot, Hot, Hot, Hot 2 FM* and a special 90-second song, *The Sound of 2FM*, written for the relaunch.

The quality of these jingles has been proven. They have stood the test of time and are still being used.

The 2FM roadcaster was another means of getting back in touch with the people, especially in the regions. It is a "studio on wheels" which travels throughout the country. Promotional material such as stickers, paper hats and t-shirts were distributed from it.

The branding of the station and its change of image were facilitated through using the roadcaster more regularly throughout Ireland.

Branding also tackled the "personality" problem. The idea of the star being the station was achieved to a certain extent by the jingle campaign. This, coupled with the roadcaster, also combated the problem of the urban-rural divide. The jingles stressed the idea that the station belonged to everybody and that it was a nationwide service. In general, the station was playing to a much more discerning and sophisticated audience, be it inside or outside the Dublin region.

This new and reinforced identity added stability to 2FM and made it a very exciting place to work in. The staff got a new lease of life. An in-house launch, exclusively for 2FM staff, informed them of the projects that were about to be undertaken, and enlisted their enthusiastic support.

PROMOTIONAL ACTIVITY

Promotional activity began approximately three weeks before the launch. It included advertising through:
- national door-to-door mail drop
- teaser radio commercials on Radio 1 and 2FM
- RTE 1 and Network 2 television carried a series of specially made commercials

To involve the public, a major competition with a first prize of a holiday a year for ten years and a new Ford car a year for ten years was launched. The prizes were negotiated through a series of "contra deals" with companies, i.e. advertising space on RTE in return for the goods.

The creative treatment theme saw popular 2FM disc jockey, Gerry Ryan becoming "disenchanted" with the sound of the station. He had discovered the formula to transform it (later to be revealed as the new jingle package). However, in exchange for the handing over of the new sound, he wanted a powerful position in RTE. He was refused. So, in high dudgeon, he decided to place the new sound in a safe, and bury the key to the safe somewhere in Ireland.

The public, to enter the competition, had to pinpoint on a grid map the exact location in Ireland where the key had been buried. A national mail drop of entry forms, along with various money-saving coupons, such as special offers in Peter Mark hairdressers, Bus Eireann, Burger King, Pepsi-Cola and Club Orange, among others, was undertaken. The contra arrangements were negotiated by Anne Davey and Colm Maguire.

A national advertising campaign on radio and television began at the start of March. The commercials were written and produced mainly by Paul Kelly and Isabel Morton. The campaign created pandemonium with the plight of the missing key even reported on the RTE nine o'clock television news !

Other DJs became involved, appealing to the public to help them find the new sound of 2FM. Clues were given on air to help the search. The whole organisation became involved. Six television and 25 radio commercials were produced. Huge excitement was created. There were more than 500,000 entries in the competition.

She found the Sound of 2FM—Eileen McGuirk with, from left: Paul Kelly, managing director, Golley Slater; Gerry Ryan, 2FM and Colm Molloy, marketing director, RTE, outside the RTE Radio Centre, Donnybrook, March 1989.

The winner, Eileen McGuirk, was chosen on the Friday before the launch. She was picked up by Rolls Royce on the day, transferred to the RTE headquarters at Donnybrook, then whisked away by helicopter to dig up the buried key on Howth Head, Co. Dublin. She returned to RTE with the key, opened the safe, loaded the sound cartridges and officially "turned on" the new sound of 2FM.

There were runner-up prizes of 8 CD midi stereo systems, sponsored by Pepsi-Cola. In order to get the DJs back to their roots there were 260 prizes of dinner for two, to be taken with the winner's favourite DJ. Entrants had to give an order of preferences—lest one DJ should end up with 260 dinners to eat.

A massive amount of organisation went into this competition. The legal side of it had to be absolutely watertight because of the laws on gaming and lotteries. As Paul Kelly said: "The RTE legal department were one of our most difficult target audiences!".

EVALUATION

The reaction was staggering. In addition to more than 500,000 people who entered the competition to find the key, song request forms, also on the entry leaflets, flooded in from all over the country. 2FM was re-launched with gusto and it still holds its market share with the independent stations. The original jingles from 1989 are still being used, their quality having stood the test of time. 2FM's listenership figures rose substantially in the immediate wake of the re-launch.

Paul Kelly says:"The real judgement of the exercise is that 2FM, five years after the re-launch, is still an exciting, vibrant station. It has not lost its market share to any great extent. It is still delivering the largest national 18 to 24-year-old audience.........Over the past five years 2FM has won the ratings war hands down".

Lisa Ryan has a BA Degree in Archaeology and Greek & Roman Civilisation, from University College, Dublin and the DIT Diploma in Public Relations.

HOT, HOT, HOT, HOT 2FM—THE BIRTH OF A SOUND

THE COURSE THAT JACK BUILT

The Opening of Mount Juliet Hotel and Leisure Estate
by John Collins

BACKGROUND

The seed for Mount Juliet Hotel and Leisure Estate was sown at Royal Dublin golf club in 1985. Toyota Ireland sponsored the Challenge of Champions between Seve Ballesteros and Jack Nicklaus. It was Nicklaus' first visit to Ireland. Toyota chairman and keen golfer, Tim Mahony, was chatting to him about the great landscapes available for golf courses in Ireland. Nicklaus, who had begun to design courses in the early eighties, said he would love to do one in Ireland, given the right terrain.

Three years later, Tim Mahony, through his company Killeen Investments, had acquired Mount Juliet Estate, situated outside Thomastown, Co. Kilkenny. As an estate Mount Juliet had existed for over 600 years and its 1,500 acres had excellent hunting, shooting, fishing, equitation and stud farming facilities. There was also the historic Mount Juliet House. Killeen bought the estate from Major Victor McCalmont whose family had owned it since 1914.

Mount Juliet was ripe for development as an idyllic leisure retreat aimed at both the home and international market. It is home to the Kilkenny Hunt, has a pheasant population of over 7,000 which is kept carefully stocked and two renowned salmon and trout rivers pass through its grounds—the Nore and its tributary, the King's river. The estate also has an impressive equine pedigree in the shape of Ballylynch Stud—home to The Tetrarch who was once described as the fastest horse in the history of the turf.

Tim Mahony knew that if these facilities and suitable accommodation could be developed, the addition of a Jack Nicklaus signature course would complete an excellent package. The call was made to Nicklaus that the right terrain had been found. Slattery Public Relations, who worked for Toyota Ireland, were engaged to oversee the press and public relations of the development.

PLANNING

The Jack Nicklaus connection gained Mount Juliet a lot of easy coverage in its early days. Although helpful, it was clear that hyping this aspect would not keep Mount Juliet in the public eye at home and abroad during the two-and-a-half-year refurbishment and development, before the golf course opened.

It was decided that a long-term view was needed to maintain a profile. "From a real positive it went to all the negatives (as rumours began circulating) and that was when we started to put out a long-term view - four phases", explained Padraig Slattery.

FROM JOHN PAUL TO SAINT JACK.....

- Phase One: the purchase of the land and the refurbishment and opening of Mount Juliet House as a 32-bedroom hotel with conference facilities.
- Phase Two: the design and construction by Nicklaus of an 18-hole golf course and a three-hole golf academy.
- Phase Three: the development of the leisure complex beside the golf course known as The Hunter's Yard. This would complete the equestrian and shooting facilities as well as offering swimming, a golf professional's shop, a restaurant, two bars and further conference facilities.
- Phase Four: the construction of low density self-contained properties throughout the estate.

Mount Juliet clearly had a message that could be communicated through different groups of journalists—property, golf, feature, gossip, diary, food, lifestyle, tourism. There was something for all of them at Mount Juliet and a planned, precise programme was targeted at each group, including visits to the site. Slattery knew the product well and were able to explain to each group where it fitted for them and when it would be on stream. On another level, as Padraig Slattery puts it, the business writers were being told "this place is not for sale. The sums add up".

As the time to open approached, a professional sales team would be in place but there was also the need to launch Mount Juliet on the European, American and international stages. Networking with consultancies in Scandinavia, Germany, France, Italy and Holland was planned. Slattery's previous work with Bord Fáilte also came to bear. They would be able to bring Mount Juliet to foreign audiences that logistically Slattery could not. This fitted in with Bord Fáilte's strategy of increasing the number of golfing holidays taken in Ireland.

IMPLEMENTATION

Jack Nicklaus first visited the site in July 1988. A leak at the British Open where Nicklaus had been playing, resulted in a huge press turn-out when he arrived at Waterford Airport in his own jet. Although not planned, this was a perfect launching pad for Mount Juliet. Nicklaus is considered one of the top designers in the world and this was to be his 80th course and his first in Ireland. Mount Juliet was firmly in the media spotlight and a plan was drafted to ensure this continued.

Local audiences were not neglected. The McCalmonts had been very facilitating to the local people and it was said that everybody in the Thomastown region learnt how to drive in the grounds. Things would change now, as security guards were posted and building went ahead. The local papers, especially the *Kilkenny People*, but also the *Nationalist and Leinster Times* and the *Munster Express*, were targeted. The message was clear—anybody would be welcome at Mount Juliet but they would have to pay. It would be expensive but it would be value for money. The estate also provided over 200 jobs during construction and another 200 when completed. The local towns of Thomastown and Inistioge were given a major economic boost and this was made clear by everyone involved.

Slattery attempted to be in the papers every week without resorting to advertising.

The message was going out that this was a quality leisure estate, second to nothing else in the country.

The "big house", now refurbished, was opened as a hotel by the then Minister for Tourism & Transport, Seamus Brennan, TD, on 21 October 1989. The hotel stood on its own with the other facilities not yet ready. Critical stories began to appear in the newspapers. Slattery were fire-fighting but continued to hype the Nicklaus connection. On each visit further information was released, e.g., he would not be designing any further courses in Ireland for at least another five years. The project was given a major boost when Mount Juliet was chosen as a location for US TV show *Good Morning America*. The sun shone, the Taoiseach, Charles Haughey, arrived and the presenters said "we are sitting here in one of the most beautiful places on earth".

The date for the opening, Sunday 14 July 1991, was to coincide with Nicklaus' attendance at the British Open. The media had attempted to build up a rivalry between Mount Juliet and the K Club, a somewhat similar development at Straffan House, Co. Kildare, that featured a course designed by Arnold Palmer. They had set their opening for the following day, 15 July, because Palmer also was only available around the British Open.

For the opening, a short golf clinic and match between Nicklaus and one of Ireland's greatest-ever golfers, Christy O'Connor, Snr, was to be the centre-piece. The referee was Joe Carr, Ireland's best-loved amateur golfer from the 1950s and incoming captain of the Royal and Ancient at St. Andrews.

Media facilitation was a priority. Most of the major Irish, UK and European writers had already enjoyed press trips to the estate. A coach was organised from the Shelbourne Hotel in Dublin on the day. The guest list, which was a who's who of Irish politics and business, provided plenty of pictures for social columns on Monday morning. Couriers were provided so that photographers' film would be back in Dublin for the first editions. The fact that Sunday is a "dead day" for the national papers also helped increase coverage.

Now that the visually impressive course was opening, television pictures were more important than the print media. A video was commissioned about the opening, on which RTE would collaborate, but it would be owned by Mount Juliet. Nicklaus, O'Connor and Carr were wired for sound as the opening round was played. This added to the interest for those attending and also provided excellent documentary footage. Nicklaus explained the thinking behind each hole as they went around the course. The video became *The Course that Jack Built* and was licensed to RTE, Sky Sports and an American video channel. Sky received good feedback after the first showing and it went on air another 12 times at no extra charge. The phone number for information on Mount Juliet was also included. This video has since been pirated, but nobody is objecting, and Slattery have now lost track of where it has been screened. They are aware it has gone as far afield as Australia.

Guests were well-catered for, being wined and dined in two gigantic marquees. Mahony even insisted on traditional Sunday roast beef. In his speech he spoke of the golf course being "the focus of a retreat for our wearied and harassed European neighbours". Local dignitaries were numbered amongst the guests as well as national celebrities.

Amidst the visiting celebrities, the local people and golf enthusiasts were not forgotten. Six hundred tickets were sold for the event at £25 each, the proceeds going to a Kilkenny charity for the mentally handicapped. The addition of the golf clinic meant these people were well catered for. The stewarding for the match was carried out by a group of 50 golfers from the nearby clubs of Kilkenny, Callan, Carlow, Castlecomer, and Borris. As a further gesture of good will the caddies were junior golfers from Carlow and Kilkenny. Even the music in the marquees was provided by a local big band. The security and catering was provided by Kilkenny firms. Besides ensuring favourable coverage in the local media and the creation of numerous angles for stories, these moves allayed fears that Mount Juliet would merely be a playground for the idle rich of the UK and Europe.

The entire operation, with 1600 people in attendance, went without a hitch. Nicklaus was in contention for the Ryder Cup that year—an added bonus as the sports journalists turned out and gave the match their attention. It was won by O'Connor, 72 to 74.

Since the opening Slattery have striven to keep Mount Juliet's high profile and quality reputation. "It is a kind of monster, Mount Juliet, in a sense. The nature of the beast is that it needs to be fed— it has to be fed publicity", explains Padraig Slattery. The fact that Mount Juliet was the venue for the Irish Open Golf Championship in 1993 and 1994 has helped. Over 70,000 visitors attend and corporate hospitality and associated sponsors are carefully catered for. Added to that, television pictures of the course are transmitted around the world and the golf professionals have voted it their favourite tournament of the tour.

Mount Juliet has a strong corporate identity, based around the logo of a pheasant silhouetted in front of an old fanlight window. All of its signage reads "Hotel and Leisure Estate".

Mount Juliet exploits as many different angles as possible. For the sporting fraternity, a number of successful horses run in the Mount Juliet colours and Darren Clarke originally represented the club on the European golf tour. The estate also facilitates fashion shoots, fashion shows and car launches. All of this works effectively as a form of reminder exposure.

EVALUATION

Slattery's work has been almost a text book example of how to exploit the angles around a project and create a quality reputation in people's minds over a period of time. The fact that they have managed to do this abroad as well is remarkable.

Typical angles presented to different media included charity donations by Nicklaus, Mount Juliet being the only course of its type to have a female director of golf, and the non-discriminatory nature of the membership. These were fully exploited and ensured that Mount Juliet stayed in the media spotlight.

A quality product is not always a guarantee of success and a number of difficulties, such as the 86 miles distance from Dublin, were successfully overcome. Bad publicity about receiving European funding for a private development was also turned on its head. The EU will only fund clubs that do not discriminate and in Ireland's case there are only a handful of courses that do not discriminate against women. This was made abundantly clear to those trying the rake up dirt on the development.

The Course that Jack Built was a tremendous success. Many visitors have mentioned it as their reason for coming to Mount Juliet. Americans were captured by the footage on *Good Morning America* and many of them have referred to it. Slattery's stated aim of making the national papers every week was also met and this has surely contributed to the estate's success with Irish golfers and sportsmen. The obvious trap of not stressing Nicklaus' credentials as a designer, but hoping his playing credentials would carry the course, was avoided.

The test in a development like this is whether it is attracting visitors. Despite some early difficulties, the Estate has been virtually full since the opening of the Hunter's Yard. During 1994, Michael Knox Johnston, director of operations, reported a 79.8 per cent occupancy.

There are around 50 corporate members of the golf club—each obtaining ten memberships for an annual fee of £12,000. There are no individual members, but everybody is welcome to come and play for £60 green fees. Green fees topped £600,000 in 1993, the third highest in the country. This fact was picked up by all the national papers.

An unexpected spin-off has been the large number of Jack Nicklaus "groupies" who travel to every one of his courses, mainly from the US. There are an estimated 50,000 of them and they provide a continuous business at Mount Juliet.

Slattery themselves put their success down to the fact that they were working with a quality product, were involved fully from the start of the £25 million project, and that Killeen Investments were aware of the importance of public relations. It is clear that public relations advice was asked on a number of issues that other companies would have left purely to internal management.

FOOTNOTE

In 1994, Murphy Brewery became the new sponsors of the Irish Open Golf Championship, taking over from P.J. Carroll after nearly 30 years. They brought fresh life and enthusiasm to the event and record crowds to Mount Juliet. Also, David Leadbetter, one of the world's leading golf instructors, has opened a golf academy at the club.

John Collins has a BA Degree in English & Philosophy from University College, Dublin and the DIT Diploma in Public Relations.

LEADING THE RACE INTO EUROPE

Ireland's Entry into the EEC
by Sinéad O'Toole

BACKGROUND

Ireland applied for membership of the European Economic Community (EEC) in 1961. The United Kingdom and Denmark also applied in 1961 and Norway in 1962. Following the French veto on British entry in 1963, action on the applications of Ireland, Denmark and Norway were suspended. All four reactivated their applications in 1967. No progress was made until the end of 1969. The negotiations with Ireland and the other three countries for the enlargement of the EEC were opened on 30 June 1970.

By early 1971 the negotiations were making good progress and they were concluded successfully in January 1972. Engineering the agreement for Irish entry and positioning Ireland properly in the enlarged community called for considerable diplomatic and negotiating skills. The Irish media had two big stories—accession and the Northern Ireland troubles. The international media concentrated on the troubles.

Pro-active public relations had not previously been engaged in on a continuous basis by the Irish civil service but it was now clear to the Minister for Foreign Affairs, Dr. Patrick Hillery, that a special information effort would be needed through the negotiations and the referendum. In December 1970, he invited Eilish MacCurtain, press and information officer in the Department of Posts & Telegraphs, to head a publicity/information unit as first secretary in-charge in the economic division of the Department of Foreign Affairs.

Foreign Affairs saw the information unit as an instrument to profile its leadership in the EEC campaign. The unit was up and running within a month. Eilish MacCurtain had two other first secretaries working with her. The team reported to Robin Fogarty, counsellor-in-charge, who with assistant secretary, Sean Morrissey, and Dr. Hillery were the principal Irish negotiators in Europe.

CHALLENGE

Eilish MacCurtain had worked in the public relations department of Bord Fáilte and as senior assistant in the Government Information Bureau before joining Posts & Telegraphs. She had built up wide community contacts with voluntary organisations and non-governmental agencies through her previous jobs as Irish national secretary of the European Youth Campaign and as national secretary of Macra na Tuaithe (now Foróige). She had also established good relations with the media.

The Government realised the need for a constant flow of reliable information to the

---

media and to the opinion formers as the negotiations progressed. Once the package was agreed in January 1972 the implications had to be addressed directly to the public as well as to the media in preparation for the referendum in May.

As negotiations for Irish entry to the EEC were at an initial and delicate stage, it was decided that Robin Fogarty would act as chief spokesperson to the media, particularly as the corps of five diplomatic correspondents, including RTE, accompanied the official party led by the Minister for Foreign Affairs. MacCurtain's main job was managing the unit and keeping a watching brief on how things were unfolding and to advise the Minister and Fogarty on all reactions and issues arising. While she recognised the dangers of not being totally in control, she realised that it was unrealistic for Foreign Affairs to put her in a role that was highly sensitive and technically new to her. In practical terms it would have been difficult to manage both roles anyway and Fogarty's communications skills were second to none.

There was no precedent in the civil service for such a campaign and there was anxiety lest the civil servants become politicised or be perceived to be aiding the Government in the spread of propaganda. The strategies of the campaign were therefore far from clear. There were to be a number of elements, including media relations and monitoring, and information had to be distributed to various sectors and to the general public, but it was not clear how this was to be achieved.

The Government realised that getting information to the opinion leaders and the public was extremely important. Particular attention had to be paid to the members of the Dáil and Seanad and the anti-EEC lobby groups.

THE CAMPAIGN

The campaign was in two stages:
- from January 1971 to the successful completion of the negotiations in January 1972
- from January to May 1972 when the referendum was held.

Special features of the campaign, in summary, included:
- publication of information booklets every few months, explaining how the EEC worked and the implications of Irish entry for different sectors and interest groups. Some leaflets were introduced to counter specific controversies, e.g. fisheries policy;
- distribution of these booklets to as wide a readership as possible
- limited advertising of the availability of the booklets
- constant liaison with the media, especially the diplomatic correspondents
- written reports presented by the Minister for members of the Oireachtas
- facility visits for journalists to the European institutions
- a commissioned survey of public opinion on proposed Irish entry
- liaison with bodies such as the Irish Council for the European Movement (ICEM) to spread awareness of the EEC and build up support for Irish entry
- meetings for special interest groups and the general public.

Publications

The first part of the campaign therefore, while the negotiations were still in progress, contained an important media element and also the beginning of the informational element. However the information was not definite at the time because negotiations were still taking place. It was important to portray an element of stability because if there were a gap someone would have filled it with anti-propaganda. The Government and the civil servants were the main promoters of the campaign; the Labour Party was against joining, as were the trade unions.

The information unit, as one of its first priorities, visited the European institutions in January 1971. The Irish negotiating team had just secured the translation of the Treaty of Rome into Irish. The Irish language was an important issue and the fact that Ireland had successfully negotiated a full version of the amended Treaty of Rome in Irish was very important politically at home.

The information unit then decided to publish a very basic document, which would tell people how the Common Market worked. It would be advertised on national television and would be widely available.

The Common Market and How it Works was issued in May 1971. It explained the Common Market, why it had been set up, how it worked, the institutions such as he European Parliament, the Council of Ministers, the Commission, the Court of Justice, the Economic and Social Committee, how decisions were taken, and what the Common Market had achieved since it was set up in 1958 in terms of economic growth, trade, increased wages etc. It had a nominal cover price of 3p (pre-decimal money) which allowed it to be sold through the Government Sales Office and through Easons.

There were no precedents. This was an entirely new departure for the civil service which had been extraordinarily inhibited and conservative about any kind of campaign advertising. One of the first things that Eilish MacCurtain did was to draw up a budget for the campaign, as this would help to focus people's concentration on the objectives of the programme. It also helped in reaffirming her professionalism to those in the civil service who didn't believe in public relations. The budget, about £16,000 for printing in a full year, seems tiny by to-day's standards.

The first booklet was difficult to produce as the writers were unsure of their brief. They had no experience in writing this kind of publication. As civil servants they were used to critical screening for everything they wrote so as to avoid any political controversy.

Booklets featuring special areas were published over the following months, for example, *Industry and Employment*, October 1971; *Agriculture*, December 1971 and *Regional Development*, January 1972.

The design of the booklets was very important. Again the civil service at that time had no idea of the relation between design and public relations. Therefore, any deviation from the normal literature produced by the civil service had to be conservative, yet eye-catching. There would be accusations of spreading propaganda if anything that looked like promotional-type literature was produced. Eilish MacCurtain chose The Kilkenny Design Workshops to design the booklets because they were avant-garde, but in a formal, corporate sense and not promotional. It was a good choice as their fastidious design approach was ideal and quelled the uneasiness and apprehension of the civil servants. Also, it was a state body and therefore tenders did not have to be sought from other suppliers.

The advertising campaign operated on a stop-start basis. Each time a new booklet was launched and sent out the advertisements would appear, giving the impression that information was emerging continually over a number of months. Negotiations were still in progress as the booklets were being published, so that there was going to be further need for more publications to address special issues and answer specific questions.

One difficulty in the advertising campaign was the sensitivity of Radio Telefis Eireann. The Broadcasting Act does not allow anything to be advertised on radio or television that has direct religious or political aims. RTE judged the EEC advertisements to be political, but only after the first one. The solution was to keep running the original slide each time a new publication was released.

Media

As has been pointed out, the campaign was able to prevent a volatile media coverage because the story was virtually exclusively covered by the diplomatic corps. This small group of five, or at most six journalists, had, perforce, to follow the negotiating team closely. This fact was effectively a clear channel of communication for them and thus reduced the workload of the information unit. This, in turn, released resources for other areas of communication. The role of public relations officer, at that time, was to discuss the public's reaction to press coverage, to inform the Minister what to be wary of and generally to analyse what was going on through the diplomatic correspondents and also to monitor the foreign journalists. Negotiations for UK and Danish entry were going on at the same time and UK papers like the *Financial Times, The Guardian* and *The Times* were very important for Ireland. The Irish campaign was of particular interest to the British and was reported fully.

UK coverage was sometimes negative and reflected an idea that Ireland was not sufficiently developed for full membership. The information unit had to be alert in reversing such trends through judicious briefing done, in the main, by Robin Fogarty.

Another exercise was to bring sections of the media to visit the European institutions. It was essentially a psychological exercise but it served its purpose. The information unit briefed all of the journalists in advance of their visits. The EEC paid for the trips so it cost the taxpayer nothing, but gave a supply of useful information for the journalists to write about. It resulted in priceless newspaper columns.

The first group to be brought out were the economic journalists and then women journalists. Eilish MacCurtain says it was "a shrewd move to involve the women journalists because they all wrote about it and women were 51 per cent of the electorate; so you had to get women readers' attention". Then there were the agricultural correspondents, the broadcasters from RTE, the education and industrial correspondents and so on. Denis Corboy was at that time the EEC representative in Dublin and he facilitated this activity.

Special reports were drawn up by the unit and circulated by the Minister to inform the members of the Dáil and Seanad. These helped to de-escalate the controversial aspects of the information campaign. Dr. Hillery's speeches on the EEC, at home and abroad, were fine-tuned to reflect policy and widely circulated to the media.

A plan was devised for securing platforms for speakers on EC membership which could be used by the media. There were constraints, however, because civil servants could not be linked with public meetings and government spokespersons were scarce. Labour and the trade unions were officially opposed and Fine Gael, the main opposition party, were in favour of entry but aloof.

The Attitude Survey

An attitude survey was commissioned by the Department of Foreign Affairs and issued in December 1971. Eilish MacCurtain saw it as a very significant feature of the campaign because it influenced the strategy in the final months to the referendum. There were no opinion polls at that time, so that the information was of vital importance. As it was an internal document it could not be published. It cost around £7,000, expensive for those times.

It was unlikely that the civil service had ever before used an attitude survey to gauge public opinion. It showed that a two-to-one majority of the population were in favour of Ireland's entry into the EEC. However, it also highlighted a large number of people who were undecided about which way they would vote in the referendum.

The primary purpose of the research, carried out by Irish Marketing Surveys Ltd was "to provide the government with information on how the public view the prospect of the country entering the European Economic Community".

In summary, 57 % of the Irish people were in favour of entry, with 24 % opposed and 19 % without any opinion. With such a floating vote the issue was wide open. The majority of people felt, in varying degrees, that Ireland would join the Common Market; indeed many saw it as almost a fait accompli. 87 % felt that Ireland could not afford to stay out, 84 % expected Ireland to join, 65 % felt there was really no alternative and 55% felt the Government would take Ireland into the EEC even if the referendum went against it.

Support for entry was strongest among the middle classes and the farmers. Opposition was strongest among the working class, especially in the cities. The survey also examined attitudes on how entry would affect Ireland—cost of living, standard of living, impact on industry, unemployment, welcome for foreigners, influence on "conservative" Irish way of life, prosperity of farmers. Many people felt that Ireland's entry to the EEC would enhance rather than hinder prospects for the unification of Ireland, but that was in December 1971, a month before the Bloody Sunday killings in Derry. The survey also showed that most people wanted more information on the EEC.

Irish Marketing Surveys recommended that in the remaining months before the referendum the Government promote the EEC concept and monitor shifts in public opinion.

The Referendum

Negotiations for the full membership of Ireland, the UK, Denmark and Norway to the EEC were completed in January 1972. Ireland, Norway and Denmark had to hold national referenda before entry could take place.

The information booklet, *Into Europe—Ireland and the EEC,* explained why the referendum had to be held. It stated: "Joining the European Communities will make it necessary to amend the Constitution so that we can undertake all of the obligations of membership. The proposal to amend the Constitution will be put to the people in a Referendum.

"As a member we shall be accepting the Treaties establishing the three Communities as well as the laws enacted by the Communities which give effect to the Treaties. The obligations of membership will arise for us in applying and implementing the Treaties and community laws. The amendment of the Constitution is necessary to avoid any incompatibility between the provisions of the Constitution and these obligations".

There was fear in Government circles that the anti-EEC lobby might get too strong. Some ministers wanted to attack them but the advice of the information unit was to keep cool. There were, however, some embarrassing moments, as when Dr Hillery said at Dublin Airport on his return from a visit to Brussels, that those who were against entry were unpatriotic. Then Brian Lenihan, a Government minister, accused opponents of being supporters of Castro's Cuba. Eilish Mac Curtain's advice was that the anti-EEC people should not be countered on their own terms. It would have put the Government on the defensive. For instance, the European Movement wanted to react when anti-EEC graffiti went up. They wanted to pull them down, but Eilish said not to. "People couldn't understand why I was advocating the idea of leaving the graffiti there and not putting up pro-EEC graffiti".

At the same time the anti-EEC lobby was getting stronger. The pro-EEC lobby needed to gain every column inch that they could. With the help of the Irish Council for the European Movement, mainly, and the Irish Countrywomen's Association, a series of public lectures and meetings were launched. The campaign got even more column inches as the principal speakers always made sure to say something newsworthy.

Polling day was 22 May 1972. The final campaign ploy to sway those who were still undecided was a full-page advertisement on the previous Sunday in the two newspapers in the form of a very simplistic comic strip. However this could have been misconstrued as propagandist if published by the information unit. It was agreed that the advertisement would be written and prepared by the Irish Council for the European Movement and Fianna Fáil who would jointly place it, pay for it and be fully responsible. MacCurtain advised on the choice of copywriter for this project.

On the same Sunday the final booklets were distributed free at the church gates. They were in both English and Irish. They were also available in post offices and shops.

The then Taoiseach, Jack Lynch, gave a press conference the day preceding the referendum to a representative group of international media in addition to the national media. This had been set up through Ireland's diplomatic missions abroad, concentrating mainly on European countries. The main objective was to set the stage for a probable victory for the Government in the referendum and to reinforce Ireland's right to full membership. In the event of a 'no' result, at least Ireland's claim to membership would have been spelt out to the international media. On the day following the referendum a press centre was set up in Iveagh House for the results as they came in. This was an essential exercise and the international press corps followed it on TV monitors and radios set up in the press centre.

EVALUATION

The referendum resulted in an overwhelming vote for EEC entry. The Yes vote was 83.1 per cent. No further evaluation of the campaign took place; it had been an outstanding success. This was in contrast to referenda in other countries which were only passed by narrow margins. Norway voted against, stayed out and were to do the same again 22 years later.

As a result of the campaign attitude surveys were used more extensively in the civil service and the place of design in publications began to be recognised.

During the campaign there was constant evaluation, especially of media reaction to the negotiations, and the attitude survey was an accurate evaluation of attitudes which influenced the later stages of the campaign.

Eilish MacCurtain was retained in the post-referendum period and during 1973, Ireland's year of accession. Her work now evolved around keeping the domestic and foreign press briefed on the progress within the new community. At the end of that year she married Brian Pearce and went to work in Ethiopia. She now runs a public relations consultancy in Dublin.

FOOTNOTE

In 1971 pro-active public relations was a new idea for the civil service. There was fear

Dr. Patrick Hillery, then Minister for Foreign Affairs (left) and Jack Lynch, then Taoiseach, sign Ireland into the European Economic Community, 1973.

that the civil service would be politicised and that information on an issue that the people were divided upon would be seen as propaganda. There was concern at Government money being spent to promote one viewpoint.

There had, however, already been a major public relations and information campaign in 1969 involving public relations people from state companies, to promote Ireland's case in the Northern Ireland troubles. This campaign had some problems. Also, Markpress, an international public relations company, got a government contract around that time and this, too, ran into some problems with the home media. Eilish MacCurtain had not participated in the 1969 campaign.

There do not seem to be any scruples now about pro-active public relations, but there is some concern. In 1994, the Government announced its proposal to spend £500,000 on pro-divorce advertising in the coming referendum campaign. Bishop Brendan Comiskey of Ferns said that this was not in accordance with the principles of democracy and even those who took an opposite line on divorce had to agree that his argument about democracy was correct.

Said John Waters in *The Irish Times:* "There is more at stake than fair play. The proposed expenditure of the taxpayer's money to advance what for the moment remains a partisan argument on a constitutional issue represents a profound breach of natural justice.......It surely cannot be right for the Government to use the people's own money to browbeat them into changing an article of their own Constitution. It is entitled to make a polite request, explain its position, and no more......It is clear, therefore, that the government should either place equal amounts of money at the disposal of both sides of the argument, or, better still, refrain from spending any public money on such advertising at all".

Senator Shane Ross, in the *Sunday Independent,* voiced the same view in support of Bishop Comiskey: "A dangerous principle is slowly crawling all over us. A politically partisan government is now setting out brazenly to use Irish people's money to advertise its . point of view. None of the groups opposed to divorce is conceivably capable of matching such a large sum in the coming campaign.......We are about to witness an uneven battle. No level playing field here".

Sinéad O'Toole, has a BA Degree in Psychology from University College, Dublin, and the DIT Diploma in Public Relations.

THE TASTE OF THE MEDITERRANEAN

The Olive Oil Information Campaign
by Francis Xavier Carty

BACKGROUND

In April 1991, the European Commission started a two-year information campaign to promote olive oil in Ireland. Similar programmes were run in the other EU member states.

The campaign came under the Common Agricultural Policy (CAP) and was designed to supplement the low incomes of the two million families who work in olive oil production in Spain, Italy, Greece, Portugal and France. It was the fifth European campaign for olive oil, but the first for Ireland.

Olive oil has an ancient history as rich and classic as its pure flavour. Dating back to the days of the Phoenicians and Egyptians in 500 BC, it is one of the oldest and most natural ingredients in the world. The earliest reference to olive trees is in the Bible where the dove returns to Noah's Ark from Mount Ararat with an olive branch in its beak. The story marks an important event in the history books, symbolising peace and harmony in the world.

Olive trees can live for a long time, often between 300 and 600 years. Some of those from the Garden of Gethsemane in Jerusalem are believed to have been there since the time of Christ.

Small family-owned industries still account for a lot of the production in Europe. It is labour-intensive but yields an income that is usually lower than national averages. The olives have often to be hand-picked because machinery cannot be brought up the rugged hillsides. Also, they perish rapidly.

It was a generic campaign for olive oil and not for any particular brand. It encompassed all grades of oil—Extra Virgin, Virgin, Olive Oil and Olive-Pomace Oil, although Extra Virgin and Olive Oil are the only grades normally seen in Ireland. Grades are based on quality of oil and level of acidity. Extra Virgin is the top quality, usually darker in colour and with a more distinct flavour. The ordinary olive oil, or 'pure' olive oil grade, more common in Ireland, is lighter in colour.

The Irish campaign was at two levels:
* dissemination of scientific and nutritional information to health professionals
* information for consumers about the gastronomic and taste properties of olive oil, and its nutritional qualities as a healthy fat alternative in a balanced diet

Grayling handled the public relations for the Irish campaign. Working for Grayling with managing director, Jim Rowe, were Sandra McDowell, Gillian Fanning and, for briefer periods, Fiona Walsh and Barry Ahern. Sister companies of Grayling handled the campaign in other countries, including the UK. This facilitated close co-operation including the common use of some promotional materials.

Grayling's client was the European Commission in Brussels which laid down strict guidelines to ensure co-ordination and consistency in the national campaigns. Everything had to be approved before publication and care taken that findings were based on proper research. There was concern that over-elaborate claims might be made for the benefits of olive oil, especially as regards heart disease. There was a common logo and corporate identity for literature and promotional materials.

The public relations budget for the two years was £300,000.

Olive Oil Information Bureau
A central feature of the campaign was the Olive Oil Information Bureau that was based at Grayling's offices in Dublin for the two years of the campaign, April 1991 to March 1993. However, as is common in such campaigns, it was the Bureau rather than the public relations company that was referred to in all dealings with the media and the health organisations.

The Bureau was the umbrella organisation for all activity and the source for all information. It had an advisory panel spearheaded by a consultant dietician, Ursula O'Dwyer, and included a leading cardiologist, Professor Ian Graham, and a general practitioner, Dr. John Cox, with a special interest in the role of fat in the diet.

The Commission supplied a considerable amount of research material and scientific information but each country also did its own local research.

CONSUMER INFORMATION CAMPAIGN

The public relations and the advertising campaigns were complementary in the consumer information campaign. Advertising was handled by Arks, which, with Grayling, is a member of Lopex plc, an international group of communications companies.

Key objectives
- to encourage trial of EU olive oil and increase consumption
- to educate consumers to be in a position to make a well-informed choice
- to develop awareness of the gastronomic and health qualities of olive oil

Target audiences
- all adult consumers, with the core audience of women in the ABC1 social category
- chefs
- restaurateurs
- opinion-formers in women's consumer organisations and the catering industry

Retailers were not a specific target, the idea being that, if a consumer demand were created and the product was already there, the trade would soon start buying more.

Public relations strategy

A number of elements were combined including:

- positioning olive oil as a tasty, healthy fat alternative and a premier oil for all culinary use, while differentiating between the various grades
- communicating the wide variety of flavours in all grades of olive oil, as well as aromas and colours
- generating awareness of the versatility of olive oil, linking it to not only the finest of Mediterranean cuisine, but also traditional-style Irish dishes for all occasions
- conveying the health benefits of olive oil in simple terms that could be easily understood
- providing the media and consumers with the skills to introduce olive oil to their diet, such as attractive recipes and serving suggestions, aimed at stimulating trial and increasing usage

There was sensitivity towards the dairy industry and suggestions that the campaign was taking sales away from butter. Grayling had a holding statement that they were promoting olive oil as complementary to butter and not as a substitute for it.

The Olive Oil Information Bureau display stand which was used at medical and paramedical meetings and conferences.

IMPLEMENTATION

Olive Oil Information Bureau
The Bureau was responsible for:
- acting as an information source about EU olive oil
- providing both media and consumers with generic product information, covering general interest, gastronomic and health aspects, via a series of handouts titled: *Olive Oil —A Gastronomic Delight; The Versatility of Olive Oil; Olive Oil—A Healthy Alternative; Olive Oil— Growing, Harvesting and Production;* and *The Olive Oil Information Bureau— Answering Your Questions*
- media relations, both initiating activity and responding to enquiries
- supplying olive oil ingredient recipes, with colour transparencies, from salad dressing, appetisers and entrées through to desserts, cakes and breads, to national, female interest and provincial media. Recipes also formed part of the information pack for consumers
- distributing leaflets about oils and health in general, as well as olive oil

Competitions
These emphasised the health properties and taste qualities of olive oil. They were run on local radio stations and in consumer magazines as well as provincial and national newspapers.

Chefs' competition
There was a national competition for chefs, run in conjunction with the Panel of Chefs in Ireland and its 138 members. Six finalists were chosen from mailed-in entries to compete in a grand final at DIT Cathal Brugha Street. The adjudication panel included the chairman of the Panel of Chefs and journalist Helen Lucy Burke who was known to be a great fan of olive oil.

Launch press reception and teach-in
The media event to launch the Olive Oil Information Bureau and familiarise the press more fully with olive oil included:
- tasting a variety of EU olive oils (Extra Virgin and Olive Oil grades)
- an address by a leading dietician on the nutritional qualities of olive oil
- an address by an EU representative regarding the objectives of the campaign
- a presentation by a top chef on the versatility of olive oil as a recipe ingredient
- fine Mediterranean cuisine with olive oil used in each dish
- generic product information covering the growing, harvesting and refining procedures; gastronomic details; health story etc

Press visit
Honor Moore, a leading consumer food journalist, was brought to Italy to visit an olive-growing region and see the harvesting and pressing procedure. She joined an Italian press group with an interpreter.

Leading chef John Cooke, proprietor of Cooke's Café, at the launch of the EU Olive Oil information campaign, April 1991

"Happy Heart Eat Out" promotion

At the end of the campaign there was a week-long restaurant promotion to focus attention on healthy eating. It was run in conjunction with The Irish Heart Foundation in Dublin and in those parts of the country where the IHF had representatives and volunteers available to promote it.

An information pack containing Healthy Eating Guidelines, recipes incorporating olive oil and door and menu stickers featuring the Happy Heart Eat Out logo, was sent to participating restaurants (they were advised of the promotion by letter and replied if they were interested in participating).

Media relations in a campaign like this is challenging because for a lot of the time there is not anything new happening and it is difficult to develop fresh angles. Activity at the Olive Oil Information Bureau came and went in bursts. At the beginning a media relations schedule was drawn up and all relevant journalists informed and given press packs. Whenever there was a competition in a provincial newspaper, especially, there was an increase in enquiries from that part of the country for a couple of weeks. Each piece of publicity, not just a competition, but an editorial piece, or an offer for a recipe booklet, led to approximately 200 enquiries at the Olive Oil Information Bureau.

HEALTH PROFESSIONALS PROGRAMME

The programme for health professionals used public relations activity only. Operated through the Olive Oil Information Bureau, it involved dissemination of scientific data to:
- general practitioners (GPs) who were a primary audience
- dieticians and nutritionists
- medical consultants such as cardiologists, hospital practitioners etc
- public health nurses
- health-related organisations
- opinion-formers in the health sector

The programme also addressed secondary school students through home economics teachers.

The key objective was to communicate the messages so that health professionals would be well-informed of the nutritional value of olive oil as a major source of monounsaturated fat and of its role in the prevention of coronary heart disease, as well as its benefits for early bone development and for people with diabetes and cancer.

IMPLEMENTATION

- Media relations focused on the medical media—medical magazines, health correspondents in national newspapers, health programmes on television and radio.
- Briefing sessions for journalists, and others, usually involved Ursula O'Dwyer and one or two representatives from the health organisations.
- A four-page quarterly newsletter, *Oils & Health Update,* for health professionals, focused on olive oil and its contribution to a healthy diet as a major source of monounsaturated fat. It published scientific research studies and reports, and gave the latest scientific thinking, such as the role of monounsaturated fat in the prevention of coronary heart disease, diabetes and cancer. Some of the material was shared with similar newsletters in the other countries.
- Participation at medical and paramedical conference exhibitions. These involved olive oil sampling and distribution of scientific information. Care had to be taken not to promote individual brands in the samplings. The solution was to mix different oils of the same grade, say French, Italian and Spanish, and serve them in decanters.
- Participation at faculty meetings of the Irish College of General Practitioners (ICGP). There are 2500 GPs and groups of them often have meetings sponsored by pharmaceutical companies in different parts of the country. The Olive Oil Information Bureau basically sponsored selected meetings, bringing a dietician to give a slide presentation and talk about olive oil. Again there were samplings and distribution of literature.
- A leaflet for consumers, *A Guide to Oils and Health,* was produced and distributed through general practitioners—50 for every waiting room in the country.
- Diet sheets were produced and distributed to consumers via general practitioners—20 pads for each waiting room or surgery so the doctor could tear one off for a patient if recommending a change in diet.
- An educational programme for secondary school students was initiated within the home economics course. Kits were distributed with olive oil information, full-colour recipe cards incorporating olive oil and an entry form to a competition which offered crystal olive oil decanters and Olive Oil Information Bureau branded aprons and kitchen appliances as prizes.

EVALUATION

Consumer programme

It was difficult to confirm increase in sales because importers/distributors were reluctant to divulge the information.

Figures from the Central Statistics Office (CSO) based on imports of olive oil into Ireland from Europe are:

1990: £500,000

1991: £1,223,000

1992: £1,691,000

These figures show a tripling of olive oil imports over the two years of the campaign. Some other market details were sought through an informal survey among importers/ distributors. The research method was not very scientific and limited credence was given to it, but it suggested that from April 1991 to the end of 1992 there were increases of:

- 59 per cent in the total retail market
- 58.5 per cent in the supermarket sector
- 67.5 per cent in the catering market
- 100 per cent and more for some importers/distributors

There was limited evidence that between June 1991 and June 1992, the number of consumers purchasing olive oil in a specific period increased from 3.1 to 5.3 per cent; many bought two bottles where previously they bought one; the frequency of purchases also increased as did the money spent per litre, indicating a shift to the more expensive brands.

Health professionals programme

Surveys through informal interview were carried out among a sample of 40 general practitioners, nutritionists/dieticians and public health nurses to assess increased awareness of the health qualities of olive oil. They were at the beginning, middle and end of the campaign and, wherever possible, the same people were contacted on each occasion.

Results indicated that awareness of the nutritional benefits of monounsaturated fats, and olive oil in particular, had risen significantly over the two years. This was especially evident in the case of general practitioners and dieticians/nutritionists, who now seemed to be recommending olive oil far more often to their patients.

Francis Xavier Carty has a BSc Degree from University College, Dublin, an MA in Irish Politics, also from UCD and a BSc (Econ) in Government from the University of London. He is Course Director for the DIT Diploma in Public Relations.

MAXIMISING HEALTH AND SAFETY AT WORK

The Extension to the European Year of Safety, Health and Hygiene at Work
by Michèle Aboud

INTRODUCTION

The European Year of Safety, Health and Hygiene at Work 1992 ran from March 1992 to March 1993. Co-ordinated by a National Liaison Committee for the European Year, the programme of activity culminated in the signature of a Statutory Instrument, SI number 44 of 1993, bringing more than 20 EC Directives on health and safety at work into Irish law. The provisions cover general safety and health, the workplace, work equipment, use of personal protective equipment, manual handling of loads, VDU workstations and the use of visual display units, use of electricity, first aid and the notification of accidents and dangerous occurrences, as well as a range of measures relating to dangerous substances and preparations.

Workplace health and safety is a serious issue in Ireland—it has been calculated that the economic costs of accidents at work are running at more than £300 million a year. There were 2779 non-fatal accidents reported in 1991 and 2874 in 1992. But these figures are known to be conservative because of the prevalence of under-reporting.

The National Authority for Occupational Safety and Health, known as the Health and Safety Authority (HSA), in conjunction with the social partners, undertook a major programme for the European Year supported by EC funding of £250,000. A calendar of events was drawn up for each month of the programme, addressing specific topics or sectors. Activities included conferences, seminars, lectures, surveys and special promotional initiatives in line with the objectives for the Year, which were:
* to increase awareness of health and safety at work
* to improve the information available on the risks and necessary safeguards to ensure safe and healthy working
* to improve dissemination of the information to each of the sectoral target audiences.

The Statutory Instrument—the Safety, Health and Welfare at Work (general application) Regulations—was signed into law by the Minister for Enterprise & Employment on 22 February 1993.

Following its assessment of the achievements of the European Year, the European Commission decided that funding would be made available for a continuation programme in four countries—Denmark, Greece, Ireland and Portugal. *Extending the Impact,* running for the six-month period to October 1993, was structured around a programme to raise awareness of the new legislation and its implications for all workplaces.

FROM JOHN PAUL TO SAINT JACK.......

BACKGROUND

The Health and Safety Authority is an Irish government agency, having both educational and enforcement functions. Officials from the HSA were members of the National Liaison Committee for the European Year, which authorised the levels of funding for the Irish programme, both for the year and its extension. The theme of the Year itself was *Getting the Message Across*; the extension to the Year aimed at consolidating and building upon the awareness created.

Setanta Communications were engaged to handle public relations for the continuation of the European Year. While the day-to-day client for Setanta was the Health and Safety Authority in Dublin, their ultimate client was the European Commission through Infopublique, a subsidiary of Shandwicks in Brussels. Infopublique was charged by the Commission with overseeing and co-ordinating activities throughout Europe. Working on the account for Setanta were Michael Moloney, managing director, with executives Vincent Quinn and Sinéad Ó Duinnín.

Unlike the year itself, the continuation was not an imposed programme, as sometimes an international or pan-European programme may be. Setanta and the HSA worked with the EU on a broad parameter, but made local decisions to fit local needs. Although the Commission specified that certain issues should be addressed, latitude was allowed in the way that they were handled.

The continuation only applied to Ireland, Denmark, Greece and Portugal. Ireland was included amongst the four countries as the Commission regarded proposals formulated by the HSA during the Year itself as innovative and promising.

THE CHALLENGE

To build on the activity undertaken during the European Year itself and to create awareness of the 1993 legislation on health and safety in the workplace—the Safety, Health and Welfare at Work (general application) Regulations, 1993.

PLANNING

Since the HSA is an 'expert' client with ready access to statistics and information, Setanta did not have to engage in primary research. The objectives of the continuation programme were also clearly defined. Setanta's primary area of activity was media relations and publicity and in this they were given an wide-ranging brief.

In general terms, the audience to whom the programme was directed was 'everybody at work'; more specifically, there were a number of key audiences, including employers, employees and the self-employed, all of whom required a set of specific messages.

While numerous news and feature angles were developed for news, general interest and specialised publications, Setanta viewed the local media as especially important. Practically all Irish companies fall into the small and medium enterprise (SME) sector, employing from 5 to 100 people. Because of their small size in European terms, work practices (including health and safety provisions) may not be formalised to any great extent. Many companies have no structured programme of internal communications and it is not as easy as in other countries to communicate with the workforce through internal newsletters. Companies may not be unionised, closing off another avenue for information. Therefore there is an increased need for the effective use of the media to bring across the message.

In common with the situation in several other EU member states, the local print media in Ireland are extremely important. Local newspapers remain in the home (or the workplace) for an extended period, being read and re-read. Thus, for it to be fully effective, the programme had to have local as well as national news angles—the stories had to have a local resonance for everybody to feel involved.

This attention to local media was to bear fruit in the campaign. One-to-one briefings were held in advance, a tactic not usually appreciated by Dublin-based bodies in national campaigns.

IMPLEMENTATION

Prior to the Health, Safety and Welfare at Work Act, 1989, some 20 to 25 per cent of workplaces in Ireland were covered by health and safety legislation. Within four years, with the signature of the Statutory Instrument in 1993, every workplace had been brought under the legal framework. However, even in workplaces that had been covered by the law previously, there was a lack of knowledge of the legal requirements.

The first objective therefore was to let everybody know that fundamental legislation had been passed. Central to the awareness-raising activity was getting people to understand their new obligations.

The keynote message was:
* increasing workplace health and safety is in everyone's interest.

The problem of under-reporting was highlighted, since this maintains a false sense of security and disguises the real cost to the national economy of lax health and safety standards.

There were some key issues to be stressed. Every workplace is required to have a Safety Statement and it is the responsibility of the employer to draw this up. It is, essentially, a safety checklist, identifying the hazards in the workplace and how they are to be tackled. An important concept is that of risk assessment—the safeguards that are to be put in place (such as eliminating the hazard entirely through changing the manufacturing process, isolating dangers by physical devices such as guards, or decreasing the danger by improving staff training and awareness) must be appropriate and directly related to the nature of the hazard itself.

Another central tenet of the legislation is that of employer/employee consultation. Employees must be consulted on any matters dealing with health and safety in the workplace—this includes bringing health and safety issues into the worker participation process in companies where participation structures exist. Employees have the right to appoint their own safety representatives, with whom the employer must consult. Where the risks justify it, health surveillance must be made available to employees. Linked with these provisions is the requirement that employees must co-operate with the employer in implementing health and safety measures, making proper use of all tools, machinery and substances and wearing the personal protective equipment that the employer is required to provide.

Some of the changes in legislation might surprise some people. For example, there is no longer any maximum limit on the weight that a man or woman can lift—the legislation now says that where possible there should be no manual handling at all and, if this must take place, there must be proper equipment to ensure that it is done without risk.

There is a whole series of provisions which are either extensions, or completely new, to Irish law. For example, where the work or the nature of the workplace warrants it, there must be rest areas for workers, facilities for pregnant women, for nursing mothers and for employees with disabilities.

The law now sets out conditions for the use of visual display units (VDUs). The employer has to assess the environment of every VDU workstation for space, background light, noise, heat and humidity and the workstation itself for reflection and glare off the screen, the type of keyboard and the software used. The desk, chair and operator's positioning in front of the VDU must also form part of the assessment. Employees are entitled to adequate breaks from screen work and to eye tests and spectacles if needed: both of these are to be paid for by the employer.

The first task was to illustrate aspects of the legislation to a whole series of audiences, effectively covering everyone at work. Furthermore, manufacturers are now responsible for the safety of the equipment that they supply, including substances such as chemicals and packing.

A further need was to alert persons in charge of any workplace that they are now responsible for injuries done to non-workers on the premises or to passers-by and they must introduce procedures to, as far as possible, prevent such injuries from happening.

The announcement of the regulations coming into force was handled through a press conference at the headquarters of the Health and Safety Authority. Setanta devised news stories for trade and consumer publications to communicate these points. It was important to make it clear that primary responsibility was being placed upon the employer, defined to include persons who are self-employed.

National Conference

In March 1993 there was a national conference at the Royal Hospital Kilmainham to highlight the new regulations. It was attended by all of the concerned interests, including industrialists and trade union representatives. There was emphasis in the keynote statement by the Minister for Labour Affairs, Mary O'Rourke TD, on the £300 million annual cost of accidents at work.

Peter Cassells, general secretary of the Irish Congress of Trade Unions (ICTU), gave a paper on consultation between employers and employees. John Dunne, director general of the Irish Business and Employers' Confederation (IBEC), dealt with the commitment of management to safety. Setanta developed several news angles from this conference, both for the national and the regional media.

Step by Step

An interesting project which formed part of the programme was the launch of the CD and tape *Step by Step—Workers' Songs on Safety*. The idea grew out of a series of three concerts held during the European Year itself and the recordings were supported by the EC from a separate budget, the object being to make the package available throughout Europe.

The package was a combination of new and old songs and Setanta undertook the launch and the following promotion. There was a very good response from the radio stations—six programmes on national radio carried interviews or discussion and *Step by Step* made the playlist of twenty local stations, with more than half of these also carrying interviews.

Safety on the Farm

Farmers (both as employers and as self-employed) and farm workers were first covered by the Health, Safety and Welfare at Work Act, 1989. The 1993 legislation introduced new requirements (such as the need to provide adequate first aid facilities) in common with every other workplace.

Because of the close connection between work and family life on the farm, farmers' families and children may have a daily exposure to a whole series of hazards, ranging from dangerous livestock and farm machinery to slurry gas and chemicals. Strong emphasis was therefore put on the need for effective health and safety measures in the agricultural sector.

The European Commissioner for Social Affairs, Pádraig Flynn, undertook a dual announcement of the HSA programme for the health and safety of children on farms and the video and training pack on safe tractor driving commissioned by the Irish Farmers' Association Farm Family Committee. The difficulty in generating media coverage of this event lay in the fact that it had to be scheduled for 5 pm on a Friday—not normally a good time, but in this case the only time that the Commissioner was available.

A tractor was brought into Dublin city centre and photographers from three of the national papers turned up to see Commissioner Flynn demonstrate the danger areas—particularly the power take off (PTO) shaft.

Photographs were used in the *Irish Independent* and *Irish Press* and the three other national papers ran it as a news story. Coverage was given in all the agricultural supplements as well as the regional press, farming publications and a broad range of magazines. The *Irish Independent* found the press release, which was titled "Irish farms—killing fields for our children?" newsworthy in itself—an article in its praise said that, at first, they had thought it 'a bit over the top', but on close reading, they agreed the theme had been well-chosen.

Consultation

One of the main themes of the legislation is the requirement for consultation between employers and employees. The first of an annual series of seminars for trade unionists on employer/employee consultation and co-operation was held to mark May Day. Emphasis was placed on:

- the need for employers and employees to talk to each other to solve problems in the workplace, and
- the right of employees to be consulted on health and safety matters and to select their own safety representative who will work with the employer in planning health and safety and eradicating hazards.

The seminar was used to publicise the presentation of the first "Safety Representative of the Year" award, reinforcing its messages.

Awareness weeks

As part of the local media campaign, Health and Safety Awareness Weeks were organised in two regions—the Midlands (mid-June) and the North West (early September).

A common format was adopted, with a programme of seminars and news events/ stories involving the Health and Safety Authority's regional office, employers' organisations, trade unions, the local authorities, health boards and government bodies. However, the focus of each week differed, to reflect the industrial bases of each region. In the Midlands (counties Longford, Offaly, Roscommon and Westmeath), the awareness week stressed health and safety in agriculture. That in the North Western region (counties Sligo, Leitrim and Donegal) focused on the fishing industry.

Both weeks included a series of events, advertised in the local press, which highlighted the type and frequency of local accidents. Setanta did not organise the events— that was usually the responsibility of the HSA working with bodies such as SIPTU (Services Industrial Professional Technical Union) or the IFA (Irish Farmers' Association).

Setanta were responsible for generating and maximising media coverage. They briefed all of the local media in advance and supplied detailed programmes and materials. This led to good publicity and such headlines as "The Life Savers are Coming". Photographers even covered the briefings. The Midlands week was launched at Elan Pharmaceuticals in Athlone by Mary O'Rourke who is the local TD and was then Minister for Labour Affairs.

During each of the weeks, the HSA sent a team of inspectors to a wide range of companies and organisations, including farms, industry, offices, schools, hospitals and fishing boats, to identify problems and give advice on safe working practices and eliminating hazards. The inspectors gathered baseline date for the programme at the same time.

In each region they found wide variations in standards of health and safety. Although there had been a general increase in awareness since the introduction of the legislation, not all of its areas were understood. Inspectors found a general lower awareness in the North West than in the Midlands. There was lack of knowledge of the Safety Statement and a reluctance of seamen to wear protective clothing. There was a high attendance at the Safety Events during each week—many of these events being aimed at employees in the local community and open to the public.

The North Western week involved more seminars and demonstrations than in the Midlands. For instance, there was a tree-felling demonstration, showing the safe use of chain saws. The launch was conducted by the Mayor of Sligo and included an inspection of the factory with the best safety record in the region.

One key target for this week was the fishing industry. Minister O'Rourke was again involved, launching a safety seminar at the major fishing port of Killybegs and, later the same day, a safety video for Bord Iascaigh Mhara—The Irish Sea Fisheries Board, at Greencastle, Co Donegal. The Killybegs seminar was featured by RTE in a review of the week's activity on the 9 o'clock evening news.

Launch of HSA Annual Report

The launch of the HSA Annual Report was used to highlight some of the themes emerging. It took place against the background of an unexpected increase in fatalities during the summer and a heavily-publicised explosion at the Hickson chemical factory in Cork. Both were used to draw out news angles around the annual report and helped to put flesh upon its statistics.

National Ploughing Championships

There was a renewed push towards the agricultural sector at the time of the National Ploughing Championships in September, the biggest event in the year for farmers and suppliers of farm equipment.

This led to further features in the agricultural and farm press highlighting the statistics of dangers on the farm. The *Irish Farmers' Journal*, the most widely read publication for farmers, ran a substantial piece on some of the less-obvious health and safety risks, including the manual handling of loads and first-aid, covering all of the messages which the campaign was concerned with bringing across.

EVALUATION

Monitoring of health and safety at work is ongoing, with the HSA evaluating the situation and compiling statistics. This research was available to Setanta Communications at all stages in the planning and implementation of its media campaigns.

The success of such a campaign is judged not only in the quantity and quality of press cuttings, but in the change in attitude which is created. And that will only happen slowly.

During 1993, the year which covered the Extension, workplace inspections increased by 13 per cent, enforcement notices by more than 45 per cent and prosecutions by 72 per cent, with enforcement actions in 26 cases. The main causes of accidents, according to Tom Walsh, Director General of HSA, were "slips, trips and falls". These accounted for 30 per cent of accidents, and they were due "mainly to poor housekeeping and untidy workplaces".

Under-reporting of workplace accidents and occupational diseases was still a major problem. "We were expecting the accident figures to rise substantially during 1993, since 20 pieces of legislation were introduced. Reported accidents went up by more than 20 per cent but studies indicate that 80 per cent of all workplace accidents and 95 per cent of ill-health caused by work are still not being notified."

There are, therefore, signs that, as a result of the Year and the Extension, more accidents are being reported, but it will be some years before attitudes shift sufficiently so that all accidents and injuries at work are reported. For instance, it is hard to believe that there was only one non-fatal accident in agriculture in 1991 and three in 1992, but that is the picture that the reported cases present.

As reporting improves, there will inevitably be an increase in the number of incidents and this will distort comparisons with earlier years.

For the health and safety legislation to be really successful, it has to change standards of behaviour—how people approach situations, such as ensuring that the machinery being installed is safe and that all workplace hazards are eliminated, rather than allowing bad practices to persist and expecting people to behave safely.

Many things have to change. The European Year and Extension are only a beginning. People should expect to be safe at work. Workplace Health and Safety programmes can perhaps be compared to the drink-drive campaign, in that it has taken a long time and forthright public debate to change attitudes. People now say, "No, I am driving and not drinking". There are people doing that naturally nowadays, who twenty years ago would not have dreamt of taking a taxi home.

Speaking at the launch of the HSA annual report in September 1994, Minister O'Rourke said it "may be time to take a sterner line" in enforcing the law. "Enforcement notices and prosecutions both rose last year", she said, "signalling a clear warning that the authority's inspectors will not hesitate to use their powers if people are heedless of hazards, dangers and their responsibilities towards others".

The Irish media are receptive to the safety issue. They have taken it seriously and reported it positively. They have not seen coverage as free plugs for any commercial organisation.

The Extension of the European Year ended in October 1993, but certain important areas will continue to be addressed through build-on activities run as part of the Health and Safety Authority's information functions for the foreseeable future. Areas for emphasis include under-reporting in the construction industry, with a directive due soon from the EU. Another directive will concern pregnant workers.

Michèle Aboud has a BA Degree in Sociology & Economics from St. Patrick's College, Maynooth and the DIT Diploma in Public Relations.

CIDER FIGHTS TO CLEAR ITS NAME

The Role of the Cider Industry Council
by Barry Kenny

BACKGROUND

Cider is one of the most traditional and natural alcoholic drinks. Apples are crushed, the juice is left to ferment, and that is the product. It has been a popular drink for centuries, particularly in rural Britain and Ireland. With this type of history it seems inconceivable that it could be a product with a very serious "image" problem, but it is.

Through the 1980s, cider became associated with underage drinking and social unrest and was branded as a "cheap" drink. This was largely due to media coverage of drink-related incidents, mostly at concerts, celebrations for results of school examinations and other lively gatherings of young people.

Showerings of Clonmel produce Bulmers and all other Irish cider brands, accounting for 90 per cent of the market. In 1988, they approached Gilmore Communications, the Dublin public relations consultancy, for help in improving the image of cider, and winning it an equal footing with other products in the beer market. Cider had a credibility problem among mature drinkers and was competing poorly with rival products.

Showerings were worried about the association with rowdiness and underage drinking. Cider had a mere 5 per cent of the beer market, yet was being given 95 per cent of the blame for any incident that occurred. An audit of the previous six months' media coverage was carried out by Gilmore and the situation was horrific. Expressions like "cider-crazed youths" and "cider parties" and "cheap cider" were rampant in newspaper reports and features.

THE CHALLENGE

"To counteract and minimise the extent of negative publicity about cider per se, and to promote a positive promotional platform for improving the market for Bulmers and other Showerings products".

STRATEGY

It was decided that this was not just a Bulmers or a Showerings problem—it concerned the entire industry. Gilmore Communications investigated some of the more damning reports from the media. It transpired, as had been suspected, that cider was being used as a convenient cliché when journalists covered drink-related incidents and underage drinking. Rarely was cider exclusively to blame—lagers and cheap vodka, amongst other

FROM JOHN PAUL TO SAINT JACK.......

products, were as much, if not more guilty, but they were seldom mentioned.

All of the cider producers became involved, forming the Cider Industry Council (CIC), under the aegis of the Confederation of Irish Industry. Showerings, Taunton Cider, Wm. Gaymer & Son and Symonds Cider Company were founder members.

In the first CIC newsletter, Autumn 1989, Chairman Brendan McGuinness of Showerings outlined its objectives:

- to examine and address the question of underage abuse of any alcohol and
- to encourage more widespread appreciation, among responsible adults, of cider.

Members had to abide by a philosophy of responsible marketing and responsible promotion. The industry would not be taken seriously if this was not done. In practical terms it meant:

- no extra fill—part of cider's "cheap" image was based on promotions run in off-licences where the already sizeable two litre bottles included 20 per cent extra free. This was actively discouraged by the CIC on the basis that it promoted over-indulgence in alcohol.
- product repositioning—the product had to be placed at the top end of the market. This meant premium lager prices, which could be a sacrifice for the industry and could lose customers. It meant encouraging increased consumption in pubs, where there is a controlled environment.
- new forms of advertising. Previously, cider advertisements were "heavy metal" and youth-oriented, including a famous Strongbow "arrows in the counter" campaign. This did not conform to the new perceptions that the CIC wanted to create. The change has subsequently been very evident in Bulmers' "nothing added but time" promotion.

These measures hurt the industry financially at first, but they were deemed necessary to prevent total collapse. The industry could not afford any accusation of tacitly approving abuse of its product.

RESEARCH FINDINGS

Since its establishment, the CIC has laid emphasis on research, publishing results of work commissioned both by itself and other independent sources.

The Autumn 1989 newsletter summarised the Economic and Social Research Institute (ESRI) report, by Grube and Morgan in 1986, which showed that by comparison with other alcoholic beverages, cider was the least prevalent amongst younger drinkers.

	Cider	Beer	Wine	Spirits
13 years or younger	16.7 %	26.2 %	26.2 %	15.8 %
14 years	23.5 %	39.2 %	38.4 %	25.9 %
15 years	36.8 %	51.5 %	42.5 %	40.8 %
16 years	44.4 %	59.5 %	53.5 %	49.9 %
17 years or older	48.7 %	67.4 %	59.7 %	57.2 %

CIDER FIGHTS TO CLEAR ITS NAME

Another survey, in Tullamore in 1988, conducted in six schools, showed that the pupils made the following choices: beer 58.5 %; spirits 15 %; cider 17 % and wine 7 %.

The Spring 1990 issue of the newsletter revealed alcohol abuse among people as young as twelve years, emerging from a Galway survey. Conducted by psychologist, Neil Johnson, Director of Combined Action, it found cider to be the least popular drink among teenagers.

The poll of 1,359 first and second year boys and girls showed that 68.6 % preferred beer, while 44 % chose wine, 29.3 % chose spirits and only 26.2 % cider.

The Autumn 1993 newsletter mentioned an Eastern Health Board study on alcohol use by post-primary school children. Cider, again, did not feature as their regular drink. Beer was the most common drink with boys, whereas girls had a more even spread of preferences with beer, wine and spirits all featuring. Boys were now starting to drink at 11 years, girls at 12. The study involved just under 300 pupils from single sex and mixed sex schools in south County Dublin.

These successive research findings show that the CIC has been basing its campaign on facts rather than aspirations and that cider is not the problem in underage drinking.

Research commissioned by CIC and carried out by Lansdowne Market Research in 1988 showed that 91 per cent of parents were in favour of a change in the law which would require young people to carry and show an ID card when purchasing alcohol.

IMPLEMENTATION

The first project undertaken by the CIC was a half-hour *Drink Talking* video in 1988. It was aimed mainly at 15 to 18 year olds and distributed to secondary schools, youth and community organisations, welfare and health professionals. It featured people who were prominent in the public eye, for example, boxer Barry McGuigan, broadcaster Carolyn Fisher and musicians Brush Shields, Don Baker, Dave Heffernan and John Sheehan. They viewed alcohol from a number of standpoints—abstinence, moderation and alcoholism.

Drink Talking took on all of the messages of the Government's Health Promotion Unit, namely that younger people should not be afraid of alcohol, but if they wished to use it, to do so in moderation and if they did not want to drink, to stand up and say so. It is still available and remains the only audio visual resource on the subject available to schools. The CIC also looked into the studies that had been done on underage drinking, such as those mentioned above. They were helped by the work of Dr. Mark Morgan of St. Patrick's College, Drumcondra, Dublin, who believed the problem had to be tackled by the whole community together and that it was not just an issue for the industry. Parents, the trade, schools and gardai all had to get involved.

This led to the Wexford Community Action Programme, a pilot programme in Wexford, carried out in association with the CIC. It was a risk for the CIC because they went into the programme not knowing what the results would be—they could have shown that cider was a significant problem in the area. However, it was a risk that paid off. Cider was not the demon and the project got wide support in the Wexford area, particularly from the Mayor, Alderman Padge Reck who made it the special mission of his year in

The Cider Industry Council presents a report on underage drinking to the then Minister for Education, Seamus Brennan, TD. From left: Peter McKimm, chairman, Cider Industry Council; Dr. Mark Morgan, author of the report; The Minister; Tadhg O'Sullivan, chief executive, Vintners Federation of Ireland.

office, and from the county council. It resulted in a series of guidelines for any community confronted with the problem and recommendations for what needed to be done both at national and local level.

The Community Action Programme now tours the country, visiting areas that request its help and volunteering its services to areas identified as having an underage drinking problem.

Other initiatives undertaken by the CIC have included:

- Publication of a booklet, *The Cider Industry of Ireland*, by Anne O'Curry, detailing its history, benefits, varieties and how it is made
- Donation of a library on the subject of underage drinking to the Garda College Training Centre, Templemore, Co. Tipperary
- Publication of a newsletter detailing the ongoing work of the CIC. It is distributed to gardai, the licensed and off-licence trade and to professional and voluntary people with an interest in the area
- Support and promotion of ID card schemes for pubs and off-licences, which have massive support among parents. CIC has sponsored a number of voluntary schemes in communities
- Support of the tightening of laws on drinking in public places
- A campaign to encourage the responsible use of cider among mature drinkers. This includes cider cuisine press releases and leaflets, taste-testing in the summer months in supermarkets and strict self-regulation
- Cider companies wishing to sponsor events have moved into rugby, golf and the arts, more upmarket areas than the industry had previously been involved with.

CIDER FIGHTS TO CLEAR ITS NAME

The latest step, last year, was the introduction of the Community Action Awards in association with the National Parents' Council Post Primary. Grants of up to £1000 are given to community groups to fund innovative projects in local areas and to develop plans to combat alcohol abuse in underage drinkers.

An ongoing aspect of the CIC campaign has been thorough monitoring of the media to ensure that cider is not treated unfairly as the sole cause of alcohol-related unrest. Anne Dowling, of Gilmore Communications, acts immediately on every derogatory reference to cider, checking first if it is true and if it is not, then taking the matter up with the source of the story. At this stage, the media have become very co-operative and frequently check with Gilmore before they publish such stories. Generous coverage has been given to the CIC initiatives.

This part of the campaign has been extremely successful, with positive mentions of cider in the media now outweighing negative ones. Files of press cuttings are also kept on underage drinking in general, ID card schemes and trade news.

EVALUATION

As mentioned, there has been a dramatic decrease in negative publicity about cider, despite the occasional lapses. One such lapse was by *The Irish Times* (30 July 1994). A preview of the fifth and last Féile music weekend in Thurles, by Brian Boyd, started: "Sex, drugs and rock 'n roll ? Yes please. Everyone knows rock festivals are all about drinking crateloads of cider, stuffing tabs of E down your throat, and getting off with whoever strays your way".

Stories from the CIC have led frequently to positive and informative features on aspects of the drink problem. The CIC have been the only drinks industry group to undertake such a plan of action, and it has gained great credit and praise from the media, gardai, parents and schools.

The repositioning of the product has been largely successful without affecting long-term sales. Indeed, indications are that the cider market is expanding in public houses.

The cider industry has spent £500,000 in the first five years of its campaign. It seeks no obvious commercial gain but by putting its money where its words are, it has gained enhanced credibility for itself and its product.

The CIC is committed to the campaign for at least another five years. It was a risk. It could have backfired. It might have been regarded as a cynical marketing exercise, but this has not happened. It has had a genuinely educational value and this has been appreciated by all involved.

Cider is the least-preferred drink amongst teenagers, but it is gaining market share in the adult sector. Sales have increased and it is moving up from five per cent of the beer market, going towards six per cent. This represents a considerable jump for an industry that is one of the oldest in the country and employs 400 people.

Barry Kenny has a BBS Degree in Business Studies (Marketing) from the University of Limerick and the DIT Diploma in Public Relations.

FROM JOHN PAUL TO SAINT JACK.......

DO BRILLIANT CAMPAIGNS WIN ELECTIONS ?

Fianna Fáil and the General Election of 1987
by Barry Roche

"The 1987 General Election was the best planned campaign that I was involved in"—
P.J.Mara, Fianna Fáil Press Officer.

"A watershed election by any standards, it was the most volatile contest in post-war Irish history."—Michael Laver, Professor of Political Science & Sociology, University College, Galway.

BACKGROUND

By February 1987, Ireland was facing a severe economic crisis. There were 240,000 people unemployed (more than 18 per cent of the civilian work force) and the current budget deficit was £1,180 million (6.4 per cent of GNP).

The Fine Gael/Labour Coalition had been in office since 1982. It had suffered two very controversial referenda: one, imposing a constitutional ban on abortion, already forbidden by law, was passed in 1983; the other, removing the constitutional ban on divorce, was defeated in 1986.

Following a record overall majority of 20 seats for Fianna Fáil in the 1977 election, there had been three rapid elections in 1981 and 1982. The Fine Gael/Labour Coalition emerged in November 1982 to restore stability. Then, in 1985, a Fianna Fáil split led to the formation of the Progressive Democrats.

Through 1986 the strains in the Coalition were evident. Fine Gael, the larger party, were pressing for tougher budgetary measures than the Labour Party were willing to accept. On Tuesday, 20 January 1987, Labour Leader, Dick Spring, and his cabinet colleagues Ruairi Quinn, Barry Desmond and Liam Kavanagh, resigned from the Government and the Coalition collapsed. Unable to command majority support in the Dáil, Taoiseach and Fine Gael Leader, Garret FitzGerald, had no option but to call a general election for 17 February.

- **Party organisation**

Fianna Fáil are the largest political party in Ireland. In 1987 they had an estimated 89,000 members, over 3,000 branches (cumainn) and at least one TD in every constituency. This gave them a very considerable advantage over their opponents who could not match such organisational resources.

The Progressive Democrat defectors consisted of some who had been among the party's most able politicians. They also commanded significant resources and members.

Most important, the socio-economic profile of the PD supporters matched the areas where Fianna Fáil were to suffer losses, namely the upper, upper middle and middle classes (the ABC1 groupings).

Fianna Fáil operates a branch system of "cumainn" within constituencies. At election time the cumainn are mobilised as electoral machines to campaign and canvass on behalf of the party. However, the Irish electoral system throws up a curious quirk. The intense competition for votes and the multiple-seat nature of Irish constituencies, along with the Proportional Representation Single Transferable Vote (PRSTV) electoral system, combine to ensure that a candidate's greatest competitor may be from the same party. In these circumstances candidates attempt to "sew up" as many cumainn as possible in an attempt to maximise manpower and resources on their behalf. It gives the public relations manager an invaluable network countrywide.

OBJECTIVES

As with any political party, Fianna Fáil's immediate objective in February 1987 was to become the party of government. Given the fact that they have been the largest party in Ireland at every election since 1932, they have persistently regarded themselves as the natural party of government.

British Labour MP, Peter Mandelson, MP, formerly head of communications and campaigns for his party, outlining the operating parameters of a political party's communications policy, has said: "Communications means throwing your net much wider than publicity. It means deciding what we say, how we say it, and which spokesmen and women we choose to say it."

Michael Laver contends that "election campaigns acted out in the media become a series of attempts by parties to increase favourable coverage of their strong policy suits and reduce coverage of their weak policy suits. It is the relative success of the parties, in achieving this manipulation of the issue 'agenda', as much as anything else, that affects the outcome of campaigns".

It would be fair to assume that this was the intention of Fianna Fáil and by 28 January a Market Research Bureau of Ireland (MRBI) opinion poll, in *The Irish Times,* gave them a 22 per cent lead over Fine Gael.

• Audiences

"The critical battles of Irish politics were fought for the support of the volatile middle class, bourgeoisie and large farming sectors of the electorate" - Michael Laver.

The following table illustrates the failure of Fianna Fáil to capture this support in the 1980s:

Fianna Fáil support, by social class:

	Total	AB	C	C2	DE	F1	F2
1982	40	32	38	42	40	37	51
1987	38	26	32	45	41	30	48

Fianna Fáil identified Dublin as an area where future gains could be made.As a result they initiated Operation Dublin, in essence a root and branch reform of the party organisation in Dublin, including the targeting of individual constituencies.

In mid-1985 they established a committee to prepare a marketing plan well in advance of the next election which had to take place no later than 1987. It was to be presented to the party front bench.

Members of the committee were: Martin Larkin, chief executive of Saatchi & Saatchi Advertising (Ireland); Michael Laffan, chief executive, Thorn EMI; Paul Kavanagh, chief executive, Irish Printers; Brendan O'Kelly, former chief executive, Bord Iascaigh Mhara (Irish Sea Fisheries Board); Des Byrne, head of the market research company, Behaviour and Attitudes Ltd.

The co-ordinator of the group was P.J.Mara, Fianna Fáil press officer, with Seamus Brennan, TD, a former general secretary of the party, also involved.

"This untitled and highly secretive committee carried out the function of a communications committee. It was given a specific brief to produce initial plans for Fianna Fáil's message and tactics in the election", writes David M.Farrell.

The committee first conducted detailed market research of a qualitative and quantitative nature.This was done with the aim of better focused strategy and tactics that could be used by front bench spokespersons. It found that unemployment and not taxation was the issue of primary concern to the voters, who were also weary of leadership difficulties that had troubled Fianna Fáil in the years since Charles Haughey succeeded Jack Lynch. Research showed that the voters wanted a strong leader and Charles Haughey fitted this profile. Fianna Fáil concluded that they should therefore opt for a positive and presidential-style campaign. In addition, it was revealed that working class voters feared a PD/Fine Gael Coalition.This also would be highlighted.

• Nuts and Bolts

Paddy Lalor, the senior MEP for Leinster and a former minister, was chosen in early 1986 to chair a 'nuts and bolts' committee that would finalise strategic preparations.As a result, Fianna Fáil, for the first time, attempted to achieve standardisation of their publicity materials.The committee would also oversee the design and production of artwork, stencils, leader posters, issue leaflets and party stickers. Some of the more imaginative ideas included the renting of time on the "scannervision" sign on O'Connell Bridge, helium balloons and the rental of two planes to fly over Lansdowne Road during the Ireland/England rugby international.

The advertising strategy was to centre around a number of themes—unemployment/employment, emigration and the state of the national health services. These were all developed for front bench approval.Added to this was the slogan: *There is a better way.*

Martin Larkin and Frank O'Hare were to take charge of the advertising; Des Byrne, market research; Tom Savage and Terry Prone of Carr Communications, media training and James Morris of Windmill Lane would produce the party political broadcasts.

Two days prior to the dissolution of the Dáil, Haughey attempted to define the electoral battleground and seize the initiative. FitzGerald was to opt for a long four-week campaign in an attempt to give the electorate time for reflection on the issues. He hoped they would not be distracted by Fianna Fáil electoral tactics which he believed to be misleading. The PDs and Sinn Féin were deemed to threaten Fianna Fáil's middle class and republican support respectively. Haughey therefore said that a vote for either would be wasted and only further contribute to the endemic political instability.

On the economy, Haughey maintained that "prudent fiscal management" could bring a two to three per cent growth rate over a four or five year period. Northern Ireland was a negative area for Fianna Fáil given its commitment to renegotiating the Anglo-Irish Agreement. Subsequently Haughey attempted to ensure that Northern Ireland would not become an electoral issue.

Fianna Fáil attempted to offset Fine Gael's strategy of a long campaign by refusing to campaign seriously until one week after the campaign had started. This had the added bonus of diverting attention away from the other parties' efforts as the media speculated on the content of the Fianna Fail manifesto. The manifesto was called *The Programme for National Recovery*.

It committed Fianna Fáil to:
* contain expenditure at 1986 levels
* not to increase taxation or borrowing
* reduce the standard tax rate to 35 per cent
* place growth at the centre of economic policy

The manifesto was vague on the issue of cuts in services.

Haughey maintained that a Fianna Fáil victory would generate the confidence to secure a consumer boom. This was in common with much conservative economic thinking at the time. In an effort to attract trade union and working class votes, Fianna Fáil reiterated its commitment to the concept of social partnership.

* **Attacks on Fianna Fáil**

Fine Gael attacked "the hidden cost of the Fianna Fáil manifesto", using half-page advertisements in *The Irish Times, Irish Independent* and *Cork Examiner*. Fianna Fáil denied the claims, but committed itself to clarifying its tax and spending policies. Ironically this enhanced Fianna Fáil's attractiveness, whereas Fine Gael appeared negative.

Fine Gael tried to offset its weakness on economic issues by proposing the idea of an economic forum that would be an all-party attempt to solve the economic troubles. This could have entrapped Fianna Fáil but it was skilfully side-stepped by Haughey who rejected it as a negation of democracy.

Fianna Fáil was trying to retain its specific identity and remain above the scramble of the other parties to be seen as the only party that could hold forward the alternative of single party government.

FROM JOHN PAUL TO SAINT JACK.......

- **Television**

Television is very attractive to the political parties, as they believe it is neutral and has more authority than the press which is seen as more partisan and less regulated.

In addition to the opportunities for news coverage, Fianna Fáil had their quota of party election broadcasts. RTE, the national broadcasting service, allocates these on the basis of a party's current representation and the number of its candidates. Fianna Fáil were given five broadcasts of five minutes each.

Following the Kennedy/Nixon Debate of 1960 much importance has been placed upon the "Great Debate". On 12 February, Garret FitzGerald and Charles Haughey met for such a debate. Carr Communications had been employed to train Haughey before the debate.

As Garret FitzGerald was perceived to be ahead of Haughey in terms of personal popularity, Fine Gael stressed Haughey's authoritarian streak. FitzGerald also had the advantage over Haughey's weakness on the Anglo-Irish Agreement which Haughey said he would renegotiate. The strategy worked as the next opinion polls showed a 3 per cent jump for Fine Gael. Haughey then sought to steer the discussion onto the economy where Fianna Fáil held the cards.

- **Advertising**

Fianna Fáil ran several newspaper advertisements during the campaign. They were typically half-page, with a headline and a photograph (not of Charles Haughey), a hundred words of text and the party slogan, *There is a better way*. The regular theme was that coalitions do not work. It was encapsulated in the words: "To restore stability requires the strength of single party government and that's something only Fianna Fáil can deliver."

Some of the headlines employed were:
- All coalitions are bad news
- Working hard and overtaxed ?
- Sowing the seeds for national recovery
- We have the will, we have the way
- We have the will, we have the way to get things going.
- Why our realistic tax plan will work for you.

In the last days of campaigning, in response to fears of a possible PD/Fine Gael coalition, Fianna Fáil played on their single party strength: *There are two choices* and *Don't risk coalition*.

- **Posters**

There was a specific attack on Labour with: *Labour isn't working; Labour's tax bombshell*. Fine Gael had conceded that they would introduce widespread spending cuts if re-elected. Fianna Fáil promptly tied this in with the perennially emotive issue of healthcare provision: *Health cuts hurt the old, the sick and the handicapped*. However, when Fianna Fáil came to power, they were to introduce even more severe cuts than Fine Gael had proposed.

- **The Haughey factor**

Haughey's benefit to Fianna Fáil was his ability to motivate the rank and file and to attract long-term supporters. He was regarded in a regal fashion, given an aura of mystique which was played upon by the media. John Cooney in *The Irish Times* (23 December 1986) had characterised him as "the once and future king" and his reticence during the campaign was described as "studied detachment and pointed immobility" under the headline "Haughey factor and Elba".

EVALUATION

The general election of 17 February 1987 brought Fianna Fáil back into power after four years and three months in opposition. The state of the parties was Fianna Fáil 81 seats, Fine Gael 51, Progressive Democrats 14, Labour 12, Workers' Party 4, Others 4.

In the case of a general election it is comparatively easy to evaluate the performance of the party. Did it fulfil its expectations? Did it hold its position in the polls or gain during the campaign? In this case it becomes more complicated. Common wisdom has it that Fianna Fáil's public relations were excellent, yet they did not receive the elusive overall majority which they sought so hard and their standing in the polls was lower by the end of the campaign than at the start.

There appear to be a number of reasons for this. Ireland has multi-seat constituencies, a mixture of three, four and five seaters. In 1979, an independent commission rearranged the constituencies. The number of four and five seaters, which favoured smaller parties, was increased at the expense of the three seaters. Therefore it became increasingly unlikely that any party would receive an overall majority.

The emergence of the PDs hit Fine Gael and its middle class support harder than Fianna Fáil. They captured nearly 12 per cent of the vote and 14 seats. With high profile Fianna Fáil defectors such as former ministers, Desmond O'Malley and Bobby Molloy, as well as Mary Harney, retaining their seats, these could have given Fianna Fáil their majority.

What was the result of Operation Dublin? Fianna Fáil gained three seats in the Dublin City and County area, winning 21 out of 48 in 11 constituencies. The Progressive Democrats took five Dublin seats, three of them with ex-Fianna Fáil members as candidates.

P.J.Mara believes there was another contributing factor: "There was not an overall majority for Fianna Fáil. But there probably could have been if we had had a candidate-based strategy side by side with the marketing strategy which had been very well developed. On the candidate side of things it was the same story as the early 1980s. The party leadership and the National Executive did not impose their will on the constituency organisations. The result was that in key marginals we lost out where we should have made gains."

CONCLUSION

With 81 seats out of a possible 166, Fianna Fáil were able to form a government when the new Dáil assembled on 10 March 1987. Haughey won the vote for Taoiseach with the support on one independent member, former Fianna Fail minister, Neil Blaney and the casting vote of the Ceann Comhairle (speaker), Sean Treacy. One independent Dublin deputy, Tony Gregory, abstained.

The minority Haughey Government, 1987 to 1989, is regarded as one of the better of recent years. It survived through the acquiescence of both Fine Gael and the Progressive Democrats.

Fine Gael, with a new leader, Alan Dukes, following the resignation of Garret FitzGerald, supported Fianna Fáil's budgetary strategy on the grounds of putting the nation first. Dukes termed it the Tallaght Strategy and the PDs were in full agreement. It worked and between 1987 and 1989 there was a reduction in current expenditure by £900 million in real terms, or 8 per cent. Opinion polls found that 50 per cent of the people saw the budgetary strategy as "good for the country".

There was other evidence of improvement. By 1989 the current budget deficit was down to £263 million, which was 1.2 per cent of GNP—a transformation from 1987. Unemployment was still a major problem, but it was only down slightly, to 202,000 (15.7 per cent of the civilian work force).

Charles Haughey called another general election for 15 June 1989 following a Dáil defeat on a private members' bill to grant £400,000 to haemophiliacs who had contracted AIDS. Haughey did not have to call the election, but again he wanted the overall majority. He did not get it and for the first time ever, Fianna Fáil went into coalition. Amazingly, it was with the Progressive Democrats, many of whose senior members had either left or been expelled from Fianna Fáil in 1985.

APPENDICES

Percentage of vote to main parties since 1981

	FF	FG	Lab	PD	WP	DL
1981	45.3	36.5	9.9	na	1.7	na
Feb 1982	47.3	37.3	9.1	na	2.2	na
Nov 1982	45.2	39.2	9.4	na	3.1	na
1987	44.1	27.1	6.4	11.8	3.8	na
1989	44.1	29.3	9.5	5.5	5.0	na
1992	39.1	24.5	19.3	4.7	0.7	2.8

FF—Fianna Fáil; FG—Fine Gael; Lab—Labour; PD—Progressive Democrats; WP—Workers Party; DL—Democratic Left.

Percentage of party support January - February 1987

Tabulated from Irish Marketing Surveys (IMS) and Market Research Bureau of Ireland (MRBI) polls

	Jan 28	Feb 4	Feb 5	Feb 13	Feb 14	Feb 15
Fianna Fáil	40	43	40	41	40	38
Fine Gael	18	20	19	22	20	25
Progressive Democrats	12	15	11	14	13	11
Labour	4	5	4	6	5	4
Others	5	6	5	6	5	6

•   Bibliography

Bew, Paul; Hazelkorn, Ellen and Patterson, Henry: *The Dynamics of Irish Politics,* Lawrence & Wishart, London, 1989.

Coakley, John and Gallagher, Michael: *Politics in the Republic of Ireland,* Political Studies Association of Ireland Press, Dublin, 1993.

Farrell, David M and Wortmann, Martin: *Party Strategies in the Electoral Market: Political Marketing in West Germany, Britain and Ireland,* European Journal of Political Research, 15(3), 1987.

Laver, Michael; Mair, Peter and Sinnott, Richard (ed): *How Ireland Voted, 1987,* Poolbeg Press, Dublin, 1987. (Special attention to Chapter 4: *Campaign Strategies: The Selling of the Parties,* by David M. Farrell.)

Nealon, Ted: *Nealon's Guide to the 25th Dail & Seanad, Election 1987,* Platform Press, Dublin, 1987.

Ryan, Tim: *Mara PJ,* Blackwater Press, Dublin, 1992.

Barry Roche has a BA Degree in History & Politics from University College, Dublin and the DIT Diploma in Public Relations.

A TRIUMPH OF STYLE AND SUBSTANCE

The Election of Mary Robinson, President of Ireland, 1990
by Ian O'Doherty

BACKGROUND

The President of Ireland is elected by popular vote and may serve two seven-year terms. President Patrick Hillery, elected unopposed in 1976 and 1983, completed his final term in December 1990.

The Constitution defines and limits the role of the President. In a sense it is the same as the role of the monarch in the United Kingdom. It is very different from that of an executive President, as in France or the United States of America.

Since the enactment of the Constitution in 1938 the Presidents have been Douglas Hyde, unopposed 1938; Sean T. O'Kelly, opposed 1945, unopposed 1952; Eamon de Valera, opposed 1959 and 1966; Erskine Childers, opposed 1973; Cearbhall Ó Dálaigh, unopposed 1974 after the sudden death of President Childers; Patrick Hillery, unopposed 1976 after the resignation of President Ó Dálaigh.

In 1990, the Labour Party, led by Dick Spring, decided to put forward their own candidate, despite being a small party holding only 15 of the 166 seats in the Dail, to 77 for Fianna Fáil and 55 for Fine Gael. It seemed to be a futile exercise. Fianna Fáil had, since the 1989 General Election been in coalition government with the Progressive Democrats who held six seats.

To run for President one needs the nominations of at least 20 members of the Oireachtas (Dáil and Seanad). The Oireachtas is the elected legislature of a lower house of deputies (Dáil) and an upper house of senators (Seanad). The President may not be a member of either House of the Oireachtas. Alternatively, a candidate for the Presidency may be nominated by four county councils or county borough councils. The President is above politics, but the path to the Presidency is essentially political.

Labour wanted a contest and they wanted the office of President to take on a useful and meaningful role. On five of the previous nine occasions, the political parties had agreed on a consensus candidate. Fianna Fáil, being the largest party, was always in a good position to win a contested Presidency.

The Presidency was perceived and commonly accepted as a job for an elder statesman who had served a long political apprenticeship.

Labour's nomination of Mary Robinson in April 1990 was a departure from tradition. At 46, she was not the typical Presidential candidate. She was young, female and liberal. The other two candidates were Brian Lenihan (age 59), nominated by Fianna Fáil and Austin Currie (age 49), the Fine Gael nominee. Both of these candidates were perceived by some as fitting the traditional job description for President of Ireland. Although they were not as old as some former presidents—Eamon de Valera was 77 when he started his 14-year term of office—they had had long and distinguished political careers. Lenihan had served in several ministries with Fianna Fáil governments and was currently Tánaiste (Deputy Prime Minister). Fine Gael would have preferred their former Taoiseach, Garret FitzGerald, but he was not willing to run. Austin Currie had been nearly 20 years with the Social Democratic and Labour Party (SDLP) in Northern Ireland, but came south in 1989 to win a seat for Fine Gael.

It was Dick Spring, former Irish rugby international full-back, who first put forward the idea of a new style of President. In January 1990 he announced that the Labour Party would be contesting the November election and if necessary he would run himself. Spring, with his advisers Fergus Finlay and John Rogers (a former Attorney-General), set about finding a candidate to suit their job description which was different from the traditional one for President. They decided on Mary Robinson. When Spring approached her she initially dismissed the idea but out of politeness said she would consider it over the weekend.

She had been an independent senator for Trinity College, Dublin, from 1969 to 1976 and 1985 to 1989. She had been a Labour party senator from 1976 to 1985. She stood unsuccessfully for Labour in the 1977 and 1981 Dáil elections, but was elected to Dublin Corporation.

Robinson was a senior counsel and had a very successful and frequently controversial career as a constitutional lawyer. She specialised in civil rights and had been involved in some of the most controversial, historic and high-profile cases in the history of the State. She had also lectured in law at Trinity College, Dublin. She resigned from the Labour Party in 1985 over its support for the Anglo-Irish Agreement.

Mary Robinson was at first not interested in running. She had withdrawn from political life. However, the idea caught hold of her and she agreed to run if selected. She was nominated as the official Labour party candidate in April and, on May Day, long before any other candidate, she started a long, gruelling, six-month 30,000 mile, nationwide campaign tour, visiting practically every part of Ireland.

Some elements in the Labour Party had wanted the veteran left-winger, and former Minister for Health, Noel Browne, to be nominated.

Once Mary Robinson was nominated the Labour Party closed ranks around her. They wanted the President to be elected by the people and not merely to be a gift to Brian Lenihan who was being promoted as the traditional, ideal candidate. There was a lot of sympathy and admiration for Lenihan who had recovered from a serious illness and liver transplant in 1989.

OBJECTIVES

Labour had several objectives in the 1990 Presidential election. They wanted to contest the election, to have a candidate in "the race for the Park" (The old Vice-Regal Lodge in Dublin's Phoenix Park, now called Aras an Uachtaráin, is the official residence of the President); they wanted Mary Robinson to win, despite the odds against her.

They looked for a development and expansion of the role of the President. They wanted the people to elect the President and not for the Presidency to be a retirement job for an ageing politician. They wanted to change the traditional role of the President into a more active and working one.

In reality, the President has very few powers. She cannot travel abroad, nor even make a public speech without the permission of the government. Her traditional role has been to dissolve the Dáil on the request of the Taoiseach, sign bills into law, receive ambassadors and heads of state and to perform other ceremonial duties.

At the very worst, the decision to run a Presidential candidate was a vote-getting exercise for the Labour Party.

PLANNING AND KEY MESSAGES

Dick Spring planted the seed for a new kind of President in a RTE radio interview with Shane Kenny on 5 January 1990. He announced, to the amazement of all, including Labour party members and advisers, that if necessary he would run himself to ensure an election took place, rather than the job just being given to an agreed candidate. Spring was criticised in the media for making such a suggestion. They said he was too young at 39 and still had a bright political career ahead of him. They said the Presidency was for a politician who had served a long apprenticeship and was ready for retirement.

The Labour party was committed to running a candidate; and so the search began to find the right one. Spring, with Fergus Finlay and John Rogers, drew up a job description for their President. The person who best suited their requirements was Mary Robinson. They realised that, if they were going to win, they would have to take a different approach than the traditional role of President dictated. Brian Lenihan's name was already being mentioned. Labour realised that they could not beat Lenihan with a Lenihan-type clone, i.e. an elderly politician with a long distinguished political career. Robinson and Lenihan were radically different.

While Mary Robinson fitted the Labour party's job requirements, she did not fit the traditional job description of President of Ireland. She was young, female, feminist, liberal and a lawyer.

The process of obtaining the Labour party nomination for Mary Robinson then began. Some resistance was encountered with certain members wanting the old hero, Noel Browne. Robinson, approached initially in February, was selected on 26 April. It was decided that if she was to have any chance of winning, an intensive six-month nationwide campaign was essential. Brian Lenihan had a much higher national profile.

Voters had to be educated to Mary Robinson, to see and hear her, to know what she looked like and what she stood for. She was promoted as the alternative to Lenihan and later to Austin Currie. Robinson had to paint a picture of how different the Presidency could be. She supported the idea of making fuller use of the office.

IMPLEMENTATION

The campaign was gruelling and physically exhausting. Virtually every city, town and village in Ireland was visited. The Robinson team lived in buses as they travelled the country in all directions. Whether on the trail or at home it was non-stop. Every morning there were 7.30 meetings which ended at 9 with everybody already exhausted. There were no yes men or women. Everybody in the campaign team had strong views and was able to defend them.

The Labour Party candidate, coming from behind, had to be the first on the campaign trail. Robinson kicked off in early May at Allihies, the most south western point of Ireland.

At first, the media took only a limited interest in the Robinson campaign. She was seen as the complete outsider. They felt she would poll well on election day but that she would come in third, in line with the party voting in the 1989 General Election.

However, media attention increased dramatically as the campaign developed and the other two candidates started their campaigns. It was not until near the end that the media rated Mary Robinson with any kind of a chance of winning.

Brenda O'Hanlon, a public relations consultant with Wilson Hartnell, who had come aboard the campaign in August, played a substantial part in the media relations at the later stages. She orchestrated an interview for Mary Robinson in *Hello !* magazine, which had considerable impact. When the idea of doing the *Hello !* interview was suggested several members of the Labour Party were apprehensive, but it worked well and portrayed Mary Robinson favourably, particularly to voters who might not have known a lot about her. It did not turn into an ostentatious display of wealth that several members of the Labour party had feared.

There were many TV, radio and newspaper interviews and profiles on Robinson and most of them worked to her advantage. However, she made some unwise comments which could have seriously damaged her had Fianna Fail taken her seriously.

Robinson's appearance was important. The analogy put to her was that she was going for a job interview. She needed to adjust her appearance and presentation because her clothes and hairstyle led to her being perceived as severe, harsh, aloof and intellectual. She had dressed like a lawyer prior to the campaign but now her clothes and appearance were developed and changed. She began wearing Irish-designed clothes, and changed her hair style. She was apprehensive about these changes at first, but soon came to appreciate their value. She was not an unapproachable kind of person, but her appearance made her appear so. The changes she made were of great benefit to her, and still are. She began to be seen as approachable, attractive, intelligent. Her true self was more visible after the changes had been made.

Her manner of speaking was another problem, not her accent, but her habit of giving long intellectual answers to questions, 3000 words when 30 would be sufficient. As the campaign progressed she got into the habit of shorter answers. The reason for her long answers had been her legal training and habit of developing answers as she spoke. This was changed so that she no longer confused or bored her audiences. It meant that she avoided misinterpretations and people, no matter who they were, understood her message and what she was saying.

EVALUATION AND REFLECTION

Mary Robinson was elected President of Ireland on 9 November 1990. On the first count Austin Currie had 267,902 votes (17.0 %); Brian Lenihan 694,484 (44.1 %) and Mary Robinson 612,265 (38.9 %). Under the Irish system of proportional representation, Currie was then eliminated and his votes transferred to their second preferences. On the second count, Lenihan moved to 731,273 votes (47.2 %) and Robinson reached 817,830 (52.8 %) to win. Robinson won 25 of the 41 constituencies in the country.

In an age when election campaigns are costed in millions of pounds, it is of interest that the Robinson team spent the grand total of £220,000, and raised only £140,000 in the course of the campaign, leaving a deficit on polling day of £80,000. "But what price should you pay to make history?", asks Fergus Finlay.

In Ireland, elections usually become Fianna Fáil versus the rest so that a non-Fianna Fáil candidate in second place after the first count often does well on transfers. Austin Currie's votes transferred to Mary Robinson at a rate of six for her to one for Lenihan.

Evaluation of the campaign shows that it was a success for Labour because Mary Robinson won. There was also a skilful use of public relations. It was non-public relations people, Dick Spring, Fergus Finlay and John Rogers, who did the essential public relations work at the start. They created the idea of a new kind of presidency, decided how they wanted to communicate it and then found the right candidate and communicated brilliantly. They decided the message and the strategy. When it came to the implementation there were many people willing to give a hand, including public relations people.

There is no doubt that there was a Labour party camp and the Robinson camp, and the grand mediator was Ruairi Quinn, Director of Elections. The fear of the Robinson camp was that they would only be identified with Labour and not with a broader electorate. Bride Rosney, a teacher who was Mary Robinson's closest adviser, played a forceful part in the campaign. Some felt she pushed Robinson too hard, leading at times to exhaustion. Mary Robinson's husband, Nick, was a power behind the scenes, ever supportive and ever protective. Brenda O'Hanlon, the public relations consultant, used her expertise and experience for general organisation and media relations in the last few months, but from a public relations point of view the message and the strategy had been decided before she became involved.

One controversial adviser was Eoghan Harris, broadcaster and former activist with the left-wing Workers Party. According to Emily O'Reilly in her book, *Candidate,* Harris thinks he was critical to the campaign, "the catalyst that fused the chemistry of Mary Robinson with that of the electorate". O'Reilly quotes Harris as saying "Well Mary and Nick's nickname for me was God".

Harris wrote to Robinson on 6 April, congratulating her and offering "to give some practical help". In a long letter he told her how she should approach the campaign, and many of his recommendations were taken on board. He dealt with issues of style—clothes, photographs, language, and substance—divorce, abortion, the Constitution. He recommended which newspapers to go for and which to avoid. He warned her not to "run a poverty campaign", but a caring campaign.

"My view", he told her, "is that you can win the campaign, or come so close as to give you a famous political victory, by presenting yourself as a democratic rather than a liberal candidate and never as a liberal-left candidate".

Fergus Finlay says in his book, *Mary Robinson—A President with a Purpose,* that Harris had "a considerable influence on the way she and Nick prepared for the early phases of the campaign, although some of the claims made on his behalf subsequently, suggesting that he exercised a virtual 'Svengali' influence over the campaign, were totally inaccurate, and seen by many as demeaning the strong and independent person that Mary Robinson is".

The final reflection comes from Fergus Finlay, quoted in Michael O'Sullivan's book, *Mary Robinson—The Life and Times of an Irish Liberal:* "The Presidential election of 1990 was a triumph in many ways. It was a triumph of dedication and commitment over the huge resources and bigger machines of the largest political parties in the State. It was a triumph of imagination and energy over the stale ideas of stuck-in-the-mud, complacent organisations. It was a triumph of style and substance."

DISCUSSION

This is an interesting experience for public relations because it was not just communication of a message but the actual way the message was created and then how the right means was found to win support for that message. Robinson started as the complete outsider without a chance of winning. Public relations played a key role as it identified the need to start campaigning early, before the other candidates. Every audience in Ireland had to be addressed. The changes in appearance and the shortening of the Robinson answers were all identified as necessary to get the message across effectively and without distortion. The media coverage was always helpful. The key messages were communicated and the candidate was identified. Mary Robinson was elected despite the views she held rather than because of them. The idea of a real alternative to the traditional Presidency became a reality.

The role of President has changed as a result of Robinson's election. She is a President with a purpose, with a direct mandate from the people.

There are some elements of the campaign worth mentioning because had they gone differently, the result could have been different. Obviously the six-month campaign was crucial to success, as also was the slow start by Fianna Fáil and Fine Gael. If Garret FitzGerald had run instead of Austin Currie the Robinson campaign would have faced a far more difficult task. She would not have gained as much Fine Gael support.

One incident which caused her great embarrassment was an interview with the political and musical magazine, *Hot Press.* She was quoted as saying she would open a condom stand in the Virgin Megastore in Dublin if she were President. As the sales of condoms were regulated at the time and not permitted in stores like Virgin, this meant she would have been breaking the law. Her defence was that when asked a question she always nodded and said, yes, meaning that she had understood the question and was now going to answer it. This was borne out when the tape was replayed. However, there was controversy and her opponents made the most of it. Some believed she misjudged and deliberately said yes. However, the issue of *Hot Press* came out just after the first opinion poll of the campaign had been conducted and before it was published. It showed her in a commanding position, not in the lead but in what to many was a very surprisingly strong second place. Newspapers quickly lost interest in the *Hot Press* interview because they had a new angle, that Mary Robinson was riding high.

Then there were derogatory comments made about her on a radio show less than a week before the election. Fianna Fáil minister, Padraig Flynn, implied in a discussion that she was not a proper family person, that she had never claimed to be a "great wife and mother'" and that it was only at this late stage she had started talking about family values. He apologised and said he was misunderstood but it is certain that he won her votes from Lenihan.

Lenihan hit disaster in his campaign but it is believed that if the election had been delayed a week he might have won. He was recovering from the fall-out of the controversial "Duffy tapes".

At the peak of the campaign, Jim Duffy, a research student from University College, Dublin, produced a tape of an interview in which Lenihan admitted he had phoned President Hillery on a night in 1982 when the Government was about to fall and that he had tried to influence the President's decision to dissolve the Dail. Lenihan had always denied this and so had Taoiseach Charles Haughey. Lenihan denied the Duffy tapes and said he must have made a mistake. He afterwards admitted that he was under heavy medication at the time of the interview due to complications following his liver transplant and that he did not even remember meeting Duffy. During the campaign he did not want to say this because voters might have doubted his fitness for office, so he just insisted it was not true, even implying that he pretended to the student to have made the phone call.

The tapes controversy was badly handled and Lenihan was poorly advised in his response. Most people were convinced that Lenihan was lying and the controversy did not die down. The survival of the Government was even threatened. Finally, at the insistence of the Progressive Democrat wing of the Coalition, Charles Haughey sacked Lenihan as Tánaiste and as Minister for Defence. All of this when Lenihan, the most popular man in the Fianna Fáil party, was seeking election to the highest office in the land on the Fianna Fáil ticket !

Robinson then made a serious mistake on the *Today Tonight* television programme when she attacked Lenihan over the Presidential phone call and all that it implied. It was uncharacteristic of her; she came across as severe, harsh and ruthless. Her approach on this occasion was attributed to exhaustion. Some blame Eoghan Harris for it, because he phoned her as she was leaving her house for the studios. He advised her to go for the jugular and she did.

FOOTNOTE

From her initial hesitancy when asked by Dick Spring to accept the nomination, Mary Robinson warmed to her new public role. "As I went around the country I became more and more convinced that this was one of those rare opportunities, first to listen very carefully and then to represent and encourage and energise and, I suppose, inspire", she said. Four years into her Presidency Mary Robinson has kept her promises. She is certainly the most visible and active President Ireland has ever had. She has effectively kept up the pace of her campaign and become a national and international figure.

Journalist Fintan O'Toole, writing a 50th birthday tribute to her in *The Irish Times,* in May 1994 said: "No politician in the history of the State—arguably none since Parnell in his prime—has commanded such wide respect".

Political friends and opponents alike agree that she is an excellent ambassador for the country but, as all equally agree, she is her own person. Nobody handles or manipulates Mary Robinson. She would not have run for the office if she and Nick and their family and friends had not been convinced by the message that Dick Spring brought to her.

BIBLIOGRAPHY
*   Finlay, Fergus: *Mary Robinson—A President with a Purpose:* O'Brien Press, Dublin, 1990 (published the week of President Robinson's inauguration).
*   Lenihan, Brian: *For The Record;* Blackwater Press, Dublin, 1991.
*   O'Reilly, Emily: *Candidate—The Truth Behind the Presidential Campaign;* Attic Press, Dublin, 1991.
*   O'Sullivan, Michael: *Mary Robinson—The Life and Times of an Irish Liberal;* Blackwater Press, Dublin, 1993.

Ian O'Doherty has a BA Degree in Economics, Sociology & Political Science from University College, Galway and the DIT Diploma in Public Relations.

THE FUTURE COMES TO TALLAGHT

The Opening of The Square—Ireland's Largest Shopping Centre
by Nicola Whelan

BACKGROUND

The idea of a shopping complex for the new town of Tallaght, west of Dublin city, was conceived as far back as 1974. The original plan was that Dublin County Council and Dublin Corporation would build a large shopping and entertainment centre and subsequently lease out commercial space to retailers and investors. However, after years of discussion, and no action, the people of Tallaght were increasingly irate with what they considered to be Government complacency.

The census figures show the spectacular growth of Tallaght. In 1950, the old village had 352 people. By 1971 this had grown to 7,405 but then came the massive housing development and the 1991 census reported a population of 62,786 for the old village and the surrounding neighbourhoods that now comprise Tallaght.

But, there were problems associated with such rapid growth. Tallaght lacked a focal point, there was no sense of community or belonging in the area. Facilities and amenities had not developed at the same rate as the population. It was the most under-shopped area in Ireland and, until 23 October 1990, it was serviced by a small shopping precinct, with one supermarket in the village. As a result, many residents had to travel to the city centre, more than seven miles away, to get their weekly provisions and basic necessities. Because of the high level of unemployment in many parts of Tallaght, and the associated levels of car ownership, many people had no alternative to the inadequate bus service to and from the city centre.

There was also a lack of leisure and entertainment facilities. This was reflected in the country's highest level of video recorders per household.

The residents, therefore, got together to improve their locality. Several committees and associations were set up aimed at forcing the Government to realise the need for commercial and recreational developments in Tallaght. One of the most prominent of these groups was Tallaght Community Council. Their main objective was to have Tallaght designated as an urban renewal area, thus gaining various tax incentives.

A British company, London & Clydesdale Holdings, had won the contract to develop the complex which was later to become known as The Square but, in 1984, Monarch Properties bought them out for £500,000. Monarch Properties had previously developed nine other shopping centres nationwide, all of which had been commercially successful and usually innovative.

Monarch insisted on full ownership of the complex. They did not want to have to answer to the County Council or the Corporation. After negotiation it was agreed that

THE FUTURE COMES TO TALLAGHT

Monarch (and its silent partner, GRE Properties) would pay £2.7 million to the County Council and the Corporation. £700,000 was to be paid on signing the lease, with the remaining £2 million on completion of construction.

The County Council and the Corporation were satisfied in that they still had some say in the construction of the complex, if the need arose. However, they did not have to take responsibility for it afterwards.

Monarch were also satisfied. They had put much energy into researching the commercial viability of such a complex and they realised its potential. They found that:

- 70,000 people lived within a five minute drive of the site
- 170,000 within ten minutes
- 440,000 within 20 minutes
- More than one million within 30 minutes.

There was, therefore, a huge potential market, as yet untapped. Tallaght also had one of the youngest population profiles in the country, 69 per cent of the population being under 35, compared with 62 per cent for the whole of Dublin. A large proportion of the population were married with children.

However, Monarch's interest in the development of the complex hinged on one critical factor, the designation of Tallaght as an urban renewal area. Once this was achieved and announced by the Minister for Finance in the 1988 Budget, Monarch got the ball rolling on what was to be known as The Square.

THE SQUARE

From previous experience Monarch, as Ireland's largest developers of shopping centres, realised the importance of finding suitable anchor tenants as soon as possible. Securing big-name major tenants would encourage smaller retailers to join The Square early on in the development, thus ensuring success.

The chairman of Dublin County Council, Ray Burke, TD, "turned the sod" on The Square on 12 December 1985. Simultaneously Quinnsworth supermarkets announced that they would be one of the large anchor tenants.

Construction did not begin in earnest until after the announcement of urban renewal status in the 1988 Budget. Once started, it took a mere 22 months to complete. Monarch had the assistance of FÁS—The Training and Employment Authority to ensure that as many local people as possible were employed on the construction site. Everything was kept to a strict budget and The Square was completed within its deadlines and on budget.

Fact File on the Square
- £85 million to develop
- built on 28 acres of land
- 135 shops
- nine restaurants
- three carparks (one for each level)
- a 12 screen cinema complex

FROM JOHN PAUL TO SAINT JACK.......

- four major anchor tenants—Dunnes Stores, Roches Stores, Quinnsworth and Clerys
- serviced by 1,700 buses per week
- facilities for a full stage (including dressing rooms) which can be transformed to host gala events
- 57 closed circuit television cameras—the largest CCTV system in Europe
- a thousand fire alarms
- more than 4,000 light fittings in the mall area alone
- 15,000 square feet of glazing in the glass pyramid
- a forty-foot waterfall

The Square is "Ireland's largest and most spectacular shopping centre" (to quote from *The Blue Book*, the advertising and public relations manual prepared by Quinn McDonnell Pattison advertising agency and Pembroke Communications). It is larger than the combined size of the Stephens Green and ILAC Centres in Dublin city.

The idea of having a carpark for every level (the carparks are on slopes) means that, effectively, there are three ground floors in The Square. Thus, the rent is approximately the same for each level. It varies from £45 to £60 per square foot, which is the going rate in Dublin.

Approximately 200,000 shoppers pass through its doors each week. Monarch no longer service the shopping units but have retained management of the common areas. All of the anchor tenants are trading well and about 80 per cent of the 2,000 staff are from the Tallaght area.

The Square is a national attraction with 50 per cent of the shoppers coming from outside the Tallaght area of Dublin 24. The busy coach park is testimony to the shoppers who come from all over the country for a day out.

Eamonn Furlong, general manager of The Square, has developed this trend to make it an international attraction, a cheap corridor across the Irish Sea to compete with the Channel Tunnel. Coachloads are now coming from England and Wales, some of them for as little as £4 a trip to enjoy the special experience of Tallaght. It is estimated that in 1994 they were bringing in £500,000 worth of business (the average weekly spend is between £200,000 and £300,000).

THE CHALLENGE

The public relations challenge faced by Monarch was significant and involved all of its key audiences.
- to distinguish The Square from the original, ill-fated complex
- to distinguish Monarch and GRE Properties from Dublin County Council and Dublin Corporation
- to raise public support within the Tallaght community
- to elicit the support of the Government
- to convince Dublin Bus to extend bus routes to The Square
- to attract reliable anchor tenants and investors
- to maximise the profile of The Square and to keep it in the public eye

THE FUTURE COMES TO TALLAGHT

The public relations preparations started as far back as 1984 when Monarch bought the development rights from London & Clydesdale Holdings. The project was handled by John Butterly of Pembroke Communications. He estimated that he had at least one member of staff (and up to four members at peak periods) working full-time on the project.

The public relations budget was £133,000 and, to quote John Butterly, "it was all done very much to a budget; there were no free lunches."

The public relations team worked closely with the advertising agency, Quinn McDonnell Pattison; the Irish commercial property consultants, The Phelan Partnership and the Monarch management team. Every morning during construction, the teams met in an on-site office, to update each other on developments in all four areas. This, says Butterly, was one of the reasons for the smooth running of the programme.

Taking each of the public relations challenges:

- **To distinguish The Square from the original, ill-fated complex conceived in 1974**

Monarch realised the importance of dissociating The Square from the original complex with all its inherent negative connotations. Their first step was to build up an entirely different corporate identity with which people could associate positive values. Thus the complex was named The Square—the traditional market place and focal point in most Irish towns.

With this new name came an eyecatching logo which was featured consistently on everything associated with The Square, from the construction billboards to the door-to-door leaflets. Next came two catchy and optimistic slogans:

- *The Future comes to Tallaght*—presenting The Square as a complex so advanced that it really belongs in the future, and
- *The Dream becomes Reality*—aimed in particular at the Tallaght community who had indeed dreamt of having such a complex on their doorstep.

The two slogans were used consistently in advertising and promotional material. The headline on the front page of *The Square Times*, specially published for the opening in October 1990, was *The Future comes to Tallaght*.

The overall image presented was fresh and optimistic, a real break with all past connections.

- **To distinguish Monarch and GRE Properties from Dublin County Council and Dublin Corporation**

Again Monarch realised the need to separate themselves from the County Council and the Corporation, and indeed, from the Government, in the eyes of the public, but most importantly in the eyes of the people of Tallaght. They wanted the support of the community but had to ensure from the outset that the community would not look to Monarch as a surrogate Government to solve all of their problems. They had to stress that there would be no handouts, but mutual co-operation and consideration. Thus media attention was given to the negotiations between Monarch and the County Council and the Corporation. This was highlighted in the signing of the lease and the handing over of the initial £700,000.

In addition, Monarch presented a personal face to the people of Tallaght in the form of two personalities, Philip Reilly, general manager of all of Monarch's shopping centres, and Bill McMunn, the head of security in The Square, who spent a considerable amount of time liaising with the community. They were seen as trustworthy and dependable, and this reflected favourably on The Square.

- **To raise public support within the Tallaght community**

Both Bill McMunn and Phil Reilly became well-known within the community. Phil was later made Tallaght Person of the Year and Bill, a former garda superintendent in the area, became Mayor of Tallaght, a striking testimony to the success of this approach.

Monarch emphasised their intention to employ as many local people as possible. For many years the people of Tallaght had heard various people commit themselves to reducing the high unemployment rate in the area, but Monarch were the first to carry their rhetoric through to action. They sought the help of FÁS to ensure that as many local people as possible got work on the construction site. When The Square was completed they stressed to tenants the importance of hiring local people. Approximately 80 per cent of the people working in The Square are from Tallaght. This received much media attention.

Sponsorship played a large role. From the beginning Monarch committed themselves to various forms of sponsorship within the community. Local schools, sports clubs, drama societies, social clubs, etc. benefited from the sponsorship to different degrees. There was also more formal sponsorship such as education awards, given to students from each of the six local schools, entitling them to free third level education. This showed Monarch's commitment to the future of Tallaght, although the awards have now been discontinued due to high cost. However, they served their purpose when most needed.

- **To elicit the support of the Government**

It was necessary to lobby the Government to obtain the crucial urban renewal designation. A lot of the lobbying was carried out by the Tallaght residents themselves. The Tallaght Community Council was especially effective, aiming its efforts at the Minister for the Environment and subsequently European Commissioner, Padraig Flynn, TD. The Monarch approach was more subtle, but equally persuasive. The co-operation between Monarch and the community was the key to success in achieving this objective.

- **To convince Dublin Bus to extend bus routes to The Square**

From the outset Monarch had envisaged attracting customers from all over Dublin. This hinged, to some extent, on convincing Dublin Bus to run buses right into The Square. The company complied and 1,700 buses now run directly to The Square each week. "Our base research showed that 50 per cent of all of our shoppers were from outside the Dublin 24 area", says Noel Murray, Monarch.

THE FUTURE COMES TO TALLAGHT

- **To attract reliable anchor tenants and investors**

Monarch realised from past experience the importance of getting reliable, well-known anchor tenants, i.e. the large chain stores that can make or break a shopping centre. A marketing budget of approximately £600,000 was concentrated on this alone ! Hillier Parker were the agents in London and The Phelan Partnership in Dublin. This marketing programme needed support from the public relations team to maximise its effect.

The media had to be kept up to date on all developments, particularly any news that would encourage investors. The public and, in particular, the financial audiences, needed to realise the scale and prospects of The Square.

Much media coverage was achieved. Top stores Quinnsworth/Crazy Prices, Dunnes Stores, Roches Stores and Clerys are all in The Square. Winning over Dunnes was particularly important because they are more known for building shopping complexes around their stores than for buying space in other companies' ventures.

- **To maximise the profile of The Square and to keep it in the public eye**

Public relations played a supporting role to advertising and marketing in this area.

Media coverage was vital and much effort was put into it. Key journalists were updated regularly on all new developments.

The Square Times was published to explain to prospective customers what services were provided and where they were located.

Radio played a large part. RTE's Radio 2FM agreed to broadcast regularly from The Crow's Nest— a studio suspended from the ceiling in the atrium of The Square. Within 30 seconds of seeing the location, Bill O'Donovan of RTE had realised the potential of The Square for 2FM and vice versa. He was quick to acknowledge the importance of the large Tallaght listenership and he understood the benefits that could be achieved by harnessing it. From Monarch's point of view, this was ideal; they knew this constant source of attention would prove vital to the success of The Square. For instance, DJs regularly mentioned that "we are coming to you live from The Square......", and The Crow's Nest is visible from almost every part of The Square.

Various promotions were undertaken to attract attention to The Square once it had opened. These included: millionth customer, laser and fireworks display, celebrity visits, hosting RTE television's *Bi-Bi Show*, a visit by the Irish football team to raise money for charities, Santa Claus arriving, Christmas parties for families of media people and for local old folks, Christmas shopping night for the disabled, Christmas busking show, What's Cooking at The Square cookery promotion, Fill your Basket shopping competition, parachute jump, and much more......

THE LAUNCH, 23 OCTOBER 1990

The date for the launch of The Square was 23 October 1990 and all of the elements, public relations, advertising and marketing, had to be timed precisely to peak on this date. Co-ordination was vital. Plans were made meticulously, months in advance, and every wrinkle was ironed out to ensure the whole event would run smoothly.

Media attention was at a high by the time The Square was ready for business. Public and journalists alike were curious to see if it would live up to its advance reputation.

Much groundwork had gone into convincing top celebrities, from all walks of life, to attend the launch. Taoiseach Charles Haughey agreed to perform the opening ceremonies. He realised the importance of the event and, of course, recognised it as a chance to win political points in Tallaght. RTE's popular *Gay Byrne Show* on radio was broadcast live from The Crow's Nest that morning and he succeeded in bringing a real party atmosphere to the event.

By 11.30 am, when The Taoiseach officially opened The Square, there were an approximate 45,000 people enjoying the festivities ! And it continued all day, and long into the evening. Live bands, both local and celebrity, played in different areas around the complex.

The country's largest-ever outdoor marquee was erected in the north carpark and it played host to the VIP champagne reception.

John Butterly had the foresight to park his car on the far side of the dual carriageway that day. Thus, he was able simply to walk across the footbridge, avoiding the chaos, when it was time to deliver the first photographs of the opening to the evening papers. This, coupled with the fact that journalists were kept fully informed from the outset and were individually invited to the launch, ensured that the event got prominent coverage in the evening papers that day and the dailies on the next morning. Even Monarch was surprised by the success of it all. Wrote Jackie Gallagher, in *The Irish Times:* "While the hype had been intense, it was not unjustified....."

EVALUATION

The Square has been a phenomenal commercial success. Community relations are excellent and Monarch continue to sponsor many events in the area.

There has been something of a chain reaction, following the designation of urban renewal status, with many companies building factories and warehouses and amenities such as a bowling alley. The new National Basketball Arena now plays host to many sporting and social events.

State investment has also advanced with the County Council's new library, the opening of the Regional Technical College and signs that the long-promised Tallaght Hospital is finally in construction.

The Square has won many national and international awards. These include: 1991 European Shopping Centre award for the best centre developed in Europe in 1990; 1991 British Council of Shopping Centres award for the best shopping centre developed in Britain or Ireland; 1991 Dublin County Council Environmental award for the best shopping centre in the county area; European Community handicapped award for commercial buildings in Europe; National Accessibility award from the Irish Wheelchair Association; Structural award from the Engineering Industry Association (Ireland); National Rehabilitation Board award for accessibility; 1992 American Shopping Centre award; International Real Estate Federation "Certificat de Selection".

It has hosted numerous gala events, fashion shows, dinner dances and charity functions, its design being such that it can be transformed from a shopping centre to a function hall, complete with stage. Gala events have included: The British Council of Shopping Centres annual conference dinner dance; The Square Wedding Fair; The Radio 2FM *Beat on the Street*; The Kenwood Sound Challenge; The 1992 *People in Need* Telethon — the biggest ever; The Square Craft Fair; The Annual Barn Dance, a staff dance celebrating the anniversary of The Square, and various fashion shows, concerts and recitals.

The well-planned and implemented mix of public relations, advertising and marketing, can claim much of the credit for the successful launch of The Square.

Monarch's foresight and experience also played a major role. They realised the effort required to achieve their objectives and they were prepared to budget for it. They spent £483,000 on public relations and advertising.

The public relations effort did not finish with the launch. It has been ongoing to ensure the continued success of the project. The final testament is from John Butterly, who was asked if he would do it the same again. Yes, he would; he felt the launch "would actually act as a blueprint for a lot of developers".

Nicola Whelan has a BA Degree in English & Economics from University College, Galway and the DIT Diploma in Public Relations.

WOOING AND WINNING THE PEOPLE OF CORK

Sandoz comes to Ireland
by Jonathan Grey

INTRODUCTION

Sandoz Pharma Ltd ranks amongst the leading companies in the pharmaceutical indus-try in the world. It is the most important division in the Sandoz Group which em-ploys over 50,000 people in 55 countries. Sandoz was set up in Basle in Switzerland in 1886 to manufacture synthetic dyes, but diversified into pharmaceuticals in 1917 and agrochemicals in 1939. The pharmaceutical division has 17,000 employees.

This experience shows how public relations was used in bringing Sandoz into Ire-land and in gaining the support of the local community in the face of stern opposition. It looks, from a public relations point of view, at the history of the Sandoz project in Ringaskiddy, ten miles south east of Cork City, from the first announcement in mid-1989 to the start of construction of the plant in August 1990.

BACKGROUND

This is the biggest single investment in bulk pharmaceutical manufacturing ever made outside Switzerland by Sandoz. The plant will produce bulk active ingredients to be sold to more than 30 Sandoz affiliates throughout the world.

In 1988, Sandoz saw the need to expand its pharmaceutical manufacturing base and a worldwide search for a suitable location started, looking in particular at its three major markets Europe, North America and the Far East. Priority was given to an EC country in view of the impending completion of the Single Market by the end of 1992.

Sandoz were shown a large number of locations by the Industrial Development Au-thority (IDA) and they examined four in detail, one in the west and two on the east coast before settling for Ringaskiddy. It was an eight year project, starting with a worldwide location survey in 1988 to full capacity utilisation in 1996, allowing assessment from the US Food & Drugs Administration.

The IDA had been trying to attract Sandoz for a number of years. In addition to the normal incentives, Ireland offered a positive tax regime and a country with a well-edu-cated and well-qualified workforce.

The new facility was designed to be a low volume, high technology operation. As there was a well-established grouping of pharmaceutical companies in the Cork area a framework for ancillary support services already existed. At Ringaskiddy, in Cork Har-bour, there was a large, industrially-zoned site with natural gas, power, water supply and

WOOING AND WINNING THE PEOPLE OF CORK

water discharge services already on line. This, in combination with a well-developed road infrastructure and communications network, made the location most suitable for the proposed new Sandoz plant. The project had to move from concept to design, from site selection to layout, the obtaining of planning permission and the necessary emission licences.

The project outlined in the planning application in October 1989 was for a £200 million pharmaceutical production plant. It would provide over 250 permanent jobs in the area with an estimated 150 jobs in indirect services to the operation.

Having chosen the Ringaskiddy site, Sandoz had to face many obstacles. The first one was whether the people of the area would want the plant as the Cork Harbour area already had the highest concentration of chemical industries in the country. Cork was seen by some as a dumping ground for 'dirty' industry.

There was legitimate fear of pollution as for many years there had been a problem with bad odours due to emissions from chemical factories. Some years previously a bus-load of children had been affected by gas as they passed a chemical factory in nearby Cobh.

Also, the people were very aware of the well-publicised fire at the Sandoz plant near Basle in 1986 which caused extensive pollution of the Rhine. In addition, another pharmaceutical company, Merrell Dow, was facing considerable public opposition at that time to its proposed new plant in another part of Cork, and was eventually to move out.

Sandoz, therefore, realised the importance of gaining the public's support before setting up. They saw public relations and communications as the best way to do this and realised the importance of having people in Cork at all times to communicate with the public and all interested parties.

Initially the company engaged Forman Dove Public Relations of Dublin and the Cork firm of O'Sullivan Public Relations. Inside the first year, O'Sullivan PR became, first the lead consultancy and, thereafter, the sole public relations consultancy, and has continued to work for Sandoz since 1989. Sandoz had brought the local residents association to Basle before the consultants came in.

OBJECTIVES

The objective was to gain public support for the project and so enable Sandoz to set up in Ireland.

IMPLEMENTATION

To achieve this objective an 'open door' policy was adopted whereby Sandoz tried to answer every question that was put to them and to be accessible to all enquirers.

It was important not to be seen by the public as an unapproachable large corporation trying to buy space in the media to get their message across. From the start Sandoz decided to gain support for the project through public relations rather than advertising.

EOLAS—The Irish Science and Technology Agency, and Sandoz put together an information caravan in Cork where all interested groups could find out about the history of

Sandoz, the fire in 1986, the drugs produced and the details of the proposed new site.

Sandoz were committed to gaining public support and said they would withdraw if they could not get it. They promised that they would not come if they were not wanted and agreed to let the matter be decided by a vote of the Ringaskiddy residents.

This brought out the opposition groups even more as the vote was an opportunity to stop the project before it even started. The main opposition groups in 1989 were the East Cork Environmental Group, RICH (Responsible Industry for Cork Harbour), Friends of Cork Harbour and Greenpeace.

In October 1989, one month before the vote, while the consultants were in Basle with a group of journalists, Sandoz formally applied for planning permission and for emissions licences. These applications were accompanied by a £150,000 environmental impact study, one of the most comprehensive ever undertaken in Ireland. It examined in detail the nature of the project, the active substances that would be produced and the processes involved, both in production and in waste treatment. Copies of the study were made available immediately to all interested groups and a "Layman's Summary" was also provided with copies being made available in local libraries to ensure full public access.

Sandoz was confident that the information contained in the study would meet all the legitimate environmental concerns about the project.

Project Director, Winfried Pedersen, said the plant would meet the highest standards of safety and environmental protection and that the company's commitment in this re-spect was underlined by the fact that it planned to spend £27 million solely on these aspects of the project.

The study showed the state of the environment in the Cork Harbour region at the time and assessed the impact the proposed Sandoz plant would have on it. It also out-lined the environmental and protection features offered by the company and how all emissions from the plant would meet not only Irish requirements but also the then stricter EC standards.

Public meetings were then held for questions and opinions on every aspect of the project. Newsletters and fact sheets were distributed. Press releases highlighted the scale of the project and the environmental safety measures that the company would take.

It was stressed that the drugs to be produced were drugs for saving lives, and that it was unfair to describe the whole thing as 'dirty' industry. Speaking on television, on the popular *Late Late Show,* top surgeon Maurice Neligan described Sandoz' flagship prod-uct, Sandimmun, as the second epoch-making stage in transplant surgery following the first heart transplant. It is the drug of choice for the suppression of rejection reactions.

In their reports, committee members from the Ringaskiddy Residents Association (RRA) who were taken to Basle to see the operation there, emphasised the fact that the plant was in the centre of the city surrounded by urban areas. The residents' representa-tives were also told about the huge clean-up operation mounted by Sandoz after the fire and pollution spillage of 1986.

There was constant contact between Sandoz, the media and the public as well as the groups opposed to the project in the run-up to the residents' vote in November. Organ-ised entirely by the RRA and not by Sandoz, it brought a 60 per cent verdict in favour of the project.

Cork County Council decided to grant planning permission and emissions licences in December. There were 57 appeals to An Bord Pleanála, the statutory corporation for dealing with appeals. As a result, an oral hearing was held in March 1990.

Again, much work had to be done to secure a favourable decision from the oral hearing. The 'open door' policy of public relations, which had worked so well for the residents' vote, again proved its value. Again, Sandoz had to make sure that they could not be accused to trying to buy their way in, either through glossy propaganda brochures or advertising. They had people available for questioning at all times and constantly provided information to the public. Another decision was not to get involved in 'slanging matches' with the opposing groups either on radio or television, but just to provide all of the facts and figures when requested. The oral hearing lasted for three weeks and there were many claims and counterclaims made by Greenpeace and the Cork Environmental Alliance (CEA), an amalgamation of the smaller groups opposed to the project.

In July 1990, An Bord Pleanála granted a favourable decision to Sandoz in respect of both the planning and air emissions licences.

Work finally began on the construction of the £200 million project in August 1990. The construction budget was £175 million, plus another £25 million for development.

MEDIA MONITOR

While one must always stress quality as much as quantity in an evaluation of media coverage, it is interesting that between April 1989 and August 1992 there were 1449 Irish media references to the Sandoz project. Coverage was monitored under the headings of court appeals and hearing; licences and planning permission; trash incinerator licence; job creation; products/awards/results/sponsorship; general articles on Sandoz, An Bord Pleanála oral hearing and miscellaneous.

The biggest category, accounting for 360 of the 1449 items (25 per cent) related to licences, environmental decisions, standards etc. General articles about Sandoz, the oral hearing and miscellaneous each provided 15 per cent of the items.

However, 15 per cent of the coverage occurred in March 1990, and related directly to the oral hearing. Of the 251 items recorded in that month, 227, over 90 per cent, related to the hearing.

There was also substantial coverage in October 1989, when the press visited Basle and the planning application was made to Cork County Council. There were feature articles, in particular, by Donal Musgrave, *Cork Examiner;* Dick Hogan, *The Irish Times;* and Síle Yeats, *Irish Press.*

The Cork Examiner provided the greatest coverage with 309 out of the total of 1449 items, or 21 per cent of all items recorded. Next were the local radio stations 96FM (12 %), Cork 89FM (11%). The three Dublin morning papers accounted for 21.9 per cent between them.

EVALUATION

The Sandoz project has been a public relations success. The task of winning the support of the people and getting the company into Ireland was achieved. The tide was turned from the people forcing the Merrell Dow factory to withdraw to accepting Sandoz with 60 per cent support.

This campaign was a fight against a hostile press and a highly motivated and organised opposition in the CEA and Greenpeace. It was a fight to gain the support and the acceptance of the people of Cork, against the odds, for the most advanced pharmaceutical production facility in the world; it was a fight which was won, an example of how the most important group to convince in such a campaign is that which is nearest to the proposed project. The Ringaskiddy residents were the ones who would be most immediately affected and once they had been convinced, other groups, operating on a wider radius from the site, could be noisy but were less significant.

A key element was the journalists' visit to Basle in October 1989 which was at their own expense, but Sandoz facilitated them and showed them everything, allowing their executives to be grilled on every detail of the operation for two and a half days. It was during that visit that Sandoz announced to the journalists that they had applied for planning permission.

Throughout the campaign people had to be convinced that the industry was not a dirty one and that every effort was being made to safeguard the environment. The facility would be the safest and cleanest of its kind in the world and would produce life-saving products.

All of this was done through the use of the 'open door' campaign, gaining the trust and respect of target audiences through simple communication and openness. An indication of local acceptance was that the first advertisement for process operators attracted 1850 applications. By the end of 1993, Sandoz was employing 175 Irish people, well on the way to the target of 250 by 1995. Approximately 25,000 people had applied for jobs, of whom 60 per cent were already in employment.

FOOTNOTE

Trial production started in 1993 and the whole plant is due to come on stream in 1996. The promises about jobs, emission levels and other environmental features are being kept. Landscaping of the 100-acre site is proceeding with 38,000 trees and shrubs, all native Irish species, designed to provide a spectacular perimeter belt for the site. The company has continued to meet the Ringaskiddy Residents Association every month and makes regular news available on details of progress in the development of the site.

Protests by such groups as Greenpeace and the Cork Environmental Alliance have continued, with a Greenpeace invasion of the site in 1993 gaining a lot of publicity.

Sandoz has been committed in meeting all the requirements of its emission licences. In particular, it has been anxious to allay public concerns about the emission of dioxins which are extremely dangerous compounds. Professor James Heffron, Department of Biochemistry, University College, Cork, has estimated that smoking a single cigarette in an enclosed area such as a living room or a kitchen can produce from 40 to 400 times more dioxins than the limit of 0.1 nanogram per cubic metre which has been set for the Sandoz incinerators.

Resources will be recycled wherever possible. Used solvents will be redirected to a solvent recovery plant where over 95 per cent will be recovered to be used again. No water, from waste to rainwater, will leave the site before being checked, and treated if it is found to be contaminated. All the air emissions from the plant will be subjected to a three-tier cleaning process. All organic vapours, which would normally be emitted when liquids are being transferred from one vessel to another, will be destroyed, greatly reducing the ultimate emission level.

Jonathan Grey has a BA Degree in Economics & Computer Science from University College, Cork and the DIT Diploma in Public Relations.

NO VAT — A GREAT IDEA FOR A BOOK !

The Removal of VAT on Books
by Amber Kehoe

BACKGROUND

The Irish pound broke with sterling in 1979. At once, there was instability in the pricing of goods from the UK, including books, because of the day-to-day change in the exchange rate. The price of books rose, and when value added tax (VAT) at 10 per cent was also taken into consideration, consumers felt the increase was exorbitant. In September 1981, VAT on books was increased to 15 per cent.

The morale of the trade, already affected by general economic difficulties, was hit further with the liquidation of Willis Books in May 1981. In September, Hodges Figgis announced they would close their shop on St. Stephen's Green at the end of the year. John F. Newman, the binders, were experiencing difficulties in servicing publishers and Clondalkin Paper Mills, the only white paper mills in Ireland, was put into the hands of a receiver.

When the VAT increase was announced by the Minister for Finance, John Bruton, the President, Dr. Patrick Hillery, wrote to him urging the introduction of a special low rate for books. Dr. Hillery cited figures provided by Clé—The Irish Book Publishers' Association which showed that all member countries of the EEC, except Ireland and Denmark, had a special low rate for books. The Minister replied sympathetically but, "given the general condition of the public finances, could not discriminate in favour of books". Clé had, to no avail, been lobbying against purchase tax (now VAT) since its enforcement some ten years previously.

In October 1981, the Booksellers Association of Ireland (BAI) employed Kent Public Relations Consultants, now part of Grayling Public Relations, to lobby the Government for reduction of the VAT rate to 3 per cent. The approach to Patrick Crane, managing director of KPRC, came through Dick Roche, former deputy editor of the *Irish Independent*. Roche had been approached by Seán O'Boyle who was involved in both Clé and BAI.

OBJECTIVE

BAI's original objective was to lobby the Government to reduce VAT on books from 15 to 3 per cent. KPRC devised a programme and presented it to a committee of publishers and booksellers who included: Sean O'Boyle, Veritas Publications; Michael Gill, Gill & Macmillan; Harold Clarke, Eason & Son; Frank O'Mahony, O'Mahony's Booksellers (chairman, BAI); Vivian Pembrey, Greene's Bookshop, and Fred Hanna, Fred Hanna Ltd.

Having researched the proposal to reduce VAT to 3 per cent, KPRC advised the committee that they could get zero-rate VAT, as in the UK.

The EC Directives which, in part, governed Irish VAT laws, stated that zero rates and exemptions "may only be taken for clearly defined social reasons and for the benefit of the final consumer" (Article 17 of the Second VAT Directive). The UK maintained a zero rate by claiming that VAT on books was a tax on knowledge and thereby satisfied both the social (education) reasons and the benefit of the final consumer. This same argument was proposed by Patrick Crane— "VAT on books—a tax on education, a tax on knowledge".

Crane's proposal was accepted by the committee.

THE CHALLENGE

To eliminate VAT on books, to convince the Government that VAT could be removed from books without rocking the boat and without significant cost to the Exchequer, but with considerable political gain and popular approval.

PLANNING

The concept behind the presentation was straightforward and it became the basis of the campaign. Crane believed that the Government would not be bullied into granting any concessions to publishers or booksellers. The issue, the removal of VAT on books, was not one of any great national significance and the BAI was not a lobby of any great importance—they were not the farmers, nor the teachers !

The BAI had wanted an aggressive campaign, they had wanted blood on their knuckles ! Dick Roche had sold KPRC to them on the basis that Crane was a no-nonsense public relations maverick who would help them to bring the Government to its knees, so understandably they were disappointed at first by his approach.

Crane believed that if VAT on books were to be abolished, the concession would be won not by blood on anyone's knuckles, but by making what was not an issue into something that was a talking point in the Department of Finance and in the Dail, and ultimately around the Cabinet table.

IMPLEMENTATION

The proposals for the campaign, which began in October 1981, fell under three broad headings:
*   canvass support of public representatives
*   submission to Government
*   sustained publicity campaign.

The title Crane devised for the campaign was *Veto VAT on Books* with the logo of a stack of books and the sub-head message, *No Tax on Knowledge*.

Three months after the lobby started, in January 1982, the Government announced in the Budget that the 15 per cent VAT band was being increased to 18 per cent. There was no concession for books. Booksellers would have borne an 80 per cent increase in the tax inside six months.

But it never happened. Garret FitzGerald's Fine Gael-Labour government was defeated on the Budget and immediately resigned. This gave KPRC the opportunity to make VAT on books an election issue—which it was not ! But it could be made a major talking-point.

Fianna Fáil were elected with Charles Haughey as Taoiseach. KPRC now decided to aim for a zero-rate VAT on books to be announced on Budget Day, 26 March. They had 17 days to begin and end their campaign.

The launch of the publicity campaign was on Tuesday, 9 March 1982, the first sitting of the new Dáil. A personal letter was delivered by hand to every deputy (member of the Dáil), requesting support in principle only for the elimination of VAT on books. If the deputy agreed he was asked to sign a declaration of support and join the Dáil Deputies Friends of Literacy League.

The second phase of the programme was a fully documented submission to the Government. This had to anticipate and answer every technical, administrative, legal and financial argument against the removal of VAT. Some of the main arguments were:
- If concession was given for books, other groups would seek reduced rates, e.g. construction goods, medical equipment etc
- The revenue loss to the Exchequer would be too big in the light of present expenditure needs
- The administrative problems and associated costs of introducing a new special rate would be prohibitive
- What was needed was simplification of the VAT system (i.e. one rate only along with the zero rate). The introduction of a special rate for books, papers etc would complicate matters for many small general traders who sold papers, books etc in addition to food and household goods
- In present circumstances what was needed was a widening of the tax yield, not a reduction

These arguments were met by a 13-point summary. VAT on books:
- was a tax on literacy
- was a tax on knowledge
- inhibited education
- inhibited cultural development
- reduced library funds for new acquisitions
- reduced reading opportunities
- had seriously reduced Irish book sales
- had seriously restricted new Irish writing and publishing
- was contributing to bookshop closures
- was contributing to unemployment in the book industry, since with the sterling differential, the increase in the price of an imported book could be up to 50 per cent
- created huge book bills for parents. For example, the parents of four school-going children could, in 1982, pay up to £300 for school books alone.

NO VAT—A GREAT IDEA FOR A BOOK !

- did not make a sufficiently significant contribution to the Exchequer—probably less than £2 million—in relation to its cultural, educational and hardship effects

At this point Charles Haughey was sensitive to VAT having toppled the Coalition government—the imposition of VAT on children's shoes was agreed to have been the breaking point.

What KPRC put forward was a VAT proposition that was not going to cost the Government a lot of money. As Patrick Crane states: "When you spoke to the Fianna Fáil Government about books, culture, tradition, reading, Irish writers and the great tradition of Ireland and the island of saints and scholars, they found it very easy to identify because, by and large, it flattered their image of themselves to be consulted about books and told how they could save the book industry which was in serious trouble".

Patrick Crane met the Taoiseach three times in those 17 days. Mr. Haughey, 13 years previously, as Minister for Finance, had made a popular decision to exempt writers and artists from income tax. By the end of Crane's third meeting he felt something might be done about the VAT on books.

The 17 days between the launch of the publicity campaign and the Budget Speech by Minister for Finance, Ray MacSharry, were fraught with anxiety. There were no marches or protests. However, much work and lobbying was done behind the scenes. The public now knew how much VAT on books was costing them—the media had been constantly informed of KPRC's intentions, with numerous news releases, including copies of the Dáil deputies canvass, and photographers were always at hand to record anything newsworthy.

The final onslaught came when the lobbyists waylaid the Fianna Fáil front-runners for ministerial posts, and the Taoiseach, at the Mass in the Pro-Cathedral to celebrate the opening of the Dáil. But this was a good-humoured, chatty occasion with the sole purpose of creating a photo-opportunity. And it did. Many column inches were generated.

On 26 March 1982, Minister MacSharry, in the Budget, announced a zero-rate of VAT on books.

EVALUATION

In this case evaluation is easy. VAT on books was reduced from 15 per cent to zero— a truly successful campaign !

Crane stresses that it was a cheerful campaign. The slogan, *Veto VAT on Books* was cheerful. It was easygoing. It was deliberately unsophisticated. It seemed to be coming from an industry group, but not a rich industry group, and Kent orchestrated from the background all the time.

DISCUSSION

The VAT concession gave a great boost to book publishing and retailing. At the booksellers AGM, the weekend after the Budget, the BAI and Clé set up a new marketing advisory body, the Irish Books Marketing Group. Patrick Crane was appointed to this group and KPRC produced all the marketing and creative work for Ireland's biggest ever books promotion. This was to maximise the sales potential of the removal of VAT.

The campaign began on 1 May 1982 and cost £100,000. The slogans were *Books are Cheaper Now* and *No VAT on Books is a Novel Idea*. Posters conveyed these messages. A special offer, *Buy Two, Get One Free*, attracted numerous customers into the bookshops.

"It really was Rinso bookselling", says Crane, "and if you got two books you got a reduction on one or got another one free. And with every book you bought you got an entry into a competition. It worked."

The whole concept of marketing books was changed. Easons, the major Irish book-sellers with several branches in Dublin and other cities, became pioneers in displaying books so the customer could see the entire cover. Previously it was more common for the spine only of the books to be visible on shelves.

Bookshops, instead of closing down, began to open again —Chapters and Waterstones were among the newcomers in Dublin. A sub-campaign, costing £2,000, was started by KPRC on 9 September 1983. It was entitled *Top o' the Irish* and promoted Irish writers.

Book sales increased by between 25 and 30 per cent in the year following the removal of VAT.

Later figures showed that the book industry continued to prosper. Between 1986 and 1992:
- Total book sales increased from £56.6 million to £80.9 million
- Sales of imported books (at retail value) increased by 26 per cent
- Sales of Irish published books (at retail value) increased by 78 per cent (educational by 69 per cent and general by 104 per cent)
- Irish publishers' market share increased from 33 to 41 per cent.

These figures come from The Fishwick report for the Irish Books Marketing Group in 1987 and the Conroy O'Neill report in 1992.

Ironically, it is now only believed to be a matter of time until the implications of harmonisation within the EU lead to a set VAT rate being reinstated on books in Ireland and in every other European country.

Amber Kehoe has a BA Degree in Economics & German, from the University of Dublin, Trinity College and the DIT Diploma in Public Relations

IF THEATRE IS TO BE........VAT IS THE QUESTION

The Removal of VAT on Theatre Tickets
by Amber Kehoe

BACKGROUND

Following the highly successful campaign against VAT on books, the Irish Theatre Managements' Association, in 1983, asked Kent Public Relations Consultants, now part of Grayling Public Relations, if anything could be done about the VAT on theatre tickets. The rate was 23 per cent.

Theatre in Ireland was in crisis. Unemployment among actors was as high as 80 per cent, much higher than in any other sector. Four hundred of the 500 actors on the books of Irish Actors' Equity were out of work. A freelance actor could expect to spend seven months of the year unemployed. The situation was twice as bad as five years previously. Audiences were down. That year the five main independent theatres had closed for periods or been threatened with closure—the Olympia, the Gaiety, the Oscar and the Eblana in Dublin, and the Cork Opera House. It was feared that even the subsidised Dublin theatres, the Abbey and the Gate, would soon have to close for periods.

Many shows in the independent theatres ran at a loss even before the curtains rose. The show, *Whose Life is it Anyway ?* expected, even on an optimistic occupancy projection of 70 per cent, to have a £15,000 loss for its five-week run at the Olympia.

The State grant to the Arts Council was $4.5 million from which the theatres got £2 million. Half of this went to the Abbey Theatre which then had to pay back £640,000 in VAT and PAYE/PRSI (pay as you earn and pay-related social insurance).

The zero-rating of VAT on books had, at this stage, been declared contrary to EC tax harmonisation policy and while KPRC reckoned, quite rightly, that the decision would hold, they foresaw little possibility of its being repeated. Zero-rating was out, but they were still prepared to aim for it, while realising that a nominal rate of 5 to 10 per cent was more feasible.

OBJECTIVE

To lobby the Government for a zero VAT rate on theatre in the January 1984 Budget and to make the public aware of the effects of VAT on theatre.

PLANNING

As initially with the booksellers, the Irish Theatre Managements' Association wanted a "bloody" campaign. They, like the BAI, had fought without effect for a VAT concession.

FROM JOHN PAUL TO SAINT JACK.......

Patrick Crane once again proposed a more subtle approach. He judged that the campaign for the theatre had something that was missing from the books campaign—it had critics and correspondents, people with access to media space. These people had a great sympathy for the campaign.

IMPLEMENTATION

The campaign was launched on Wednesday, 7 December 1983 with theatre people making a spectacular carnival march from the Gaiety Theatre to Dáil Eireann. Three hundred joined in, "with clowns, jazzbands and fellows on the backs of lorries", all headed by the country's most popular comedienne, Maureen Potter and including entertainers, Brendan Grace and Tony Kenny. The marchers wore costume and make-up to attract maximum media attention.

The event was good-humoured, a carnival not a protest. Ministers and TDs came out to meet the revellers in the street, shaking hands and even having their pictures taken. To end it all, a pair of piebald horses, pulling an old hearse, arrived from Fossett's Circus and led the marchers back to the Gaiety.

The Taoiseach, Garret FitzGerald was very supportive. Alan Dukes, Minister for Finance, was more reserved partly because, on the basis of EEC tax harmonisation, he had been critical about the zero-rate of VAT for books. A personal presentation was made to every member of the Dáil and Seanad in support of the case for the removal of VAT. Submissions were handed in to Alan Dukes and Ted Nealon, Minister for Arts & Culture. The submission had four arguments in support of removal of VAT on theatre:

1. Economically, if VAT were removed, the Exchequer would stand to lose £400,000. But if the 400 unemployed actors, alone, were put back to work, their PAYE and PRSI contributions would wipe out that loss with a return of at least £450,000 plus a social welfare saving of over £2 million. It stated that these actors could be put back to work.

2. Politically, it would be a good decision to zero-rate VAT on live theatre and an enlightened administration would be lauded by the media.

3. Legally, the only real barrier was EEC legislation regarding new zero-ratings. Even if the EEC were to take an enlightened Irish Government to law for defending Irish culture, the penalty, under 1 per cent own-resources, would amount to only £4,000.

4. Culturally, there was an argument to override all others. The real issue was the moral case, the case for the special tradition of Irish theatre, and the horrifying implications of letting it die.

A photocall notice was issued to all the national media prior to the march and press releases were sent out afterwards. TDs and Senators were invited to join an all-party Dáil and Seanad group through, once again, signing a simple declaration of support.

At this stage the public were targeted. A tongue-in-cheek slogan was devised: *If Theatre is to be.... VAT is the Question*. Support cards were placed in all theatre programmes encouraging patrons to sign and send them back to Leinster House. No stamp was required on letters sent to one's own TD. However, half-way through the campaign, An Post decided to end the concession of free postage to Leinster House, even for government departments. The post offices were inundated with sackloads of support cards with no stamps. Leinster House refused to pay and accept delivery. The campaign, run on a shoe-string, was faced with the prospect of paying the double post now due, or having all the cards returned to their senders, with double post due at that end as well.

Then, Aisling Kilroy, a Kent executive, rang Feargal Quinn, successful supermarket king, who was chairman of An Post and famous for getting things done. He was sympathetic to the case and got An Post to relent !

Meetings were held with the Taoiseach and with Alan Dukes, who became more supportive as the campaign went on. One of the many cartoons showed Dukes, a very tall man, snowed under by postcards, each bearing a different message of support from every member of the Dáil and Seanad, issued the first day the new Dáil sat. Dukes is captioned saying: "All right, all right, I get the message". And he did !

Posters were put up, presentations held, novelty New Year cards published, and daily contact with members of the Government maintained. There was extensive national press, television and radio coverage. The campaign turned the minority-interest topic of VAT on theatre into a high-profile talking point—a national issue.

Finance Minister, Alan Dukes announced in the January Budget a reduction of VAT on theatre from 23 per cent to a "nominal 5 per cent".

EVALUATION

Following the announcement, the Minister for Arts & Culture, Ted Nealon, complimented KPRC and told a press conference that "the VAT concession was won by the excellent *VAT is the Question* campaign". The Minister described it as "imaginative, good-humoured and well-argued".

There was a great welcome for the concession, with such newspaper headlines as : "VAT relief greeted with rapture"; "VAT down, curtains up in theatreland"; "Tickets concession gives theatres half a million pounds".

As with the VAT on books campaign, Patrick Crane says that a large degree of the success resulted from "a planned, unsophisticated approach. Don't look too sophisticated, don't look too organised, don't give the Government the impression that they are under pressure and that there is a big organisation behind it. And, more than anything, make submissions short, to the point and accessible. I believe all that contributed to why it worked".

DISCUSSION

A VAT campaign fighting fund was launched by the Irish theatre industry in December 1983 to raise £10,000. Based on a draw and theatre ticket discount scheme, the fund offered a one-off 10 per cent discount on theatre tickets for every £1 raffle ticket bought. There was also a private members' draw, under the auspices of the Irish Theatre Club, with a first prize of a holiday-for-two in Spain, plus other prizes including five pairs of tickets for every show at the Abbey Theatre during 1984.

Represented in the campaign were: The Irish Theatre Managements' Association, Irish

Actors' Equity, Irish Transport & General Working Union No. 7 Branch, the Irish Federation of Musicians and Allied Professions, and the Society of Irish Playwrights.

A large amount of the cost of the campaign was met by Gerry Sinnott, managing director of the Olympia Theatre who represented the Irish Theatre Managements' Association. Patrick Crane pays tribute to the central role of Sinnott, "he has a terrific heart".

In the following Budget, January 1985, Alan Dukes abolished VAT on theatre. This, however, was two-edged. It was not a zero-rate as with books; it took theatre out of VAT altogether, so that they could not reclaim the VAT they were paying.

In 1990, Kent Public Relations Consultants was acquired by Grayling, one of the Lopex companies in Ireland which also acquired Arks, Youngs and Kennys in the 1980s. Patrick Crane joined the Grayling board as creative director.

Amber Kehoe has a BA Degree in Economics & German, from the University of Dublin, Trinity College and the DIT Diploma in Public Relations

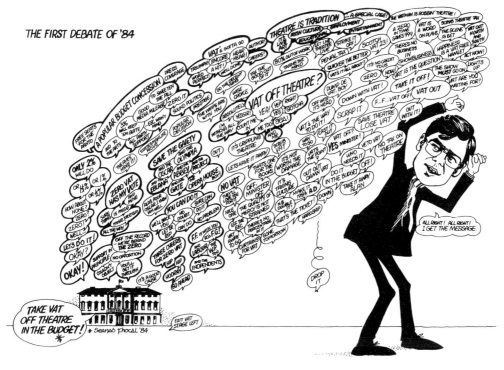

Alan Dukes gets the message !

IF THEATRE IS TO BE........VAT IS THE QUESTION

SORRY, NO IRISH SERVED HERE !

The Lobby to Allow Restaurants Serve Beer and Spirits
by Antoinette Harbourne

BACKGROUND

The Irish Restaurant Owners' Association (IROA) had been lobbying the Government for 15 years to legalise the sale of beer and spirits in restaurants. They could sell imported wines but not home-produced beers and spirits.

Sale of drink in Ireland is licensed. The licence holder can sell drink for consumption on or off the premises between given hours. Limited extensions may be granted through application to the courts. Changes in conditions or hours require new legislation. The IROA knew what they wanted but did not know how to go about getting it.

In 1981, Myles Tierney, political lobbyist and Dublin county councillor, wrote a letter to a newspaper about Irish drinking laws and their absurdity. Two or three months later he got a call from IROA president, Des Coffey. They met and the IROA were convinced that Tierney's experience as councillor, journalist (formerly *The Cork Examiner)* and lobbyist made him the man to do the job for them.

Myles Tierney, who has over the years developed his own special approach to lobbying—relying, among other things, on force of argument more than on personal introductions—said the IROA had failed in their own lobby because "they did not realise that the nature of political argument is to disturb the public repose". He holds that in a constitutional democracy people need to know the reasons for a change of law in order to assent to it. For this reason there must always be enough unrest to dramatise an injury, in other words, the "public repose" must be disturbed.

OBJECTIVES

The IROA had been seeking a series of different though related changes:
- To create a new type of licence enabling restaurants to dispense beer and spirits as well as wine
- To serve during the "holy hour" as well as one hour after the public houses' closing time. The holy hour, still in force at that time in some urban areas, forbade drink to be served between 2.30 and 3.30 in the afternoon.
- One hour "drinking-up" time
- Extension of trading hours of the licence to 1 am for restaurants in city centres or areas frequented by tourists

---

FROM JOHN PAUL TO SAINT JACK.......

The IROA ran the risk of the Government rejecting their argument on a point of detail. For example, an extension of trading hours could be interpreted by the publicans as unfair competition. So, Myles Tierney recommended a more simple approach, to limit the main objective to allowing restaurants to sell beer and spirits, as well as wine which was already allowed during a meal. The Minister could have demanded more details, in which case the Association would have had to expand its request. However, he did not.

STRATEGY

Myles Tierney offered the IROA a political lobby following the three stages which he uses with all his clients:
- Demonstrate that there is an inequality, an injury to someone. This shows that the "public repose" is disturbed. Tierney holds that all government action is directed at preserving the public repose. If there is lack of repose government acts to restore it.
- Dramatise the issue. This is necessary to maintain political pressure and win support.
- Force the issue to a conclusion, in this instance a decision by the Minister to reform the law, and then to bring in the required legislation. "In lobbying you have not succeeded until the law is changed", he says, adding that "clients often find it very difficult to understand that the Minister saying he will change the law does not mean that it has been changed".

He developed this systematic approach from his years as a county councillor when he was on the receiving end of many petitions and lobbies and saw how badly they were often presented.
       The campaign to achieve the main objective for the IROA was set out under four headings:
- preparation of the lobby
- briefings
- dramatisation
- the decision and its implementation

IMPLEMENTATION

Myles Tierney's company, PASS PR (now Myles Tierney & Associates), were the appointed consultants to liaise with the press and to assist the IROA and its members in carrying out the objectives of the lobby. But, to avoid any suggestion of "fronting", which could damage the campaign, the IROA president, or other appointed member, was to be the lobby spokesperson to make all statements and generally to be the human face of the IROA. A small committee worked with Myles Tierney and generally supervised the day-to-day running of the lobby, including such reviews as were thought necessary.

Preparation of the lobby
A committee was set up to prepare a detailed casebook and brief for those involved in the lobby. This book, an essential element in all of Myles Tierney's lobbies, formed the

basis for all briefings and was circulated to all interest groups and opinion formers. It had to relate to the background of these groups who were identified through extensive and rigorous research.

The "publics" to whom the lobby looked were:
- politicians - Taoiseach, Government, TDs, senators and local councillors
- present and potential users of the services of the IROA
- the pro-drink lobby
- the anti-drink lobby
- opinion-makers, including selected public figures, journalists, and selected social and community organisations
- foreign commentators and journalists.

The most sensitive interest groups included those concerned with underage drinking, medical organisations, churches, brewers and distillers, financial institutions, government bodies, the vintners' trade union and the Vintners Federation of Ireland. The vintners wanted to limit the availability of Irish drinks in restaurants. They feared that the increased number of outlets, and the proposed liberalisation of the law, would damage their members to the extent that many of them would have to close down. However, the vintners did not conduct a campaign against the liberalisation of the law.

The case book came to 24 pages. The cover stated: *A necessary reform* and had a photograph of a placemat, including the slogan: *Sorry, no Irish served here !*

The presentation of the argument was simple and convincing in analysing the idea of change and answering anticipated objections. It gave all the necessary arguments about injury to the IROA and the public good. It was backed up with statistics about alcohol consumption and illness and results of research from independent sources. Tierney didn't worry about his opponents. He only needed to know what they said in order to show them to be unreasonable.

There were five sections in the case book:

1. A one-page summary on why the reform was being sought and what results it would achieve.

2. The present position of the Minister and why he was objecting to the reform. His two principal objections, that the reform might lead to the opening of additional drink outlets and to more abuse of the law by underage and late-night drinking, were answered clearly.

3. A question and answer section which showed that the reforms would:
- not add significantly to the number of drinking outlets because of the heavy investment involved and the need to consume a meal.
- show the prevailing laws to be abnormal/unfair, i.e. out of step with the rest of Europe.
- not create or increase alcohol-related problems in Ireland.
- be unlikely to lead to underage drinking because the cost of using restaurants as a source of drink would deter teenagers.
- not increase driving hazards. The amount of alcohol consumed and the rate at which it is absorbed are reduced when consumed with food.

- not lead to an increase in alcoholism because alcoholics are not interested in eating and drinking together.
- help to improve Ireland's bad drinking habits. Most Irish people drink in pubs and the consumption of drink is mainly social in character and not strongly correlated with food.
- promote Irish tourism, products and jobs.
- take the elitism out of wine by associating Irish drinks with food.
- make Irish restaurants more attractive.
- create a market for the sale and promotion of Irish drinks to tourists, some of whom do not go to pubs.

The stand-up "tent" card which was placed on tables in all IROA restaurants. On the reverse it asked "So, if you want an Irish produced drink don't ask the waiter, ask the minister", and contained the petition with room for signature.

4. The final section gave more detailed comment on such topics as:
- need for reform
- elitism of the present unfair law
- anomaly of Irish restaurants only being allowed a wine licence which meant that all the drinks which they could legally serve were imported drinks—no Irish served !
- acceptance by the IROA of the need for proper control and supervision of licensed and non-licensed restaurants
- the new licence would be for restaurants and not a covert method of getting a publican's licence
- heavy drinkers would not be interested in restaurants as places to drink
- it would not be a temptation for the underage drinker
- drunken driving
- the benefits of moderate consumption of alcohol with food
- improving drinking patterns
- the effect on employment
- support for reform
- the correct timing of the campaign as the Minister was now considering a new licensing law
- the medical opinion
- the position of the alcoholic
- alcoholism in Ireland

SORRY, NO IRISH SERVED HERE !

The case book was fully referenced so that challengers could easily find their way through it.

The next stage in the preparation of the lobby was to reduce its message further to reach wider audiences. The "Tent" campaign was introduced to reach the people who go to restaurants. The tent was a piece of card in the shape of a placemat, bearing the inscription *Sorry, no Irish served here*. It was to be circulated to every IROA restaurant. Its brief and powerful message would leave little room for argument. It finished: "Endorse our campaign by signing this advertisement and return it to us or contact your TD at Dáil Eireann, Dublin 2" and had room for a signature. Between the knife and fork was a smaller slogan *Change the course of Irish drinking*.

The placemats sought support for the campaign by providing spaces for signatures. Then there were also to be "lobby support forms"—specially adapted for:
- politicians
- members of local authorities
- media
- the public

Briefings

The case book formed the base for extensive briefings with interested groups. It informed IROA members and Bord Fáilte before launching the lobby. Tierney organised separate meetings for each group at which the case book was distributed, discussed and a plan of action confirmed. All resulting plans would differ only in that each group had a different role to play. They all related to Tierney's master plan, the lobby objective of allowing beer and spirits to be served in restaurants.

The local and regional committees of the IROA were essential to these briefings and in general to the management of the lobby and its implementation.

Dramatisation

The lobby had to establish in the public mind that failure to amend the law was creating an injury. This had to be brought before the public and politicians to create the tension necessary to disturb the public repose. In the dramatisation of the issue the proposed changes had to be highlighted as helping to control excessive drinking.

The most notable steps in the dramatisation were:
- The Minister for Justice and all TDs and senators were approached personally and informed by spokesmen on behalf of the IROA. The individual interviews were imperative but time-consuming. They were reinforced by letters to all of them.
- Circulation of the case book to regional tourism organisations, and to all elected local authorities.
- inaugural press conference.
- media coverage in national and international press, radio, TV and magazines.
- meetings with Bord Fáilte and the regional tourism organisations at which the research material and the case book were presented. These meetings were often an opportunity for media functions. Apart from saying that the law should be reformed, the IROA had to show that it was possible to change it. Bord Fáilte representatives

were taken to Northern Ireland where there was a restricted right to sell drink with meals. They used this as a model to show that a change in law was possible.

- efforts to get regional tourism organisations and local authorities to pass resolutions. A specific form of resolution was circulated to such bodies or to friendly members for them to table and debate.
- publicity statements from restaurants.
- use of the "letters to the editor" columns, again based on the theme of the campaign and the case book. This had only limited impact.
- contact by IROA members with local organisations of which they were members, including clubs like Rotary, as well as social and sporting clubs, and offers to give short talks on the objective of the lobby. They were always based on the case book.
- launch of the "Tent" campaign with 100,000 placemats distributed to all members for their customers.
- lobbying of interest groups and an attempt to get them to declare their support and undertake action in co-operation with the IROA. For example, Bord Fáilte made available reference material in relation to tourism demands. They also assisted in correlating the statistics issued by the lobby group with their own, thus cutting costs.
- contact with the anti-drink lobby, ideally to win their support but, should that support not be forthcoming, to try and silence them. Every effort was made to convince the licensed vintners that the proposed changes would only have a marginal effect on their trade and its employment. They were not convinced and they remained hostile.
- invitations to TDs and senators to be guests for dinner at owners' restaurants where the campaign material was handed to them. They were asked to sign the pledge of support. Groups of TDs from the same constituencies were brought together. This was done through local or regional committees of the IROA.
- invitations to editors and tourism, industrial, social and food journalists and columnists for meals. This was handled by the national executive in Dublin, and by local or regional committees elsewhere.
- a modest advertising campaign, costing about £10,000, to reinforce the message.

The decision
The objective was to get the Government to agree to the reform and to incorporate it in a Bill which would be passed by the Dáil and Seanad and become law. To get the support of both Government and opposition parties, the IROA employed the use of the resolutions—signed statements of support from TDs or candidates, local party pledges and local party manifesto promises.

Timing and circumstance were very important in gaining a positive ministerial reaction. As the Minister for Justice had indicated his intent to introduce new licensing laws, this was the obvious time to push the reform sought by the IROA. The IROA had good luck in bringing the issue to the politicians and the public because there were an unprecedented three general elections in 18 months—June 1981 and February and November 1982, each of which resulted in a change of government. This provided plenty of opportunity to seek affirmations of support.

SORRY, NO IRISH SERVED HERE !

In another sense this musical chairs period of Government went against the lobby—nobody was in power long enough to make the changes. In all, it took two years to organise the lobby and bring it to the stage where the Minister for Justice agreed to change the law.

There were some special episodes within the campaign:

- A press conference was called to launch it in May 1981, but that was the day the Pope was shot in St. Peter's Square. There was little room for headlines about Irish restaurants and their drink licences.
- The placemat campaign generated a lot of comment and publicity. People spoke about it and asked questions. The restaurateurs were delighted and able to explain the unfair treatment they were getting.
- Government minister, Brian Lenihan, was in a restaurant with some friends and they all signed the petition. Taoiseach Charles Haughey politely declined on another occasion.
- By February 1982 the Fianna Fáil party had put it into their election manifesto. They were elected and the IROA, thinking they had achieved their goal, thanked Myles Tierney and paid him off. Little did they know.......It was to be three years before the legislation got onto the statute book and then it was badly flawed.

Without Myles Tierney the IROA wandered outside the parameters of the political argument that he wanted them to make.

He had got them to highlight the inequality of the existing legislation in answer to the arguments of the opposition, but they reverted to bargaining tactics. They volunteered to pay a licence fee. Of course, the Minister was delighted. This indicated to him that they were uncertain of success and it also helped him to meet the complaints of the publicans. Knowing this, he imposed a licence fee of £4,000 a year (£1,000 more than had been agreed) when he eventually put the Act through.

Myles Tierney claims that the IROA did not realise that, with the strength of the tent campaign and the favourable attention it had created for them, they no longer needed to rely too much on Bord Fáilte for support. "Once the message got over that no Irish was served in an Irish restaurant the opposition were gone. We had everyone's support", he recalls. But Bord Fáilte took advantage of the occasion and used it as an opportunity for a tough drive on standards. Basic criteria for licence eligibility, as set out by Bord Fáilte, were:

- only restaurants holding "Cuisine Retailers On" Licence and Restaurant Certificate, would qualify for the new licence
- Bord Fáilte would be empowered to certify as bona fide any restaurant applying to the board for such certification, provided that the restaurant:
  - was well-equipped
  - operated by a competent manager and staff
  - provided high standard catering (not snacks)
  - had a minimum of 95 per cent food consumed at tables on the premises

- had a minimum number of chairs and tables
- had a waiting area not greater than 30 per cent of the dining area
- provided documentary evidence that the premises complied with legislation on public health and fire prevention.

Myles Tierney says if his services had been retained he would have pointed out the ridiculous nature of some of the conditions as the Bill was going through the Oireachtas.

At first, very few restaurants applied for the licence. Many small restaurants couldn't afford the fee and the restructuring costs to adapt to the new requirements—knocking down walls, installing new toilets etc.

On the other hand some restaurants bought publicans' licences as they became available and there has in the past few years been a large increase in the number of pubs setting up restaurants in their premises—full restaurants and not just pub lunches.

CONCLUSION

The IROA eventually achieved its objective but it took a long time and ended up costing a lot more than the £40,000 (approximately) that Myles Tierney had estimated for fees and implementation. As for the *Sorry, no Irish served here*, Myles does not claim its authorship. It came from Ted O'Sullivan of the O'Sullivan Ryan advertising agency during a brainstorming session. "And as soon as he said it, I knew we had won", says Myles. "It was a lovely slogan. It powerfully demonstrated an obvious inequality".

Antoinette Harbourne has an MA Degree in Anglo-Irish Literature and a BA Degree in English & Spanish, both from University College, Dublin, and the DIT Diploma in Public Relations.

BANK REFLECTS IRISH HERITAGE AND GLOBAL COMMITMENT

AIB's New Corporate Identity
by Morgan Walsh

BACKGROUND

Allied Irish Banks Plc was formed in 1966 with the merger of three well-established banks, the Munster & Leinster, the Provincial and the Royal. Its name, along with its Mercedes-Benz type logo, reflected this union. However, by 1990, AIB had developed beyond its origins. This table summarises the extent to which AIB had grown in its 24 years of business.

A Confluence of Changes

AIB	1966	1990
Assets	IR£270 million	IR£16,000 million
Employees	2,600	14,000
Branches	430	650

Not only did AIB grow in size, it also expanded the range of services for both personal and business clients. It was an entirely different bank from the one that was set up in the pre-EU days of 1966. It had a different focus and had come to the point where it was no longer just a big Irish financial institution. It was operating also in the United Kingdom, the USA—where it had acquired a regional bank, First Maryland Bancorp—and on the capital markets front. Half of its profits were coming from outside the island of Ireland.

THE CHALLENGE

Corporate identity grew in importance through the 1980s to become a powerful strategic tool in the public relations and marketing of financial services. AIB is an example of how one financial institution used this opportunity.

The corporate identity of an organisation is the sum total of its characteristics, defining its personality, and distinguishing it from others. For Wally Olins, corporate identity is affirmed by a company's products, buildings, communications materials and by how it behaves. It is expressed through the names, symbols, logos, colours and rites of passage which the organisation uses to distinguish itself, its branded products and constituent companies.

Together, these expressions make a collective sense of belonging and purpose. Corporate identity and corporate image are closely bound together. Identity, as projected by

FROM JOHN PAUL TO SAINT JACK.......

the organisation, contributes to the shaping of people's perceptions so that an image of the organisation is formed.

The identity review at AIB was part of a major Marketing Action Programme (MAP) which ran from the mid 1980s. This programme was aimed at taking stock of where AIB was headed. It had to become more market-focused, more customer-driven. That required all of its staff to become more aware of selling. The MAP was really a series of programmes which included internal management courses from the chief executive, Gerry Scanlan, down and assessment of the Group's management and practices. The staff themselves evolved a lot of the measures that needed to be taken.

Changes in the corporate culture in Ireland were considered and it was decided that a more open and aggressive marketing role was needed for the post-1992 era of EU de-regulation. The move towards the single European Market was bringing about stiffer competition in the financial sector.

It became apparent that customers were not fully aware of the range of services offered by AIB. This was due to a lack of cohesion between AIB's numerous subsidiaries. It was clear, therefore, that AIB needed a new corporate identity. The old one had served its purpose well but had become outdated and failed to capture the spirit and culture of today's AIB. People, even some of the staff, no longer recognised what the old logo sym-bolised.

STRATEGY

In May 1988 a brief was drafted stating the key issues that needed to be addressed in a new identity. These were:
* AIB's longstanding Irish heritage
* AIB as a unified group
* the distinctive character of AIB as progressive, friendly and professional.

This brief was sent to three companies specialising in the design of corporate identity. Wolff Olins was appointed in September.

While Wolff Olins was recognised internationally as the leader in the business, Irish design firms were critical of AIB for not asking them to tender for the contract. AIB felt that the Irish companies had not the capacity and experience to handle a project with such a wide customer base, a world audience and large staff based in different locations.

Six months later, Wolff Olins made the following recommendations:
* Naming—AIB should act as a prefix to all of the group subsidiaries, e.g. AIB Invest-ment Managers, AIB Finance, AIB Leasing etc.
* New visual identity—to capture the AIB of the 1990s and reflect its personality and spirit
* New corporate colours—acting as a departure from the traditional "banking blue". These new colours would appear as warm and friendly
* New typeface—to correspond with the new visual identity and corporate colours

During those six months a series of presentations was made, followed by redesign work.

The final logo was inspired by one of the earliest Celtic images of the Ark and the Dove. The original was found carved onto a stone cross located near the River Killary in Co. Meath.

The use of the Ark as part of the logo serves to affirm AIB's Irish heritage. It epitomises its sense of security, while also acting as a symbol of its commitment to the global communities it serves. The corporate colours of red, blue, green and cream reflect the warmth and friendliness of the Irish, an integral part of AIB's character. These strong colours are easily recognised, individual to AIB and an important extension to its identity.

All of the above recommendations were approved by the Board of Directors in July 1989.

IMPLEMENTATION

One of the most impressive aspects of the entire identity programme was the manner in which the implementation was managed.

A corporate identity steering group was formed to oversee the development of the project for launch in January 1990. A full-time project executive and two full-time team members were appointed. They had to work with an amount of secrecy so that there would be a surprise element and the impact of the launch would be maximised. Responsibilities were carefully assigned and the progress monitored on a weekly basis.

The following areas needed to be tackled:
- stationery
- literature
- two-dimensional graphics
- external signage
- legal aspects
- communications / Launch Day
- advertising
- corporate wardrobe

In monitoring the development aspects, a computerised project management system was utilised. This involved the input of a spreadsheet which listed tasks to be performed, target dates and people responsible—so there was no escape ! It was vital that any teething problems were ironed out before the day of the launch.

LAUNCH DAY, 8 JANUARY 1990

Before the launch day an extensive series of both internal and external communications were carried out.

Internally, it was announced in November 1989 that a new identity had been approved and was being developed. A circular was sent to all staff members on 2 January 1990 outlining and explaining the reason behind the new identity. To support the circular, a staff video was produced which gave a step-by-step account of how the new identity was decided upon, and exactly what it meant to AIB Group.

All internal communication was significant in that it assured the new identity was both understood and supported by all AIB personnel.

Externally, it was announced in October 1989 that the old identity of AIB was under review. Advertising over a period indicated that a change was on the way—AIB was evolving, represented by a caterpillar turning to a butterfly. A typical piece of copy read:

"At Allied Irish Bank, we have chosen a new direction. We see our goal clearly; we intend to be the best. But ambition alone is not enough. We must provide our management and staff with the skills, systems and supports necessary to reach this goal. The beginning of this process was the simple recognition that our customers are the most important people in our organisation and to fully satisfy their needs, nothing less than the best will do."

Communication of the new corporate identity was part of the change in AIB. For effective public relations, the launch day itself was of vital importance. After so much had been put into the development of the identity, the final task was to ensure total awareness and understanding of it.

All of the new print material was delivered to AIB branches on 5 January. A total of 42 new brochures had been produced (with the theme of "natural world"), as well as redesigned stationery, cheques, cheque cards and other essential forms. Exterior signs had been redesigned at 14 branches.

On 8 January the new identity was unveiled to the public, with a 30-minute live telecast on RTE Network 2. There were 500 guests at AIB Group Headquarters, Bankcentre, Ballsbridge. They included Government ministers, ambassadors, staff, shareholders and customers. Televisions and screens were set up in branches and offices throughout the country to relay proceedings to staff and customers.

The external communications team also arranged the following:
- A letter to each shareholder from the chairman, outlining the new identity
- All corporate clients were contacted by executives
- Key customers were updated by branch managers
- Media were briefed and a news release issued
- Executives from the corporate identity steering group were available for interviews, as were the design personnel from Wolff Olins
- The opportunity was used to launch AIB's Better Ireland Awards—which over the next five years would allocate £200,000 in awards annually to projects in four categories, Youth, Communications, Heritage/Environment and Arts/Culture.

EVALUATION

Initial reaction to the new identity was positive. Irish design agencies were impressed by the strong image presented in the new logo.

John Tobin of the Visual Communications Group saw it as "a superb piece of design work that will last a long time. It is a bolder step than anyone would have expected". He added that foreign companies would be impressed. "The messages coming from the design are strength, quality and international. The logo isn't just for the little old lady with

BANK REFLECTS IRISH HERITAGE AND GLOBAL COMMITMENT

her savings account, it's pitched at a global viewing public".

Other comments focused on how AIB had separated itself from the crowd and had broken with the traditional banking image. As a result, AIB was considered more friendly and approachable than its competitors. For instance, *The Sunday Tribune* saw the logo as "a success visually and a welcome change from the usually more staid corporate imagery".

Market research undertaken by AIB's Public Affairs Department six months after the launch found:

- The new logo was instantly recognised
- AIB was perceived as being more friendly, with the important international aspect of its business recognised

DISCUSSION

This experience demonstrates the growing importance of corporate identity as a public relations tool in the financial sector.

The new identity was not just a project for AIB but a necessary step for the future success of the Group. It captured accurately AIB's personality and direction. It was therefore essential that it be closely monitored and remain consistent.

The steering group countered any anomalies within the new identity. Implementation had to be disciplined but also flexible enough to meet the changing needs of AIB Group, for example, the launch of Ark Life Assurance and First Trust Bank.

The evolution of AIB from being an Irish bank to an international financial services organisation was one that needed to be communicated to many audiences—employees, shareholders, customers and the corporate community.

Kevin J. Bourke, group general manager, corporate relations, AIB, says that Wolff Olins was not told to get rid of the "Irish" angle; the bank is staffed by Irish people and it will always be regarded as an Irish bank.

The decision to change a corporate identity is not taken lightly by a large company because it is expensive if done properly. At the time of the launch, AIB project manager, Jerry McCrohan, estimated a cost at £1.5 million to cover Wolff Olins fee, the live television transmission of the launch ceremony, the staff video and a swatch watch with the logo on it for everyone of the 14,000 staff. It did not include the renovation and decoration of the branches nor the new stationery and brochures, nor uniforms for staff, but many of those changes would have to have been made anyhow.

This might seem expensive, but not when compared with the £50 million which British Telecom are reputed to have spent on their new identity only to have it slammed for "failing to inspire".

Morgan Walsh has a BA degree in Economics & English from University College, Galway and the DIT Diploma in Public Relations.

HOW IRISH LIFE WENT PRIVATE

The Privatisation and Flotation of Irish Life Assurance plc
by Fiona O'Riordan

BACKGROUND

Formed in 1939, the state-owned Irish Life Assurance plc grew rapidly to become one of the leading life assurance companies in Europe. At the end of 1989 it had assets of almost £4,200 million invested on behalf of more than half a million policyholders. Through its subsidiary and affiliated companies Irish Life had interests in general insurance, building society operations, mortgage funding and banking. Premium income for 1989 was £598 million.

On Monday, 12 March 1990, the Government announced that Irish Life was to be floated on the stock exchange. The government was to sell the majority of its 90 per cent shareholding to private investors while retaining a 34 per cent stake.

The Minister for Finance, also retained a 'golden share' giving the power to limit the size of individual private shareholdings.

The privatisation, possibly one of the most difficult that could have been undertaken due to the complex capital structure of the company, was scheduled to take place in two phases. First, the company was to undergo a complete restructuring of its capital base, followed within two years by a flotation on the Dublin and London stock exchanges.

Privatisation is based on an assumption that increased efficiency of resources can be achieved by changing the institution's ownership and control. As a policy option, privatisation is extremely divisive, although it is supposed to represent a reform which will enable a country to obtain a higher standard of living from the resources at its disposal. This improvement across the board is far from guaranteed; indeed, the history of privatisation in the UK and the United States has shown that there are definite losers as well as gainers from the change.

In Ireland, at the end of the 1980s there had been little real discussion on whether privatisation as a policy could be pursued. To some extent, trade union opposition in principle to selling state-owned companies meant that the Government did not highlight the issue for fear of causing difficulty in getting co-operation on other aspects of economic policy.

Also, privatisation to the Irish public smacked of the 'Thatcherite policy' of Britain in the 1980s. The perception of the privatisation of companies like British Telecom was that there was little by way of discernible gains for the public either financially or in the services provided by the newly privatised companies.

THE CHALLENGE

Irish Life, as the most appealing candidate for privatisation, was a test case for the Government. The reasons for its privatisation were obvious:

- The government stood to gain substantial one-off revenues from the flotation if it could be established that it, rather than the with-profits policyholders, was entitled to the reserves in the company.
- The proposed sale could be portrayed as being a necessary step to expansion into the United States where there were difficulties in operating as a semi-state enterprise.
- There was now no compelling reason why the State should be involved in the financial sector. Privatisation takes place first in enterprises which face significant competition from the private sector.
- Management and staff at Irish Life saw themselves as being more closely aligned with the private than the public sector, except for the fact that the company was constrained from expanding by its archaic capital structure.

Prior to privatisation, the shareholdings in Irish Life were as follows:

	%
State	90.25
Irish Life Staff Pension Fund	4.72
Public	5.03
	100.00

With state ownership at over 90 per cent exchequer finances were still in no position to commit funds to the company.

Moreover, the 200 or so shareholders who owned the balance of the equity had no incentive to subscribe to new capital because of the very strict limits on the payment of realistic dividends by the company. Despite the fact that the company generated premium income of over £700 million a year on an asset base of almost £5 billion, the total dividend to shareholders, including the State, was £0.6 million in 1990.

This inability to reward shareholders clearly inhibited investment in the company and the absence of an official market in the shares meant that shareholders were effectively 'locked in' and prospective investors were 'locked out'.

RESTRUCTURING

There was to be a new holding company, Irish Life plc and a new life assurance company, Irish Life Assurance plc. The complexities of the restructuring stemmed from the company having shareholders as well as with-profits policyholders, both having a claim to the company's profits.

It was not clear how the reserves in the company would be divided between the two interest groups and how the with-profits policyholders would be treated after the flotation. Also, a proper valuation could not be put on the company without restructuring.

The company had to engage in difficult and lengthy legal and financial negotiations to establish the rights of with-profits policyholders and shareholders. Court approval for the changes had to be sought in Ireland and the UK.

Throughout this process, management at Irish Life recognised the critical role of public relations. Wilson Hartnell Public Relations were the Irish consultants, with the team led by Mary Finan and Brian Bell; in the UK, Dewe Rogerson were retained because of the simultaneous dealing with the London Stock Exchange. It was vital that the target audiences be communicated with continuously so that when approval and permission were sought, it would be granted. The public relations action plan might have seemed simple on the surface, but an enormous amount of work went into explaining what was happening to everyone concerned. Irish Life was determined to avoid, if at all possible, the controversial and highly negative publicity which had been attached to a number of high profile restructurings in the UK.

The target audiences for the re-structuring were:
- with-profits policyholders
- other policyholders
- shareholders
- staff
- financial media

It was clear, however, that the messages to each of them would have to be slightly different and would have to deal with that audience's particular requirements.

The public relations action plan centred around the establishment of a telephone hotline manned by Irish Life staff and professional recruits. The hotline dealt with every kind of enquiry imaginable from "what is a share" to the most complex financial questions. Letters were also sent to shareholders, policyholders and staff explaining the re-structuring. An annual general meeting was held for shareholders to voice their opinions. The media were briefed regularly and press releases were issued to keep the general public informed of the changes. There was also a highly-focused advertising campaign.

The enormous research and thought that went into explaining the restructuring to the target audiences paid off and the company was rewarded with endorsement from shareholders, policyholders and staff.

Media comment on the restructuring was considered informed, accurate and, in the main, positive and court approval was gained in the UK and Ireland. At all stages, however, there were strategies prepared to meet every eventuality and criticism.

FLOTATION

Having completed the restructuring by the end of 1990, the way was clear to begin serious preparation for the proposed summer flotation of the company's shares on the Dublin and London stock exchanges.

139 million ordinary shares (approximately 46 per cent of the total share capital) were to be sold by the State. A further 10 per cent of the State holding was to be put for international placing with Assurances Generales de France (AGF) and Kredietbank, two

international companies involved in joint ventures with Irish Life. The State's holding was to be reduced to 34 per cent.

The timetable for the offer was as follows:

	1991
Pathfinder prospectus	June 20
Marketing period	June 20 - July 3
Announcement of underwritten price	July 4
Offer for sale subscription period	July 4 - July 12
Announcement of basis allocation	July 18
Share dealing commences	July 23

To meet the objectives and timescales a marketing committee was set up with representatives of the company, the government, the merchant banks, stockbrokers and the public relations advisers. This committee met every few days to review progress and to assign responsibilities. The company recognised the role of public relations in the flotation and the consultants had direct access to top management at all stages.

One of the key elements of any flotation is to explain properly to the target audiences the business of the company being floated. The key elements of the public relations were as follows:
- to communicate the business of Irish Life as effectively as possible;
- to create demand for the offer across the Irish domestic market;
- to provide media support for the institutional marketing programme in the designated overseas market
- to present Irish Life positively to all identified target audiences

The public relations programme was divided into four phases.

1. The pre-offer phase
The trigger point for this phase was the posting of the policyholders' letter confirming that the share offer would take place in July. The objective was to harness and control the considerable interest from all areas of the media, not just the business area, and also to develop some human interest stories.

2. The pre-impact day phase
This phase was based around a press conference in Dublin to coincide with the publication of the pathfinder prospectus. Pathfinder provided important pieces of information with regard to likely allocations between the different market places and this phase was used to sustain and improve interest, both public and institutional through the carefully managed dissemination of important financial information.

3. The application phase
The platform for this phase was the publication of the full prospectus. This involved a Dublin press conference and the media objective was to support a public perception of demand for the shares.

FROM JOHN PAUL TO SAINT JACK.......

4. The allocation phase

This ran from the close of the offer to the listing of the shares on the Irish stock exchange. The objectives were to communicate information about applications and subsequent allocations, to ensure the relevant facts were interpreted as positively as possible, and to provide a response mechanism to any negative issues.

The public relations tools were obviously dictated by the special nature of the company being floated. They included a fact sheet, an extensive questions and answers document, a video, a management roadshow around Europe and the USA, and ongoing press conferences and briefings.

The Irish Life case was particularly intensive for the public relations team because of the simultaneous flotation on the Dublin and London stock exchanges. Clearance in both the UK and Ireland had to be obtained before the release of any statement, letter or other communication.

Finally, in any flotation there must be an element of excitement to make the shares attractive to potential investors. Irish Life made particularly good use of the photocall to add this element. On the day the company went to the Stock Exchange the then Minister for Finance, Albert Reynolds, unveiled the previously unannounced share price which hung from the outside of the Irish Life offices in Dublin.

EVALUATION

The enormous research and thought that went into explaining the restructuring of Irish Life paid off handsomely and it went through very smoothly.

However, a final objective in any flotation is the successful sale of the company's shares to the investment community and this also was achieved. It does not matter how good or how fancy the public relations programme is if it does not deliver this end result for the company.

The Irish Life shares were oversubscribed three times. On the first day of trading almost £35 million worth were traded on both the Dublin and London stock exchanges and the price rose 9p above the 160p flotation price after peaking during the day at 170p. By September the share price had topped 190p.

The media hailed the flotation as a success and the company gained its public status and 30,000 new shareholders.

FOOTNOTE

The public relations recommendation for flotations in general is to:
*   make sure the company and the business are properly understood
*   keep the media well-briefed
*   stick to the timetable
*   constantly evaluate media coverage to ensure messages are being understood
*   set up a small marketing committee and allocate responsibilities
*   make sure all the public relations tools are ready in advance

- pace the public relations action plan properly
- never lose sight of the key objectives

In 1994, Irish Life launched its new corporate identity. The company said it was changing the way it did business to meet the new demands of the future. "All our literature and correspondence has been rewritten in plain English to provide the information you need with no jargon or small print. Any projections we make of future benefits will be cautious. We want the only surprises you get to be pleasant ones......So it's not just our logo that's changed. The real difference will be a better all-round service that gives you the expert advice on the plans and policies that are right for you".

As with the share price announcement in 1991, there was a photocall for the launch of the new logo and other corporate changes. David Kingston, managing director, was shown hammering the new logo onto the wall of the head office. The corporate identity, designed by Wolff Olins and a panel of four Irish designers, is based on the Celtic legend of Aengus Óg and cost £50,000. At the same time Irish Life reported a 25 per cent rise in group new business to £328.2 million for 1993, and a 15 per cent rise in new business written in Ireland to £174.1 million.

Fiona O'Riordan has a BBS Degree in Accounting/Finance & Law from the University of Limerick, and the DIT Diploma in Public Relations

A BATTLE FOR MILK AND MONEY

The Formation of Lakeland Dairies Co-operative Society Ltd.
by Harriett Ryan

BACKGROUND

Killeshandra Dairy Co-operative Society in Co. Cavan was defeated by Goodman International in its bid for neighbouring Bailieboro Co-op in January 1988. Killeshandra then asked their public relations consultant, Pat Keating, then a director of Grayling Public Relations, to draw up a public relations/shareholder relations strategy in anticipation of further challenges from the Goodman organisation. They also saw the need for rationalisation and the role for communications in preparing for it.

Goodman International, substantially owned by Larry Goodman, is an Irish meat processing and exporting company which had a turnover of £800 million in the year to 31 March 1994.

In December 1989, Food Industries plc, the subsidiary of Goodman International which at that time owned Bailieboro Co-op, announced what in effect was a takeover bid for Killeshandra and for two neighbouring co-ops, Lough Egish and Town of Monaghan, with proposals for the formation of a new society from the merger, to be called United Dairies. Since Food Industries already controlled Bailieboro and Westmeath Co-ops, the United Dairies proposal was designed, in effect, to bring the region's 130 million gallon milk pool into 'private' ownership, with a consequential loss of farmer control.

Killeshandra stated on 19 December that its board had agreed to enter into discussions "with parties interested in the amalgamation of the dairy industry in the north-east", opening the door for merger negotiations to get underway among the region's two major co-ops, Killeshandra and Lough Egish.

The logic of Goodman's amalgamation proposals could not be denied and Goodman had a strong case. The battle between Goodman and Killeshandra and Lough Egish Co-ops had begun.

THE CHALLENGE

In January 1990, Killeshandra and Lough Egish Co-ops announced their proposals for a merger to form Lakeland Dairies. They needed farmer support and confidence, without which the merger could not take place. The alternative was that Food Industries would win the battle and control of the dairy industry in the north-east.

The challenge for the Grayling public relations team, comprising Pat Keating and Winifred McCourt, was to deliver the vote at the special general meetings of both co-ops to support a merger proposal and to launch the new co-op. They also had to execute a

---

A BATTLE FOR MILK AND MONEY

communications strategy, working in close rapport with corporate finance, legal, banking and management executives.

The challenge revolved around winning the hearts and minds of the farmer shareholders. Both Killeshandra and Lough Egish knew that in order to win they had to present a strong and united front.

STRATEGY

An aggressive public relations campaign was needed to keep Food Industries from 'swallowing' the proposed Lakeland merger. It covered all aspects: media relations, press briefings, preparation of prospectus, support literature, advertising, canvasser training, canvasser manuals and media training for spokespersons. In addition, there had to be monitoring and intelligence gathering, pro-active initiatives to expose the 'true' intentions of the takeover bid and the management of issues and response programmes as the campaign developed.

Some specific strategies were to:
- set up information centres
- groom a spokesman for the management team
- produce literature for bill-posting and direct mailing
- identify Goodman's and Food Industries' weak points and illustrate their intentions; all information to be made public
- make direct comparisons between Food Industries and Lakeland Dairies
- implement a blueprint for a vigorous canvass system for Killeshandra and Lough Egish shareholders
- develop a canvass list and identify leaders in the farming community
- devise shareholder presentations with graphic displays and audio visual back-up
- hold series of small shareholders meetings rather than the preferred mass rallies of Food Industries
- write briefings for advisory groups and put into place an effective system for analysis and evaluation.
- design a new logo and slogan
- identify relevant interest groups to provide third party endorsement of the merger proposal.

Some of these strategies were adopted immediately, others were held back for later in the campaign.

IMPLEMENTATION

The public relations campaign was centralised in the Dublin offices of Grayling. To have been based at Killeshandra or Lough Egish could have caused friction; to have been somewhere in between would have meant less support services and less access to the media. The corporate financing of the merger was driven by Gandon Corporate Finance, also in Dublin.

FROM JOHN PAUL TO SAINT JACK.......

Grayling had the assistance of senior executives at Lakeland in the implementation of the campaign. Michael Parker, now general secretary of the Progressive Democrats party, assisted in farmer liaison and training.

In response to Food Industries' request for discussions, Killeshandra and Lough Egish issued a press statement, illustrating the areas of concern:

- They denied a claim that Food Industries had met them.
- Bailieboro's financial reports indicated that they were in debt—Killeshandra and Lough Egish were not prepared to foot the bill.
- If the United Dairies amalgamation were to take place, the farmer shareholders were not certain as to who would ultimately own the society.
- The co-op boards were also afraid that some of the activities then performed by Killeshandra and Lough Egish would eventually be undertaken by Food Industries' own subsidiaries.
- In the absence of clear proposals from Food Industries the board of Killeshandra were concerned that the 'special mechanism' mentioned by Food Industries for the farmers to sell back their shares was a back-door route to a Goodman takeover.

The birth of Lakeland

On 15 January 1990, Killeshandra and Lough Egish rejected the takeover bid and announced that a legal agreement had been reached to merge their interests in a new co-operative. Merger details would be published on 30 May and special general meetings called for both co-ops on 22 June. The agreement for the amalgamation was deemed irrevocable until voted upon by shareholders.

Shareholders in both societies were told they would have their shareholdings converted into shares in the new society which they would be able to cash in at market-related value at their own discretion. The new society would also provide for the ongoing protection of the interests of shareholders and suppliers, including provisions for control of the board and ensuring that no shareholder would have a majority stake in the new society without the consent of the members.

The new society would provide capabilities for strong farm service and would operate in nine counties: Cavan, Monaghan, Leitrim, Longford, Westmeath, Offaly, Kildare, Dublin and Louth. It would have a milk pool of 60 million gallons and access to substantial financial resources for future development.

On 19 January the name of the new society was launched as Lakeland Dairies. On the same day it was announced that representatives of the Lakeland Board had met members of Food Industries in an attempt to persuade them to accept a real internal market mechanism rather than the takeover bid envisaged in their proposals. Food Industries abruptly terminated the discussions refusing to proceed on the co-op's basis of one-man-one-vote on all issues.

On 14 February, Lakeland Dairies announced the appointment of Donal Creedon, former secretary of the Department of Agriculture, as chairman-designate. His primary role would be to oversee the merger process and subsequently to ensure that the rationalisation of operations of the two societies could be achieved. He would be responsible, with the board, for the selection of the new management team. He would also help with the formulation of the ongoing development plans.

Lakeland Dairies did not have everything their own way. Food Industries were putting up a good fight. Pat Keating says: "We fought it through very tight public relations..... we learnt that it was a question of doing it with literally military precision and planning..... we fought with very professional canvassing, very well-planned meetings and very well-presented identity". Lakeland Dairies had a very strong identity and the new logo and slogan reflected it—*Unity is strength and together we're stronger.*

Public relations was an integral part of the campaign, dealing with both management and media. At one stage there were up to 20 press calls a day.

Lakeland circulated cartoons to illustrate messages and portray Goodman promising an illusion of money. One showed him with his sleeves rolled up at a small printing machine, with David Dilger of Food Industries standing outside the shed saying, "Print it faster, Larry". In another, he was sitting at the end of a rowing boat with a group of farmers doing the rowing. "Pull harder, lads", he was saying. Then he was depicted as a big Gulliver-type figure, down on bended knee poking the Lilliputian-type farmer in the belly: "You want to talk about milk price ?"

The merger details were published on 30 May, accompanied by a statement from Donal Creedon that "the co-op movement, unlike private industry, is based on democratic principle". Shareholders, interest groups and potential influencers received the documents that same day. Press conferences were held in Dublin and in Cootehill, Co. Cavan, to drive home the Lakeland message, *Together we're stronger.*

A vigorous canvass and extensive programme of shareholder meetings started immediately. Lakeland Dairies set the agenda and controlled the campaign. It was essential from the start that Food Industries be not allowed to get the upper hand at any point.

Media relations played a pivotal role. Press releases were issued as appropriate, with daily and individual briefings for key journalists and the progress of the campaign was evaluated and fine-tuned as necessary. The co-op, finance, legal and public relations executives met daily to assess progress.

Food Industries tried to undermine the campaign strategy, but feedback showed that a groundswell of support for Lakeland was steadily building. With ten days to go the focus shifted to getting the vote out on the day.

Third party endorsements started coming in. The Irish Farmers Association, Irish Creamery Milk Suppliers Association, Irish Co-operative Organisation Society, Virginia Milk Products, Avonmore Co-op and the main agricultural bodies all declared in favour of Lakeland Dairies.

On 22 June, 90 per cent of the shareholders, from an area comprising nine counties, turned out. They approved Lakeland Dairies and voted by massive majorities to form the new co-op—85 per cent at Killeshandra and 72 per cent at Lough Egish. Food Industries declared that they would accept the democratic decision of the shareholders.

The IFA and ICMSA, as well as other representative organisations, welcomed the outcome. Bank of Ireland approved a credit line of £20 million for the new society.

New crisis
All seemed well—a successful campaign had been carried out—until autumn 1990. It

then became apparent that promises made to shareholders as regards cashing in their shares at market-related value could not be honoured; an internal market in shares did not exist. Lakeland could not create such a market without encountering severe financial difficulty.

The co-op, at great cost, had borne the toll of winning the merger. Killeshandra and Lough Egish had maintained their high milk prices throughout the campaign in sharp contrast to a dramatic fall in the world market. Management had been distracted from the day-to-day business during the protracted campaign.

A new chief executive, Dan Buckley, took over in September. He was former chief executive of Adam Foods, an Irish Dairy Board operation in the UK.

Lakeland had no option but to offer the shareholders a radically revised package. If it was to survive it could not, in the short term, fulfil the financial promises made in June.

On 28 December, Lakeland announced that they could not implement the share market at that time. Pat Keating remembers: "It was a disaster. We had no credibility. Goodman had guaranteed £53 million in payment for the business. Our offer was eventually worth £50 million and based on a share market that we now said we could not implement".

A radically different package was now proposed. It involved no share market at all and no commitment to ever having one. A new special general meeting was called for 14 March 1991.

The campaign got underway with a series of shareholder meetings and media briefings. The programme for the campaign was similar to the previous one in that media relations played a central role. It addressed the reality of the situation—loss of confidence in the agri-sector due to the major financial crisis that had just struck Goodman International, the falling returns from the international market place and the prospects of GATT and CAP reforms which created uncertainty for farmers.

It was clear from initial reactions that emotions ran high among shareholders and that Lakeland was not going to be given an easy passage. Some of the farmers who voted in favour of the Lakeland merger had expected a cash bonanza. Many had made commitments in lieu of financial expectations, others saw it as a means of offsetting the problems caused by a bad year and the anticipated downturn in farm incomes.

Just four weeks before the special general meeting, Paschal Taggart, a well-known entrepreneur, offered himself as financial adviser to dissatisfied shareholders. He would auction the co-op—find a buyer for it—so that the farmers would have a market for their shares. He would work for them on a 'no fee no foal' basis. It was suggested that Taggart was acting on behalf of an interested buyer.

There were now two packages on the table for the shareholders. Taggart had a reputation for an astute business acumen, while the new team at Lakeland had yet to make their mark.

The public relations strategy was hard-hitting and forward-looking in that all issues were dealt with openly and in line with the reality of the situation. Dan Buckley had a distinct advantage because he had not previously been with either Killeshandra or Lough Egish and he had a totally new approach that many shareholders found refreshing.

It was vital to cement the fragile relationship between shareholders and Lakeland.

They were encouraged to think Lakeland rather than Killeshandra or Lough Egish separately. They were not given false hopes. It was up to themselves to decide.

On 14 March 1991, the special general meeting in Cavan, attended by 3,000 Lakeland shareholders, agreed to forego Lakeland Dairies' original commitments to share purchase. They voted 84 per cent for the new agreement. Lakeland Dairies was now finally up and running and had the mandate of its shareholders.

EVALUATION

This was one of the most highly-profiled agricultural campaigns of recent years. It received major coverage on television, radio and press. The cost, in terms of merger activities, was £2.5 million.

The campaign focused the attention of the farmer shareholders on the issue at stake—a farmer-owned, farmer-run co-op. It succeeded in merging two of the biggest co-ops in that region—one of the first steps in rationalisation there.

Throughout the campaign, public relations activity contributed substantially to the process of managing change within the business. Public relations management and strategy became a front line and high profile part of the management agenda and was a major factor in rejecting the takeover bid and ensuring the formation of Lakeland. Pat Keating and his team worked in close rapport with corporate finance, legal, banking and management executives.

FOOTNOTE

In 1990, the public relations consultancy now known as Grayling Ltd was called Forman Dove. The name was changed to Grayling in 1991 in line with a programme of building Grayling as a brand name in Europe for the public relations businesses of Lopex plc, of which Forman Dove was the Irish office. Pat Keating is now managing director of Keating & Associates and retains the Lakeland public relations account. Winifred McCourt is with McMahonSheedy Communications.

Annual turnover for Lakeland is now £113 million with profit before tax of £2.3 million. Communications, public relations, profile management remains a priority and the co-op is highly successful and effective in communicating its mission and message at national and regional level.

Golden Vale, the large County Cork based co-op, has bought Bailieboro from Food Industries and also taken over Leckpatrick, another co-op in the region. Town of Monaghan is still independent.

The milk pool in the region is now 200 million gallons, out of a billion nationwide. The Co-ops are still small compared to the big ones in the south, as are the average cowherds.

Harriett Ryan has a BA Degree in English & Philosophy from University College, Galway and the DIT Diploma in Public Relations.

"GOD GAVE US BANTRY AND WE GAVE IT TO GULF OIL"

The Betelgeuse Explosion at Whiddy Island
by Paul O'Shea

BACKGROUND

Whiddy Island, in the far south-west of county Cork, was the site of a transhipment terminal owned by Gulf Oil. Surrounded by the deep waters of Bantry Bay, the terminal opened in 1969 to serve as a storage and distribution network for Northern Europe.

The small town of Bantry, and its surroundings, were an important and unspoilt tourist attraction, but the project was welcomed by the local community and the Government. The only negative reaction was from an environmental group in the nearby village of Glengariff and from sections of the media.

The terminal generated almost £10 million a year over the next decade. At its height it handled 400 ships a year, with 82 people directly employed and a further 150 in ancillary services.

The first five years were as expected, with no reason to doubt the terminal's safety. However, local journalists were alerted to concern about unspecified amounts of oil pollution, attributed to the Whiddy Island operations.

In October 1974, during a routine unloading of the tanker, *Universe Leader,* an oil valve was accidentally opened and later closed. On noticing oil on the stern the terminal manager ordered an inspection by divers. No damage was found. The terminal manager stated that there was no evidence of an oil spill. However, over the next few days, oil came ashore at several places and there was local outrage. Eventually, it was estimated that 2,540 tonnes of oil had been discharged.

Local and national press covered the story for nearly a week and Gulf Oil came in for much criticism and political concern. Senior Gulf management were very annoyed, not only because of what happened, but because of their poor internal and external communications. The internal communications were so poor that the vice-president in charge did not arrive on the scene until five days after the incident.

Gulf Oil then decided to formulate a crisis management plan with their public relations consultants, John McMahon & Partners.

The plan was still being prepared when, in January 1975, there was a collision between a tug and a tanker, the *Altran Zodiac.* Heavy diesel oil escaped and 430 tonnes of it came ashore at Glengariff. The reputation and trustworthiness of Gulf Oil dropped to a new low.

"GOD GAVE US BANTRY AND WE GAVE IT TO GULF OIL"

PLANNING

Gulf Oil completed the crisis management plan and began intensive training throughout the corporation in mid-1975. The training dealt with all possible crises, and suitable responses. At Bantry, the crisis management team to co-ordinate the response included a vice president of the company and the Irish and British public relations consultants. The responsibility of the team was to ensure swift and efficient implementation of the crisis plan.

There were several provisions regarding the media. Press packs were assembled to inform journalists about the history and operations at Whiddy Island and other relevant information concerning Gulf Oil. Facilities were earmarked as possible rooms for press conferences and for journalists to work and meet company executives. Offices were also designated for the crisis management team. These would become the nerve centre in any crisis, co-ordinating all media relations and company personnel. The emphasis on internal communication was especially important in light of previous blunders. The lines of communication for future crises were clearly mapped out. A schedule of personnel to be contacted was drawn up, including a list of addresses and phone numbers where people could be contacted. It also identified who would have to go to Bantry in person.

The most significant feature of Gulf's preparation for the crisis was the use of Crisisport. This was a simulated training exercise developed by Burson Marsteller, the international public relations firm. The exercise involved employees role-playing various positions in a fictitious disaster. BM co-ordinators, with the full script of the crisis, directed employees at all times.

During the training Gulf's workers learnt how to react to specific incidents whether it be a phonecall from a journalist or an irate local farmer. The management had to act out hypothetical situations, concentrating on such issues as interviews with both print and broadcast journalists. Co-ordinators shaped the exercise by continually introducing new problems and giving tips on how to respond. Actors and journalists were brought in to give the exercise a more authentic feel.

Between 1975 and 1979 Gulf Oil workers had a considerable amount of Crisisport training. The terminal staff were prepared to give swift, positive responses so that the company would gain credibility with the media and the general public. Rather than catching-up from behind, Gulf Oil would, to an extent, be able to shape developments as they unfolded.

The plan was not confined to Ireland, but extended to senior personnel throughout the world in the US and the rest of Europe. It was relatively expensive but proved its worth in the correct way later incidents in the US and elsewhere were handled.

IMPLEMENTATION

Early on Monday morning, 8 January 1979, between 12.30 and 1.00 am, the 61,775 ton oil tanker *Betelgeuse*, owned by the French company, Total, blew up at the Whiddy Island terminal. It was carrying a mixed cargo of approx. 120,000 tonnes of Arabian heavy and light crude, the heavy oil in the vessel's middle tanks. The *Betelgeuse*, due to be scrapped shortly after its visit to Whiddy, was incorrectly unloaded at the terminal. This caused the ship's metal structure to twist and crack. Eventually it broke on its back and exploded. Fifty people were killed: 42 French nationals working on the boat, one Englishman and seven Irish terminal workers.

Since 1975 Gulf Oil had consistently worked to rehabilitate its reputation within the local community and the local and national press. It was now faced with a disaster bigger than anything it could have anticipated.

It was a massive crisis but, nevertheless, efficient implementation of the plan could help to limit the damage, reassure those who suffered and enable Gulf to emerge with some semblance of integrity.

However, an unsuspected factor was to negate much of the benefit of the Crisisport and other training of the previous four years.

John McMahon was more than 200 miles away, at home in bed in Dublin, when he received a phone call from *Irish Press* journalist, Andrew Bushe, looking for comment. He was hardly out of bed when he got a call from Gulf confirming that there had been a terrible disaster. Shocked, but fortunate to have a full tank of petrol in his car, he immediately contacted Bill Finnigan, the Gulf Oil chairman, in Dublin, and they drove down to Cork at high speed.

He also phoned Michael Regester, Gulf's public relations manager in London. Regester contacted his director, Peter Hamilton, who went to the Gulf office in London and delivered press packs to the London papers and news agencies through the night. This chain of communication was the routine outlined in the crisis plan. It worked efficiently to meet the immediate needs

John McMahon, MPRII, joint managing director, McMahon-Sheedy Communications Consultants Ltd.

of the British and international media for background facts about the company and the terminal. Regester went to Heathrow to hire a plane to Cork Airport.

John McMahon arrived in Bantry before dawn to see the sky lit up by a large plume of smoke. The Taoiseach, Jack Lynch, a Corkman, was already at the scene giving interviews.

The entire crisis management team had arrived by Monday evening, including a vice president of Gulf Oil from Houston, Texas and a number of executives from the UK. The offices designated for the crisis management team now became the focus of media attention. A press conference was held early on the evening of Monday, 8 January.

The statement was based on the despatcher, John Connolly's account of events. Connolly maintained the ship broke up and caused a small fire which spread and eventually caused the ship to explode at about 12.55 am. Connolly gave this account to Gulf's lawyers at Whiddy. Nobody doubted his word and an official statement was issued to the media at the press conference on Monday, 8 January.

On Tuesday, reporters began to question Gulf about the time of the explosion. Gulf believed their information to be correct, so they re-affirmed that the *Betelgeuse* exploded at 12.55 am. The press corps were sceptical, because local people claimed to have heard what they believed to be an explosion well before 12.55 am, perhaps as early as 12.30 to 12.45.

One convincing witness was Peter Tynan O'Mahony, an *Irish Times* journalist who was on holidays in a house overlooking the terminal. While looking out over the Bay from his room, he was listening to the BBC Radio World Service.

He heard thumps, saw the ship was on fire and observed further explosions and fire. Working back from the BBC 1.00 am News, he estimated he saw the fire at "about a quarter to one or ten to one". Other witnesses corroborated his evidence and indicated that the incident actually started as early as 00.31-00.32 hours "at which time sounds like distant thunder were heard" (Costello Report).

Tynan O'Mahony phoned *The Irish Times* news desk in Dublin and thus the story began its journey onto the front pages, into news bulletins on BBC and RTE and around the world within minutes of its happening.

The time discrepancies suggested something was amiss. Journalists grew angry as they believed Gulf was hiding something.

John McMahon recalls the press conference on the Wednesday. "We could not do anything. We produced the terminal manager. He was harried. The press were extremely antagonistic. I have never seen a press corps like I saw on that day in Bantry. Never before and never since. They were very, very emotional in trying to get this manager to reconcile the two different times. He couldn't do it. So, they rejected his evidence and in a sense Gulf was already being tried and given a sentence three days after the event."

Conspiracy theories and rumour abounded. Many believed Gulf was covering up for its negligence.

Gulf were now in the midst of a huge controversy. Not only had 50 people died, but media speculation suggested the company was lying about the circumstances. The crisis management plan relied upon receiving accurate information which could then be given to the press, but the press now believed their trust had been betrayed in the previous two days. As they published their stories, the reputation of the company was torn to shreds. Total had no public relations presence in Ireland and they put out no statements, nor made any effort to do so. They left it to Gulf to make all the running.

At official level, the Government passed special legislation to enable a tribunal of enquiry to be set up. The tribunal was chaired by Justice Declan Costello of the High Court. Its first sittings were held in the West Lodge Hotel, Bantry in May. Justice Costello heard evidence from both Gulf and Total personnel, as well as the relevant government departments. The inquiry, conducted both in Bantry and Dublin, heard 184 witnesses over 72 days between May and December 1979; its 488-page report was published in July 1980.

The report concluded that fault lay primarily with Total because the metal structure of the *Betelgeuse* was poor and the ship had been unloaded incorrectly.

Gulf were also indicted on a number of counts. Justice Costello felt the company should have been more concerned with safety and less with operational efficiency and economics. For example, if a tug had been on standby it might have picked up survivors in the water that night. Some crew had jumped overboard but in the freezing water they could not survive for more than about 25 minutes, even with life jackets.

The most controversial finding of the inquiry concerned the time of the disaster. Justice Costello chose not to believe John Connolly's account of events. "The tribunal concludes that the despatcher was not in the control room at the commencement of the disaster and he decided to suppress this fact, and fabricate an account of when and how the disaster occurred. With a view to supporting this version, incorrect entries were made in the logs of the control room, the Ascon Jetty security hut and the *Donemark*, which is the supply vessel taking people in and out from the island and false accounts of the events were given by Gulf employees both to their employers and to the investigating Gardai".

The twenty-minute time discrepancy meant there never was a chance of saving those who jumped from the ship.

EVALUATION

From a public relations point of view, Gulf Oil came out the disaster with loss of integrity and diminished reputation. Their reputation and credibility with local and national media was very damaged. Their crisis management plan which was to reduce any negative feelings towards the company, both during and after a disaster, may have failed in its ultimate goal. However to consider the plan an outright failure would be unfair. It succeeded in many aspects. The people were also shocked but sympathetic to the company in trying to handle a dreadful human tragedy.

Media relations in the first 24 hours were good. This was due not to luck, but to hours of training and preparation. Indeed the day after the disaster *The Irish Times* ran a headline, "Bantry people hope Gulf will stay". This success was because:

- the crisis management team arrived swiftly
- Gulf hid nothing and gave information freely, thereby establishing a good relationship with the press
- the media were provided with facilities where they could work and meet company executives
- the crisis management team had their own offices where company strategies and press releases could be formulated.
- the presence of senior Gulf executives gave added weight to the company's statements.

"GOD GAVE US BANTRY AND WE GAVE IT TO GULF OIL"

The good media relations of the first 24 hours were due to mutual trust. The media were happy to believe Gulf's story, so long as they were being given an accurate account of events. However, when they found out the truth, their sense of betrayal was great. This is the crux of Gulf's experience in Whiddy; they issued and stuck to a story that they believed to be correct, when in fact it was wrong.

Gulf may have been naive for basing its story on one man's account of events, but John Connolly was the only one to have seen the disaster happen. In addition, the company's lawyers had taken a statement from him on the first day and were against changing it. The company never changed its story and this further antagonised the media and local people.

Bantry, a very small, tight-knit community, was in a state of shock. Seven local people had died and the town was a media circus. In an attempt to ease the worry of the bereaved families, Gulf executives visited all of them within 36 hours. They assured them of every assistance they might need and initial payments were offered even before the insurance and legal experts had made any decisions. This was not an attempt to buy favour but was a genuine gesture of concern.

For up to a week the story was front page news in the national newspapers. There was further media interest in the salvage and the inquiry which followed. Pro-active public relations was impossible during the inquiry because it was felt it could be prejudicial to the outcome and might affect witnesses. Journalists made their own judgments on the evidence submitted, with the Irish public relations consultant, John McMahon, limited to merely giving background information. This did not allow the company any great opportunity to air its own views; damage limitation was all that could be done.

With hindsight one can afford the luxury of identifying the mistakes and failures made at Whiddy Island. The task of the public relations team was to ensure that Gulf Oil dealt with the disaster in a professional and effective manner. The right people, the right preparation, the right environment and the right management structures were put in place, but fate and circumstances extinguished any hope of success.

The collusion of John Connolly and his fellow-workers robbed the crisis management team of the one thing they needed most, the truth. Everybody on the island that night was interviewed, and gave a similar account of events. The company never suspected the widespread deceit that was to be uncovered by the inquiry. This was the vital mistake. Human error and negligence are common causes of this type of disaster, but they were either not considered or were ignored by the management team. It is easy to say that more stringent cross-examination of the workers should have been done. However, in such an emotionally charged time, companies expect the truth and do not want to harass their workers who have been through such a frightening and distressing experience.

The vital ingredient which Gulf lacked was truth. If they had got the truth, they would have been in a good position to execute the crisis plan to its full effect. They did not get the truth and from this point on never had a chance of coming well out of the crisis.

DISCUSSION

The Whiddy Island tragedy was the first example in Ireland of a planned management response to a public relations crisis of such magnitude. Previous disasters had been managed without this detailed preparation. Gulf brought in crisis management structures because it had its fingers burnt in previous incidents. A lack of foresight had meant that the value of crisis public relations was learnt the hard way.

Did Irish industry learn anything from Gulf's experience at Whiddy ? Are Irish companies prepared for the crises that invariably turn up, always unexpected, nearly always at a most unsuitable time when it is more difficult to organise the response ? The answer to the first question is probably yes, to the second, probably no. With tight budgets and emphasis on cost-cutting, managers are slow to invest money in preparing for a crisis that might never happen.

John McMahon says that if the Whiddy Island experience were to be repeated, the public relations advice would be not to rely on the evidence of one person, not to get into debate about such matters as the precise time of the tragedy, but to stick to incontrovertible facts. However, he warns that public relations and legal experts are often in conflict. The public relations advice is to communicate and retain control of the communication; the lawyers' advice is to keep quiet, lest future settlements be prejudiced. It is in the public interest and in the interest of the company's reputation that the public relations advice be allowed to prevail.

Gulf Oil does not exist any more. Its assets were taken over in 1984 by Chevron in a contested battle by T. Boone Pickens whose strategy was to break it up into its constituent parts. In 1985 the Irish Government announced it had got $44 million from Chevron in a deal releasing them from their lease and that the Whiddy terminal would not be re-built. The 12 storage and two ballast tanks are still on the island, now owned by the Irish National Petroleum Corporation for the Irish Government. The oil forms part of the national reserve.

The quotation at the top of this case study, that "God gave us Bantry and we gave it to Gulf Oil", is attributed to the Australian anthropologist Chris Eipper, to which he added: "The sentiment being that if the first gift was an overdue act of charity the second one was one of undue recklessness". On the other hand, the people of Bantry never experienced excessive charity throughout their history. Their misfortune has been an inability by themselves and their rulers to take economic advantage of the natural advantages of the area. Perhaps, the existence of a prosperous mussel industry nowadays around Bantry portends a better future for them.

Paul O'Shea has a BA Degree in Economics & Sociology from University College, Cork and the DIT Diploma in Public Relations.

LAST EXIT FROM BAGHDAD

PARC and the Gulf War
by Frances Keegan

BACKGROUND

PARC is a subsidiary of Aer Lingus. It was set up in 1975, prompted by an idea from the personnel department of Aer Lingus. Its formation arose from the need to make better use of personnel resources, following the example set by the catering department which spawned Aer Lingus Catering and the computer department which developed Cara Computers.

David Hanly, managing director of PARC, worked in the personnel department at the time. He felt that Aer Lingus had experience and skills in personnel recruitment and management which could be sold outside the company.

However, the Irish market was small and highly competitive and PARC were aware that if the company was to grow it would have to seek new business outside Ireland.

PARC's first overseas break came in the late 1970s when it won a contract to supply technical staff for a mining project in Zambia. Following this, PARC returned to aviation, an area that was familiar and is now its biggest. It began recruiting pilots and air hostesses for Iranian and Jordanian airlines. In 1981, the company moved into project management and received a part of the multi-billion dollar contract for reconstruction of Baghdad.

This connection with Baghdad was strengthened with an unexpected offer in 1982 from the Iraqi Ministry of Health. PARC were asked to tender for the contract to set up a new hi-tech hospital in the city.

PARC had no experience in hospital management but, with expert help from St. Vincent's Hospital in Dublin and from the Irish Department of Health, a bid was drawn up. Six months later, PARC was awarded a £12 million contract and the agreement was signed in December 1982. The hospital opened five months later.

The Ibn al Bitar hospital was Iraq's answer to the Mayo Clinic, a third level referral/ tertiary hospital. The contract was to manage and staff the hospital. The hospital employed 650 people, of whom 253 were Irish and the remainder from other countries. There was also a large administrative Iraqi staff of about 100.

The hospital was built during the Iran/Iraq war and PARC were aware of the delicate situation. Contingency plans were drawn up in anticipation of crises. Such a crisis arose in August 1990 with the Iraqi invasion of Kuwait. PARC were in a very invidious position.

Following the invasion of Kuwait it was realised that there could be retaliation either from Kuwait or from the international community through the United Nations. There was a real threat that the liberty of the PARC employees could be severely restricted. PARC were never told that they could not leave but the negotiations for exit visas for

FROM JOHN PAUL TO SAINT JACK.......

employees were long and complicated.

The Iraqi Ministry of Health were fully satisfied with PARC's administration of the hospital and indicated that PARC employees were under no threat from Iraq. They wanted PARC to remain.

THE CHALLENGE

Iran and Iraq had been at war for seven years and PARC employees had been working in the hospital throughout this time. The war had not touched them. But PARC were always aware of the situation and a crisis plan had been in existence since the early days. Two further plans were drawn up to cope with all possible changes of circumstance.

These three plans were devised by PARC on the basis of three different scenarios that could be anticipated. Each would come into operation if the preceding one was no longer viable:

- **Plan One**—to get everybody out through a peaceful negotiation process with the Iraqi Ministry of Health before 15 January 1991, the UN deadline for Iraq to withdraw from Kuwait.
- **Plan Two**—to evacuate all personnel over land to the nearest safe border. This plan had been in place since the hospital opened. There was already a supply of buses and jeeps at the hospital which had been used to transport staff to and from work. These vehicles were fully maintained and emergency supplies of petrol, food and water were kept in store. There was also a considerable supply of US dollars on hand should money be needed for any reason. If war erupted before staff had been evacuated the plan was to wait two to three days

Bill O'Herlihy, MPRII, managing director, Bill O'Herlihy Communications Group Ltd.

in bomb shelters before approaching the local military leader to request a route out of the city to the nearest safe border.

- **Plan Three**—to withdraw to the bomb shelters located next to the hospital. The Iraqi authorities had already approved of this and had given over the keys. This plan was based on the assumption that the employees could not get out. The shelters were maintained with sufficient food and water for a three-month period. In the event of chemical warfare, about which there had been anxiety, PARC had acquired chemical warfare suits from the German and Irish governments for all their staff. They would be equipped to sit it out.

IMPLEMENTATION

In August 1990 PARC held a crisis meeting with their consultants, Public Relations of Ireland (now part of Bill O'Herlihy Communications Group Ltd).The association between PARC and PR of I had been formed in 1979, so PR of I were fully aware of the situation in Baghdad and the policies that PARC had adopted.The meeting was called to decide the strategy that would be implemented.

Four PARC executives were to handle the crisis in association with PR of I.All other employees were to handle business as usual. David Hanly said it was essential that other areas of business were not neglected.

The four from PARC were David Hanly, managing director; Peter Keenan, deputy managing director; John MacSweeney and Brian Flood. From PR of I there was Bill O'Herlihy, managing director and Andrew Kelly who had recently joined the company from RTE.

Brian Flood was an ex-army officer and had worked in Baghdad for four years while the hospital was being established. He was fully aware of the networks that had been formed within the Iraqi government in Baghdad and was a strategic player in handling Iraqi officials at lower levels. It was Brian who had put into place the initial crisis plan during the Iran/Iraq war.

In early August 1990, Brian Flood flew to Baghdad with the Irish Minister for Foreign Affairs, Gerard Collins, TD, to arrange evacuation of all staff.The other plans became fully operational and were checked regularly.

The evacuation plan involved lengthy negotiation between David Hanly and the Iraqi Minister of Health.The first evacuation took place at the end of October 1990 but there was a prerequisite— a skeleton staff of volunteers would remain on at the hospital. Shortly before the deadline of 15 January 1991 these people would be flown to Cyprus, the nearest safe air base. If nothing happened on 15 January they would return to the hospital. But war did break out and PARC stayed out of Baghdad.

While the negotiations were taking place there were many other issues which had to be handled in Ireland.These involved dealing with relatives of the employees and with the media and government.

The PARC team and PR of I had an 8 am meeting every day throughout the crisis.This meeting decided the issues of the day and the strategy to deal with them. Each person was assigned to a specific area of the media.

There were also regular briefings in Baghdad with the employees at the hospital.The purpose was to keep them fully informed at all times on all developments.These briefings and the BBC World Service were the employees' only access to non-Iraqi controlled channels of communication.

Early in August the leader of each political party in Ireland was briefed on the current situation and what PARC were doing to get people out.This provided the politicians with sufficient information for their constituents. It also helped to prevent the rumour machine going into action.

With these matters under control PARC and PR of I dealt with the relatives and the media, especially the press. The relatives had set up a relatives' committee to put pressure on PARC to get people out. They felt that they could achieve success through extensive media coverage, but in reality this only delayed the negotiation process in Iraq.

Peter Keenan had been appointed to liaise directly with the Department of Foreign Affairs and the relatives. His role was to ensure that the relatives were given regular briefings and made aware of the facts. On at least two occasions, David Hanly wrote personally to the nominated next of kin of every employee in Baghdad.

When the crisis broke out in August 1990, PARC set up phone lines for relatives and employees to speak with each other every day for the first week and once a week thereafter. This was how RTE and the other media interviewed the employees in Baghdad. They had to be careful what they said and how they said it as all media coverage was closely monitored by the Iraqi embassies in London and Paris and reported directly back to Iraq. Care was necessary to ensure that offence was not given to the Iraqis as any misinterpretation could delay the processing of exit visas.

The biggest pressure on the employees in Baghdad was the misunderstanding of the situation by the people in Ireland. It was very serious and PARC had to make people understand fully that they had contingency plans and were capable of getting people out. The public relations campaign had to ensure that nothing happened to make the Iraqis change their policy on exit visas. If Baghdad misconstrued any manoeuvre the pieces of paper might not be signed and people would not come home.

However, people did start to come home and PARC were seen to be keeping their word. On arrival, PARC were there to greet them but also, in a sense, to debrief them. They were asked to bear just one thing in mind, not to say anything that was anti-Iraqi because their colleagues were still in Baghdad and their safety depended on a calm approach to the battery of press that were waiting outside. Ultimately everything worked out. All came home, on a staggered basis, and there was no loss of life, not even a cut.

EVALUATION

In hindsight, it is easy to say how well everything worked out but PARC had been in a vulnerable and dangerous position that could have resulted very differently. To evaluate how they handled the situation one must look at the objective which PARC had set itself —to get everybody out. They achieved this, so one must conclude that the operation was a success. In addition, they remained on good terms with the Iraqi Ministry of Health. They remained neutral throughout the war and after and were seen to be non-political, a difficult thing to achieve at any time. PARC may return to Baghdad at some future date, but not for the present because of United Nations sanctions on Iraq.

The hospital remains closed and will have to be virtually rebuilt. It was damaged, mainly by fire, but that was later in the war, long after the staff had left.

Other indications of how well PARC handled the situation are the countless enquiries from employees wanting to go back to Baghdad. This speaks for itself. PARC is the type of company that no matter where it was going to be after Baghdad, it would have to get people to work for it again and win new contracts. It is not easy to win contracts, especially if one's reputation has been tarnished. In the event, PARC's reputation is unblemished because in handling the crisis so capably it has shown its professionalism and dedication.

On the negative side, PARC lost a £12 million contract, that was over 50 per cent of its business. It had to start picking up the pieces. This negative was converted to a plus, in a way, because PARC is back now at about the same level as it was prior to the Gulf War, and it is stronger. Its business is now more diverse and it is less vulnerable because all of its eggs are not in one basket. It has emerged from the crisis with a stronger corporate image and financial position and is a tough competitor on the open market.

DISCUSSION

The biggest pressure on the people in Baghdad and on PARC was caused by people in Ireland who misunderstood the situation or, in some cases, did not want to understand it. It was these people who put PARC employees most at risk and hindered the work of PR of I and the PARC team.

Certain journalists covered the story throughout the whole period. PR of I and PARC took care to maintain a good relationship with them and to be seen as a source for accurate and honest information. It was an international story, of interest not just to Irish journalists but to many others from London and as far as Australia and Canada.

In most cases the press were responsible because they were getting the story and no journalist wanted to be responsible for the people not getting out. The press were responsible because they were being treated fairly. The policy was to allow a free flow of information, taking the risk that such a flow could become difficult to control.

Andrew Kelly had been editor of the *Six One News* on RTE television, joining PR of I shortly before the crisis. One of the things he learnt was that if you treat the media fairly and decently you get the response especially when it is a sensitive issue.

However, there were some journalists who were simply hungry for a story, a hunger that at times seemed to override the importance of human life.

Overall the crisis was handled by PARC and PR of I. Although employees in the hospital were from many countries, some of which were part of the UN forces, PARC put a mantle around all its staff ensuring that they were not viewed by nationality but rather as PARC employees. They were looking after all of their employees and not just the Irish. It was on this basis that the British and other embassies felt that PARC were in a far better position to negotiate the exit from Baghdad. "PARC were non-political and played things straight down the middle:", says David Hanly.

Frances Keegan has a Diploma in Business Management from DIT, a BA Degree in Marketing from the University of Glamorgan, Wales and the DIT Diploma in Public Relations..

AN EVENTFUL DAY
FOR THE 9.55 am TRAIN FROM TRALEE

Irish Rail's Crisis Plan in Action
by Brian Harmon

INTRODUCTION

A derailment or a crash can have a dramatic effect on the public perception of a railway company. Failure to handle enquiries adequately can generate speculation and hype which, in the long term, can seriously damage company reputation.

Crisis plans vary from one company to another in terms of action taken, but, always, the aim is to prevent misinformation and hearsay from becoming the perceived truth and to ensure that information is released promptly, enabling most queries to be answered spontaneously.

A rail mishap becomes news because human life is involved. Road accidents may not make headline news unless there are fatalities, but a minor rail incident does because public transport—plane, boat and train incidents are news.

BACKGROUND

The nature and structure of rail transport means that there must be an immediate, accessible crisis plan ready to be executed in the event of an accident. Iarnród Eireann (Irish Rail), the state-owned company, has had very few major accidents over many years of service and no passengers or staff have been killed for the past ten years. However, such a record does not mean that crisis management teams can ever afford to be complacent.

This experience does not deal with a major rail crash but a minor derailment which happened near Tralee, Co. Kerry, in November 1993. It highlights the importance of a public relations crisis plan and reveals how misinformation and speculation were initially taken to be the truth until swift implementation of the plan. It emphasises the public relations motto in crisis management: "Be prepared".

In this instance the crisis plan was executed under favourable auspices—there was a clear cause for the derailment and no individual could be blamed.

OBJECTIVES

Iarnród Eireann's crisis plan contains four broad objectives:
*   to have a planned emergency response covering all possible crises
*   to have roles allocated to crisis team members, so that each is aware of his/her role in the event of a crisis

AN EVENTFUL DAY FOR THE 9.55 am TRAIN FROM TRALEE

- to have additional back-up staff in case the crisis goes beyond 48 hours. These staff members are fully briefed on the varying needs of the response to the crisis.
- to communicate effectively and efficiently to all relevant publics—relatives of the victims, relatives of staff, the media and the shareholder, i.e. the Minister for Transport.

The primary objective of Iarnród Eireann's crisis plan is to inform publics of a rail incident as soon as information becomes known to the crisis team. An underlying objective in the Tralee derailment was to correct a rumour that there had been fatalities. In releasing information to the media and the public, Iarnrod did not speculate. When details were received, they were checked and re-checked before being released.

PREPARATION AND PLANNING

The public relations manager of Iarnród Eireann, Cyril Ferris, has held his position for many years. Through all major accidents and minor incidents he has constructed a crisis plan. It has evolved over time, with lessons learnt from each incident.

The variety of crises that could emerge for the company has dictated that any new emergency plan soon becomes obsolete. The public relations function, for example, is now more involved than formerly in documentation of incidents and the legal aspects. There will always be an inquiry, at least an internal one with independent board members, and everything that may be said by any company spokesperson will have to be defended. Public bodies like Iarnród Eireann have very precise procedures in relation to claims for damages that might be taken by members of the public.

As a crisis waits for nobody, preparation is the catalyst in carrying out the emergency response. While railways are the least likely mode of transport to have an incident, they are particularly sensitive because of a number of factors such as the size of rolling stock, the transportation of people and produce over long distances and the routes that trains take. Hence, the need for active preparation regardless of whether a crisis emerges or not.

When an incident occurs the Iarnród Eireann crisis team goes into action immediately. Each member acts as a node within the team network: gathering information and passing it on to Cyril Ferris. He liaises with the media and issues statements after they have been cleared by a higher authority.

ROLE ALLOCATION

Roles have been assigned to people so that in the event of a crisis, each knows exactly where to be and what to do.

The crisis team for the Tralee derailment included:
- the senior management team (the chairman and the managing director), and the accident investigation team of Iarnród Eireann, who flew to Kerry, as did the inspecting officer from the Department of Transport. This was important because the presence of the company's chairman comforting victims showed the public the human side of the company.

- an expert panel of deputy managers whose duty it was to be able to understand the way in which a crisis developed during the course of the 'crisis day'
- a product manager with an intimate knowledge of railways and of operation
- a signalling expert
- a planning engineer
- administrative assistants
- the company secretary who was present for authorisation purposes.

With such a planned and organised framework in place, the team was free to change or alter programme responses as information and details filtered through to them. They could run proposed responses past people of authority and, following clearance, have the relevant information in the public domain in a matter of seconds. This is the most important feature of the rail company's crisis plan: speed in terms of co-operation, co-ordination and communication.

IMPLEMENTATION AND EXECUTION

Thursday 11 November 1993:

10.05 am: The 9.55 am Tralee to Cork train derailed. It was a three unit train—one locomotive and three passenger carriages. Two carriages derailed, one rolled down an embankment and ended on its side. The locomotive pulled one carriage up track and had not derailed. The driver of the train climbed up onto a nearby road and decided from what he saw that there must be fatalities. He stopped a passing car and was driven the four miles to Tralee where emergency services were immediately alerted. The driver of the car contacted Radio Kerry, the local station.

10.35 am: Cyril Ferris was informed of the accident and of possible fatalities. He was not at his office at the time but contacted headquarters at Connolly Station, Dublin and called the crisis team into action. A few minutes later, he was told by his assistant that Radio Kerry had enquired about the incident and possible fatalities. He immediately rang the radio station to confirm the accident but asked them to hold on fatalities until confirmed. Through this quick action, he was able to prevent the rumour on fatalities being broadcast on the eleven o'clock news.

One of Cyril Ferris' first phone calls was to the Department of Transport to inform the Minister, Brian Cowen, TD, of what had happened. He then began ringing the relevant media in order of importance: national television and radio (RTE); the Dublin evening papers; the national daily papers and the regional papers. By contacting the national daily papers at this stage, he facilitated them with regard to organising aerial photographs, giving them enough time to hire aircraft if necessary.

11.05 am: It was confirmed that there were no fatalities, but 13 of the 35 passengers were injured. Fifteen minutes later, Ferris had contacted all the media again, giving the new details which he had just received. Again, speed and timing meant that all the relevant media were contacted, informed and corrected within the space of half an hour. It is interesting to note that all of this was carried out in the back of a taxicab on a mobile phone as Ferris made his way through snarled-up traffic to Iarnród Eireann headquarters at Connolly Station !

11.30 am: By the time he arrived at head office, a local perway inspector was on his way to the scene of the accident, as was a divisional engineer. The inspector, equipped with mobile phone, described the accident scene to the crisis team in Dublin. He noted that the rail track was broken not at the end of the rail where it might be expected to fracture, but in the middle. He also gave technical details—locomotive registration, units involved, carriage damage etc. This information was vital to all the technical people involved on the crisis team panel who started checking out the necessary details, e.g. age of locomotive, and line and unit servicing records.

11.40 am: Ferris again informed the media. The next step for him was to relate all known information to journalists for the one o'clock news bulletins. Between calls, he was told that the line of track in question was relaid during the 1970s and refitted and rebolted in July 1993. All the bolts had been tightened and 200 new sleepers were put down in this particular stretch of track. He had now learnt that the story of possible fatalities had originated with the driver.

1.00 pm: Both the national television and radio news bulletins ran the story as the third or fourth item primarily because no one had been killed. So, through Ferris' continuous updates with the media, the story was put in context. At this stage the chairman of the company had arrived by air in Kerry to visit and comfort the injured. After visiting the scene of the derailment he spoke to Radio Kerry having been briefed beforehand by Cyril Ferris.

As spokesperson, Ferris handled the informational role exclusively and was team leader throughout the crisis. In a lunch-time interview with Radio Kerry, he reiterated that the likely cause appeared to be a fault in the track and not the train itself.

During this time the product manager set up a telephone information bureau which could take 20 lines. Three phone numbers were issued to provide public information for relatives of those who may have been on the train.

A rail incident, regardless of size which initially may not be known, may require crisis teams working for up to 72 hours. Iarnród Eireann's plan caters for this fact—more people are chosen for the team than may actually be required. This is essential if the crisis spills beyond 48 hours—shifts need to be introduced. This is a simple element, yet in many crisis management plans, it is overlooked.

EVALUATION

The Cork Evening Echo, the only evening newspaper in the region, led with the incident as a lead story. The two Dublin evening papers had it on page three and not as a lead story. Later in the day a list of all the injured people was sent to the papers, having been cleared by the hospital authorities. Radio Kerry, which had been the first to break the news of the accident, had an extended 'talk back' programme during the evening. Listeners expressed their grievances about the quality of the rail service in County Kerry.

The following day, most of the daily papers had photographs of the derailed train. The photographs were larger than the coverage primarily because the details of the event itself and the identities of injured passengers had already been well-documented the evening before. The *Irish Press* had a feature on rail maintenance, incorporating the

Tralee derailment. The story highlighted how this stretch of line was going to be replaced as soon as money was made available.

The local weekly paper, *The Kerryman*, ran a story with the headline: "Irish Rail to spend £30 million on crash line". This story was important because Radio Kerry and *The Kerryman* are the principal local media in the county. Overall, the provincial newspapers gave a positive report.

Twenty-four hours after the derailment, the crisis plan was being wound down. Cyril Ferris had successfully contained and confined the entire crisis. The plan had been executed with such precision and timing that the public had been kept well-informed of all the facts from the moment the crisis emerged, i.e. the derailment was more than likely caused by track failure than a failure in the train or human error.

The fact that media coverage was subsiding did not necessarily mean that the issue of rail care and maintenance was over. Cyril Ferris turned around the negative news to take advantage of the media opportunity. He announced that £30 million was to be spent on the section of line where the derailment took place and that £275 million was earmarked for capital investment in the railways under the EC structural funds programme. Completion of rail and track investment on the Tralee line was expected by late 1994.

Television coverage outside of news items was minimal. A week later, *Prime Time*, an investigatory television programme, covered the incident by incorporating it into a programme dealing with safety standards in relation to a deteriorating rail system.

A divisional engineer, Diarmuid Ó Murchú, discussed exactly what the rail company's policy and practice is for monitoring and checking the rail network. This includes full-time patrolling of the tracks, ultrasonic testing, an electronic track-recording mechanism and recycling rails. This recycling process involves heating the ends of the rail at high temperature, thereby reconstituting or mending the damaged rail ends. It was the electronic track-recording mechanism which detected faults in this line in July 1993. The programme concluded that the company was being far from complacent when implementing safety standard regulations.

The system that is in place in Iarnród Eireann pays extreme attention to detail: every incident, including train delays, is recorded. There is a 24-hour daily incident report recorded and filed by the public relations manager.

CONCLUSION

Cyril Ferris stated from the beginning that the probable cause of the derailment was track failure. The section of track where the accident happened was checked and rechecked in the months prior to the derailment. Every rail is stamped with a registration number and year of manufacture. The rail which caused the derailment was manufactured in 1902, but experts hold that age does not automatically mean that the rail is unfit for use. However, Ferris anticipating questions, took the initiative and got two expert opinions, one from British Rail.

The British Rail expert said that a question of doubt regarding the age of rails was quite common. Both experts said that a while a 1902 rail was more likely to fracture than a 1993 one, any weaknesses would be quickly detected with continual maintenance and checks. The independent experts' report concluded what Ferris had suspected from the outset—the derailment was caused by a classic metal fatigue. The molecular structure of the rail had altered due to a combination of possible reasons, such as temperature, weather and usage as well, of course, as the age of the rail. In defence of old rails, it must be said that bridges built in 1743 still have trucks going over them and they are regarded as safe as long as they receive proper care and maintenance.

Ferris' admission to the media that he suspected metal fatigue was totally correct. He did not conceal the truth or alter his story and would have responded truthfully had he been asked about the 1902 rail.

DISCUSSION

The Tralee derailment was a good example of a well-executed public relations crisis plan. The absence of fatalities meant that the media communications dimension was simplified and less complex. However, this did not mean that the public relations function became diluted or in any way less important. On the contrary, it highlighted how clear, authenticated facts were distributed to the media and the relevant publics spontaneously and diligently without any chance for speculation to arise.

The credibility of the public relations department of Iarnród Eireann has been strengthened through the effective handling of the Tralee crisis. Its crisis plan has been finely honed over the past decade and is continually being revised. Any weaknesses which emerge from an incident are considered so that a co-ordinated, consistent and thorough plan prevails today.

It was so thorough in this instance that the Minister for Transport decided that a public enquiry, to determine the cause of the accident, was not needed.

As with any crisis involving danger to life, handling the human dimension is always a priority for a company. This was effectively done by senior management in Iarnród Eireann.

FOOTNOTE

Coras Iompar Eireann (CIE) is the main authority for the provision of public transport in the Irish State. It came into being in 1945. A 1986 Act restructured it into a holding company and three major operating subsidiaries—Iarnród Eireann (Irish Rail), Bus Eireann (Irish Bus) and Bus Átha Cliath (Dublin Bus).

Investment in railways has been a controversial issue for many years and they have faced growing competition from roads both for freight and passenger transport. The new EC investment is the first time since 1984 that railways have received any funding for infrastructural development. There is now a new integrated approach giving equal funding to both road and rail. This has occurred primarily because of the successful lobbying by Iarnród Eireann. However, the problem remains that the burden of infrastructural costs hamper Iarnród Eireann's capacity to maintain all of its lines properly. For example, the signalling system on the Dublin-Sligo line is archaic: a thunderstorm, affecting the telegraph wires, can put the line out of operation. Miles of sleepers, all over the country, are in need of replacement.

There was a public outcry a few years ago when eventual closure of certain sections of the Sligo line was rumoured. David Waters, managing director of the company, visited towns along the line and explained the realities. This helped the public to understand that due to a shortage of funds, transport provision had to be curtailed and could not improve until such time as these funds were made available. However, in September 1994, it was announced that the Dublin/Sligo line was to be upgraded and modernised.

The company requires £275 million over the next decade to upgrade the radial rail network. This is part of the Government's Operational Programme on Transport which represents the country's submission to the European Commission for funding under the Community Support Framework, including the Cohesion Fund.

The financial performance and productivity of Iarnród Eireann has improved since the restructuring. While the service continues to show a deficit which dropped from £96 million in 1987 to £93 million in 1993, there is a surplus after State grants which has risen from £114,000 in 1987 to £1.159 million in 1993. The company sees the reduced deficit as a measure of performance.

Revenue has increased each year and a tight control has been kept on expenditure. Staff numbers have been reduced from 7,090 in 1987 to 5,250 at present and this has been achieved by consensus. A measure of increased productivity has been output, in terms of passenger kilometres plus tonne kilometres, per staff member. This has risen from 115 twenty years ago to 370 in 1994.

While the roads account for 96 per cent of all internal passenger travel, the railway competes on all the major inter-urban corridors. Iarnród Eireann's market research shows that the railway has a 24 per cent market share on these corridors. The railway accounts for 26 per cent of inter-urban freight tonne kilometres and has a 17 per cent share of all freight hauled over 150 kilometres.

Brian Harmon has a BA Degree in Economics from University College, Dublin and the DIT Diploma in Public Relations.

THE HUMAN AIRPORT
WITH A WARM AND FRIENDLY FACE

The Aer Rianta Arts Festival
by Miriam O'Callaghan

BACKGROUND

A er Rianta, established in 1937, is the Irish state-owned authority which manages and develops Dublin, Cork and Shannon airports. Through its wholly-owned subsidiary, Aer Rianta International, it has become the biggest airport management consultancy in the world. It has lucrative operations including duty free shops, bars and other services in Moscow, St. Petersburg, Georgia, Kiev, Poland and Pakistan and duty free outlets now on both sides of the Channel Tunnel and most recently in Bahrain and Bangkok. It will extend its consultancy services presently, to include a new venture in Vietnam.

With core values stressing communication, open systems, equality and customer service, it is in its pursuit of excellence and humanisation that Aer Rianta's objective—to make Dublin Airport the best of its size in the world— is most clearly seen to be achieved. While operations at Cork and Shannon are integral to Aer Rianta's success, it is Dublin Airport which, according to chief executive, Derek Keogh, "remains in the key pivotal position in the company's operations".

Background figures:
* More than 1,000 Aer Rianta staff are employed at Dublin Airport
* Seven million passengers use the airport every year
* This number is expected to rise to 10 million by the year 2000

For a significant number of passengers, Dublin Airport is their first experience of Ireland. Aer Rianta is acutely aware of the enduring quality of these first impressions.

Airports are stressful places, so stressful that Kevin Myers, in *An Irishman's Diary* in *The Irish Times*, says: "It is surprising that nobody has ever set up a cardiac unit next to check-in, so that you can check your bags, your ticket and your heart".

Airports can also be intimidating. Despite increased global air travel, there are still a significant number of people for whom flying is an infrequent, or once-off experience. The attendant unease of not knowing one's way around the duty free, or a sometimes complicated boarding procedure, can easily lead to embarrassment.

But stress and intimidation are not the only negative airport associations. Delays to departures and arrivals can be extremely annoying, both for travellers and those meeting them.

Acutely aware of these issues, Aer Rianta has sought to turn them to its advantage by

FROM JOHN PAUL TO SAINT JACK.......

refusing to disappear behind bland hotel-cum-airport-speak, and by daring to care.

Its commitment to the arts grew from efforts to alleviate stress, intimidation and annoyance by humanising its airports, exploiting the distinctly Irish idea of Fáilte or Welcome. And so, what began as a Welcome Home for Christmas campaign, with trees, lights and Santa Claus, evolved to today's innovative Arts Festival.

The company's corporate mission statement aspires to making Aer Rianta "the best organisation in the world in the field of managing airports and associated commercial activities". Consequently, the company was happy to become involved with projects that reflected excellence and good taste. Artistic endeavour of any kind, according to press and public relations manager, Flan Clune, "was a natural sponsorship for Aer Rianta".

Irate, delayed passengers have been less inclined to pace incessantly to and from information monitors in the presence of strategically-placed, warm bronzes and calming, visual and tactile art.

Water, sculpture, landscaping and performance arts have grown to become a major art sponsorship scheme, worth more than £250,000 annually.

The Aer Rianta Arts Festival cannot be discussed in isolation. It is, rather, an integral part of a serious arts commitment, which sees Aer Rianta as:

- corporate donor of the Abbey Theatre
- corporate patron of the Dublin Grand Opera Society
- sponsor of Cothú Arts Awards
- patron of the Irish Life Dublin Theatre Festival
- patron of Ballymun Youth Theatre
- sponsor of Malahide and Swords Young Musician Competition

THE CHALLENGE

The challenge to Aer Rianta in establishing an arts festival was to:

- alleviate, as far as possible, the stress, intimidation and annoyance factors at Dublin Airport
- make the airport more user-friendly through humanisation
- establish Aer Rianta as a proactive and widely-recognised sponsor of the arts
- establish the airport, a location not normally associated with the arts, as a recognised and established arts and cultural venue
- balance the excellence of the exhibited art with public accessibility
- ensure that the festival be popular and participative
- ensure that it did not interfere with the efficient running of the airport
- ensure that it appealed to its many and varied publics

RESEARCH

While the arts sponsorship programme undertaken by Aer Rianta is a weighted and deliberate one, the idea of holding its first Arts Festival in 1988, according to Flan Clune, "crept up on them", growing from the policy of making the airport more user-friendly, a warmer place.

THE HUMAN AIRPORT WITH A WARM AND FRIENDLY FACE

Surveys conducted through the years before 1988 recorded comments on the friend-liness of the airport. Aer Rianta did not commission a study on attitudes to a proposed, structured Arts Festival but it did one of the most important things in public relations — it listened. People were happy with company efforts so far and would welcome more of the same.

Media and public feedback on the Welcome Home for Christmas campaign was ex-cellent. While these audiences proved receptive to a festival, the serious hurdle of con-vincing others of the viability and worth of such a project, had yet to be negotiated. Not everybody at Dublin Airport felt that the festival was a good idea, or a proposal meriting serious investment of time, finance and reputation.

Economically, the late 1980s were tough and, with tight budgets, it was difficult to sell the idea to others as the arts in this context could not be seen to make money. Staff morale, however, had benefited greatly from the Christmas theme—an increase in moti-vation and a feeling of participation which was in turn passed to the customer. The pub-lic relations department had also noted the personal development of the staff in the company's loose use of the arts before 1988.

PLANNING

Planning for the next festival begins immediately the last one has been completed. The committee is largely self-governing in terms of selection of artists, exhibition space, etc, functioning within the marketing department of the airport. Flan Clune deals with pub-licity, promotion and the media and, while the festival has a huge and calculated public relations function, this committee reports neither to him nor his department. Budget of approximately £80,000 is set in October for implementation in February.

Planning for the next festival includes, by necessity, evaluation of the last. As none of the committee is an art expert, advice is sought from the media, for example the RTE *Arts Show*, and from people in the art world, in particular those associated with the Arts Council. A relationship of trust has been built up between the committee and its advisers and, in general, Aer Rianta is happy to follow their suggestions and advice.

At the popular level, the committee notes developments and innovations within the arts and is keen to attract big names to the festival. The Woman's Heart Tour, a major coup for Aer Rianta in 1993, caused severe crowd control problems. The free concert thrilled the capacity audience. It also shut down approach roads to the airport.

The biggest problem for the 1994 festival was that, while media coverage was exten-sive and excellent in quality, enthusiasm from the critics was under par with previous years.

IMPLEMENTATION

The Aer Rianta Arts Festival has been running annually since 1988. It takes place in Febru-ary, the airport's low season, to ensure maximum exhibition and enjoyment space and minimum disruption to passenger travel. Running daily for three weeks, from 11 am until late, it is very successful with its many audiences:

FROM JOHN PAUL TO SAINT JACK.......

- Artists get a chance to exhibit and possibly sell their work to a potential audience of six million. (In 1993, more than 90 per cent of exhibited work was sold).
- Aer Rianta staff are afforded the opportunity to work in an environment where art excellence is balanced by accessibility.

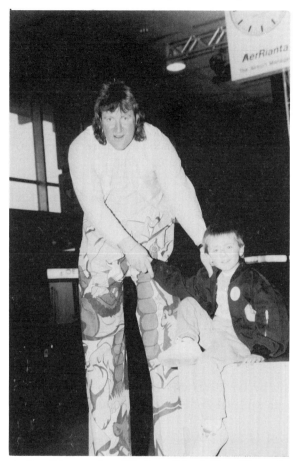

A stilt-walking member of "Audience Friendly" from Sligo makes the acquaintance of 5-year-old Patrick Gallagher from Balbriggan, Co. Dublin at the Aer Rianta Arts Festival held annually in the Passenger Terminal at Dublin Airport.

- Irish passengers take a sense of pride in the arts achievement of the airport.
- Foreign passengers have a first glimpse of Ireland in an arts and cultural context.
- People meeting passengers in a month, when the weather at Dublin and abroad can cause flight delays, pass the time viewing the exhibitions and enjoying the musical activities.
- Customers of Aer Rianta, every company operating from the airport, from the florist to the car hire, to the airlines, benefit from the increased activity.
- Local communities can view the static arts without feeling intimidated by 'high art' notions.
- Local schools get a chance not only to experience the art available, but also to perform—school choirs are invited to sing and competition for invitations is keen.
- The media have been impressed by Aer Rianta's commitment to the arts, not only during the festival, but throughout the year. This commitment has given the company great credibility as an arts sponsor which is in for the long haul, and not just the once-off stunt.
- The Government has been impressed by Aer Rianta, not only in the Arts Festival, but also in ventures such as the Kremlin Gold exhibition for Dublin European City of Culture Year, 1991, when the company was praised by the Department of Education, the Department of Foreign Affairs, the President and the Taoiseach. Aer Rianta's involvement with Cothú—The Business Council for the Arts, has also enhanced its profile with its political masters.
- Other airports have taken note of Aer Rianta's enterprise with the arts and many,

including Manchester, Belfast, Faro (Lisbon) and Gothenburg, have introduced cultural activities in their operations, but none of them to the same extent as Dublin.

PROGRAMME

The Festival successfully combines visual, static and performance arts. A copy of the programme is as follows:
- Visual and static arts—painting and sculpture, approximately 60 artists annually
- Country and western music in the evenings, as well as jazz, classical, opera, ballet, rock, folk and traditional—from Dickie Rock to Mary Black, from Don Baker to the stars of the Bolshoi. Major concerts take place in the departures concourse which holds 2,000 and is filled to capacity for all events.
- Mime artists, clowns, face painters, stilt-walkers entertain the children, particularly on Saturdays when the airport has been described as a fairyland.

All events are free to the public, with Aer Rianta staff working on a voluntary basis. Staff are not paid overtime for the many hours put in to making the festival such a success. Aer Rianta sees staff involvement as a vital feature of the festival, as it can only happen with their full participation and support.

As a spin-off from the festival there are other activities such as:
- music in the terminal
- regular exhibitions at all Aer Rianta airports by artists who have exhibited at the festival
- External sculpture with brilliant, innovative sculptures, e.g. *Ammonite*, by Niall O'Neill, and *Earth Mother*, by Dick Joint

Much exhibited work has been bought by Aer Rianta for VIP and public areas, boardrooms etc. Arts Festival spin-off is also in evidence at Cork and Shannon airports.

Cork Airport:
- art exhibitions, praised by the media, including Kevin Myers who said in *The Irish Times* that the work was worth getting to see even if one didn't have a plane to catch
- photographic exhibitions, sculpture competitions and a homage to Christy Ring, the legendary Cork hurler
- living sculpture—an orchard with horses and ponies in a paddock
- waterfall, huge fish tank and beautiful brass-canopied fireplace in the baggage reclaim hall, a welcome sight on a wet and windy night from Heathrow
- flower sculpture, Welcome Home for Christmas theme, St. Patrick's Day celebrations

Shannon Airport:
- Free open-air concerts
- opera concerts in the pier building which, until the opening of the University Concert Hall in Limerick, was the largest concert venue in Munster
- sculpture trail
- landscaping and flower sculpture
- visit of Bolshoi opera stars

Moscow:
- visit of Artane Boys' Band
- gala launch of Irish Music Week
- visit by pianist John O'Conor to perform John Field's *Nocturne*
- debut performance of *Island Wedding*, suite for instrumental and vocal soloists with chamber orchestra, composed by Charlie Lennon

EVALUATION

Evaluation of the festival can be difficult insofar as it is hard to quantify in financial terms what Aer Rianta gains from its investment. The festival has been very successful in achieving three major objectives:

- **To establish Aer Rianta as a major company with a clear, positive image**

This certainly has been achieved as Aer Rianta is now recognised as one of the major sponsors of the arts in Ireland. By emphasising the idea of Aer Rianta Kremlin Gold and Aer Rianta Arts Festival in such a high-profile manner, the company has achieved a separate identity to Aer Lingus, the national airline which has its head office at Dublin Airport. They have been totally separate companies since 1968. The fact that the two were still so often confused in people's minds was worrying for Aer Rianta, particularly when Aer Lingus was the focus of much public and media attention because of financial problems and lay-offs. The public queried arts expenditure by Aer Rianta when the company was mistakenly perceived to be losing money.

- **To enhance the company's standing with its various publics**

This objective has been dealt with under consideration of audiences. Aer Rianta enjoys the respect and understanding of all its audiences which has translated into support of its business and artistic ventures. Aer Rianta's political audience has been particularly pleased with its activity, not only in Ireland, but in every country in which it operates. It currently enjoys an excellent reputation with its Russian audiences, employee, public and political.

- **To contribute substantially to the realisation of the company's overall objective —to make Aer Rianta the best airport authority in the world.**

Enquiries regarding the arts have

Flan Clune, MPRII, press and public relations manager, Aer Rianta

---

THE HUMAN AIRPORT WITH A WARM AND FRIENDLY FACE

poured in from airports all over the world. Aer Rianta is now regarded as being the key player in humanising airports.

The overall objective of the festival is to make Dublin Airport a popular and accessible venue for concerts, exhibitions and other activities which are arts-based. With a nightly attendance of 2,000 this objective has certainly been achieved.

Media

In evaluating the festival, it is necessary to discuss media implications. Since 1988 media coverage has been wide and lavish in praise of the festival, both in content and implementation. It won a *Sunday Tribune* arts award in its first year. In 1994, *The Arts Show*, on RTE, broadcast a special programme on the festival. It has gained valuable feature and editorial space, winning two successive front pages in *The Irish Times*. Though the company was disappointed in the critics' lack of enthusiasm for the 1994 festival, it is confident that it can restore that very fine balance between artistic excellence and public accessibility.

Sales

Each year, an average of 90 per cent of exhibited work is sold. This illustrates how well the committee has chosen exhibits—the public want to buy.

Cothú

Cothú—The Business Council for the Arts, and *The Sunday Business Post*, launched The Arts Sponsor of the Year Awards in 1991. Aer Rianta has been both a winner and a sponsor of these awards; In 1992, it was highly commended for Kremlin Gold, in the Best Established Arts Sponsor category. It also sponsored the commissioning of Cathy Carman, who works from Temple Bar Gallery and Studios in Dublin, to create bronze sculptures for presentation to award winners. From 1994 the Awards are sponsored by Ernst & Young Accountants and *The Sunday Tribune*.

DISCUSSION

When it comes to arts festivals, there are many different ideas on what they should contain. *The Times* (London) arts critics, Stephen Pettit and Alison Roberts, cite breadth and appeal to various publics, in particular, the local community, as paramount. Colours, smells and vibrancy appear to be in. Hushed, unctuous gallery-tones are out. If these are the criteria for success, then Aer Rianta is a winner, but not without effort. It's not just chance, but constant endeavour, that achieves that crucial balance between excellence and accessibility.

In an interview with Paddy Woodworth of *The Irish Times*, on the arts and the Presidency, President Mary Robinson spoke of the role excellence plays in artistic expression. She also stressed the complementary role of self-expression and community involvement. Again, Aer Rianta wins with a popular and participative festival, unafraid of stressing the separate and ancient heritage of the arts in Ireland. It is fitting in this context that an arts festival take place in Dublin Airport, the site of Cloghran—Cloch Amhráin—Stone of Song where Ireland's first feiseanna occurred.

US Ambassador to Ireland, Jean Kennedy Smith, addressing the Cothú *Sunday Business Post* awards presentation in 1993, stressed that support for the arts was not charity, it must be proactive. Aer Rianta, in six years, has taken this to heart with each festival and arts sponsorship better than the one before. It has also seemed to develop an intuitive sense of what will work, not by chance but by carefully measured advice and, above all, its ability to listen.

The Aer Rianta Arts Festival is an integral part of the company's wider programme to establish a special corporate image for the company. It contributes substantially to the realisation of the company's overall objective to be the best airport management authority in the world. How ? —by reaching beyond the traditional, conventional centres for the arts and involving everyone, not just the usual cultured bunch.

Miriam O'Callaghan has a BA Degree in English and History from University College, Cork, Postgrad Advanced Studies at Royal College of Music, London, and the DIT Diploma in Public Relations.

37 YEARS ON: STILL REWARDING IRELAND'S TIDIEST TOWN

The Bord Fáilte Tidy Towns Competition
by Melanie A. O'Sullivan

BACKGROUND

In 1953, Bord Fáilte—The Irish Tourist Board, started a National Spring Festival, called An Tostal. This was an old Gaelic word for pageant, gathering, array, or display.

Communities in every part of the country were encouraged to organise pageants, parades, theatre, music, sporting and religious events. An Tostal flourished for only a few years, but it created the context in which the annual Tidy Towns Competition—a good idea that has lasted now for 37 years—took root.

The Irish Countrywomen's Association organised a National Roadside Gardens Competition as part of the first An Tostal. It was designed to brighten up approaches to, and add to the amenities of towns and villages. Bord Fáilte promoted a National Spring Clean Campaign each year from 1953 to ensure that towns, villages and resorts were made to look their best prior to the start of the tourist season. As a natural development of this campaign, in April 1958, they inaugurated a Tidy Towns and Villages Competition to find the best-kept town in Ireland. Each An Tostal council was invited to participate.

According to Aidan O'Hanlon, then public relations manager for Bord Fáilte, there was an "indifference to tourism" in Ireland during the 1950s and Tidy Towns provided the opportunity to build an awareness of its importance to the future of the country.

There were 52 entries in that first year, representing every county except Carlow, Dublin, Sligo and Westmeath. Glenties, Co. Donegal was the first winner. Entries more than trebled to 179 the following year and built to a peak of 800 in 1982, levelling out at 650 in recent years.

Bord Fáilte sent teams to all parts of the country, to explain the concept of Tidy Towns and encourage people to get involved. Aidan O'Hanlon remembers meetings in local parish halls and community centres with lectures and slides and a full house guaranteed in those days before television. Tidy Towns committees were set up and people were urged to paint their houses and shopfronts, tidy up the litter, plant flowers and erect palings. Attractive literature and other back-up material was published for nationwide distribution. This included a book, *Three Heads are Better than None....or a Recent Happening at Mile Tree,* using a fictional narrative to point out that if a town or village improved and promoted itself it would benefit in many ways. There would be increased tourist traffic, its spirit would be lifted and a concern for the environment would grow and develop.

An independent panel of assessors was set up to judge the entries, and to award cash prizes and a perpetual trophy to the national winner. Guidelines were laid down for the committees and Bord Fáilte were always on hand to give advice and encouragement. Community groups such as the GAA, the Irish Countrywomen's Association, Muintir na Tíre and An Taisce also became involved. The An Tostal councils, including local business and tourist interests, provided a potential base for Tidy Towns promotion in almost every town and village in the country.

Over 37 years the Tidy Towns concept has evolved into a concern, not only for the appearance of the Irish countryside, but also for its heritage.

Brenda King, who looks after Tidy Towns for Bord Fáilte, says it is the progress reports that provide continuity, encouraging communities to be on the lookout for new ways to improve their area, and their chances to win an award. The reports indicate performance under several headings and give advice on how improvements could be made. They are intended as constructive criticism and have also been valuable in providing the links between old and new committees as personnel change. They are confidential but the committees may publicise them if they wish.

There has been enormous coverage in national and provincial press and more recently on local radio and RTE television and radio. The last six years has also added the new dimension of sponsorship, for three years with First National Building Society and now with Super Valu Supermarkets.

PUBLIC RELATIONS FOR THE NATION

The Tidy Towns is probably Ireland's longest running, and most successful competition. From its modest beginning involving a mere 52 centres in 1958, it now has a core of approximately 25,000 voluntary helpers, annually, covering over 650 centres countrywide. It has had an enormous affect on the developmental side of tourism in working to improve what is on offer for visitors. From a public relations viewpoint, it is a twelve-month programme. The following are the main activities:

- **Search for new angles**

There has been a constant search for new ideas and events to promote the competition and retain media attention. Each year, once the awards have been presented, Bord Fáilte and the sponsor discuss the events of the previous twelve months. They note the problem areas and ways of improving them. Some events are once-off while others become permanent. Bord Fáilte are not afraid to take a calculated risk nor to drop a project which is not a success. Ideas for new events come both from feedback to Bord Fáilte and from within, especially through the preparation of the annual progress reports and reviews with the adjudication panel.

- **Media coverage**

Tidy Towns achieves Bord Fáilte's largest media coverage of the year. According to John Brown, Bord Fáilte's senior public relations officer, it generates a "massive amount of column inches" in both the national and provincial press, not just on the week of the awards presentation but throughout the year.

The September prize-giving is held on a Monday to facilitate the provincial papers,

37 YEARS ON—STILL REWARDING IRELAND'S TIDIEST TOWN

which are invaluable for informing each area about its own results and other relevant aspects of the competition. The event takes place in Dublin Castle and edited highlights are now shown on television later in the evening. The presenter, John Bowman, previously did a radio coverage. The audience figures have been very encouraging with the programme reaching the top ten for the week each time.

The growth in popularity and listenership for local radio has also been a positive development for the competition.

- **Progress reports.**

According to Brenda King, these reports, which provide a detailed analysis of the individual centres' performance over the year, have been used with great success to lobby for greater efforts in the community. Every committee is different, but they all need to be motivated and encouraged to keep up their interest and involvement in the competition.

- **Prize-giving**

Following the judging in June, July, August, points are allocated for overall effort, tidiness, presentation of buildings, natural amenities and immediate residential areas and the appearance of approach roads. The maximum score is 250 points (Keadue, Co. Roscommon was the 1993 winner with 201 points).

The major public relations focus is on the national awards ceremony in September. The 27 county winners are invited, but only the National Award is presented and the identity of the winner is a secret until the last moment.

The 1994 national winner received
- £5000 presented by the sponsor
- perpetual trophy
- bronze plaque
- grant-aid of £5000 for an approved project.

Each of the seven tourism regions has its own presentation event in October or November for local awards. This is an opportunity for extra publicity which is welcomed, especially by the sponsors. The Minister for Tourism attends the main Dublin event, and local politicians are invited to the regional ceremonies. President Robinson and, before her, President Hillery, have usually been involved in one Tidy Towns event each year, such as a visit to the winning town, another boost for local pride.

- **Sponsorship**

The first sponsor was the First National Building Society, liaising with Bord Fáilte through Niall Delaney, their public relations consultant, and Ald. Carmencita Hederman, former Lord Mayor of Dublin, and a director of First National. This partnership for Tidy Towns lasted three years and included a very successful advertising campaign on radio prior to a launch of the competition in the literary and historic Dublin suburb of Sandymount. This was a means to improve Dublin participation and it gained national television coverage.

Then came Super Valu Supermarkets in 1991, under the guidance of Patrick Crane and Grayling Public Relations. This is a very successful partnership and through the creation of a new logo, and heavy investment into promotional activities, Super Valu, with 142 supermarkets throughout the country, have become closely associated with Tidy Towns. They have also arranged a photographic calendar competition featuring entries, showing people carrying out repairs and renovations to their town or village. Super Valu have renewed the contract for another three years and Patrick Crane says that they are in for the 'long haul'. He estimates that Super Valu put approximately £150,000 into promoting the competition, and £50,000 directly to Bord Failte for the competition itself.

The need for sponsorship had been realised for some years and Brenda King now believes that Tidy Towns might not have survived without it.

EVALUATION

The fact that Tidy Towns has been running for 37 years is testament to its success and popularity. It has not been without its share of problems and criticisms but Bord Fáilte has always fought back in its defence.

Brenda King claims that Tidy Towns is 'unique' in Europe, the closest things to it being flower competitions, an angle which she hopes to highlight in the future. It has certainly contributed to the transformation of the Irish countryside. The painting, tidying and planting of flowers continues and with the growing sophistication of society, the emphasis has shifted to the restoration and renovation of old buildings and shopfronts and the burying of wirescape (telephone and electricity wires and poles).

Nowadays Bord Fáilte sees itself more as the administrator of the competition aiming to encourage and motivate the various committees through head office in Dublin and the seven regional tourism organisations.

The progress reports have been instrumental in maintaining the all important one-to-one link between Bord Fáilte and the various centres. This system encourages feedback which enables Bord Fáilte to identify problem areas and discuss ways to rectify them.

Good relations with local and national media have resulted in generous coverage. This is important for Bord Fáilte and Super Valu as it points to a well-organised and efficiently-run competition.

Sponsorship has encouraged more entries as well as a greater effort from those already involved. In addition, it has improved promotional activity and brought in some new awards. It has been an added bonus that both sponsors have had a public relations 'arm'.

Super Valu do not merely hand over a cheque, but invest time and resources in the competition. For example, they have developed a new logo which gives a uniformity to the event, appearing on everything from display material and press announcements to posters, competitions and instore promotions.

Over the years many other organisations have contributed. An Post, for example, gives an award for the best presented sub-post office. This also attracts press coverage and provides a photo-opportunity. Other awards are sponsored by such companies as Broderick's Grass Machinery, Mackeys Seeds, Harte Designs, Irish Wheelchair Association/National Rehabilitation Board, HGW Paints, Mercury Engineering, Emerald Star Line, A1 Waste, Garrison House, Bord na Gaeilge and the Irish Glass Bottle Company.

In the early days some places won several times, but this has not happened in recent years. Towns and villages now compete so fiercely that there is rarely more than a few points between the top half dozen.

Smaller villages, with less than 200 people, have won more often than others and some would say it is easier for them, but all have their chance through the six categories based on population size. In 1993 all six category winners scored between 192 and tiny Keadue's 201.

Of course care has to be taken that those who are not doing too well, but trying hard, receive encouragement to improve and aim for the top position. It is somewhat ironic that it is often the busiest tourist areas that are most in need of a gentle push.

DISCUSSION

Tidy Towns has not been without its problems, especially with suggestions, often from prominent government figures, that it has outlived its usefulness and should be scrapped. Bord Fáilte have fought long and hard to negate these feelings by constantly seeking new angles to promote and sell it.

Tourism is Ireland's second largest industry and it is essential to present the environment in the best possible condition, especially to visitors, both foreign and domestic. Tidy Towns is more than a 'fun' competition involving community co-operation and team spirit; it is also very practical and has effectively an infinite job to do in achieving its objectives.

There are four major areas of constant focus:
1. The committees and people must receive plenty of encouragement and incentive to stay in the competition and aim high. This must come from Bord Failte and the seven regional tourism organisations. The tasks are:
* to set an example for the kind of action required
* to create an awareness of the competition and its importance to the country
* to promote and encourage participation
* to keep existing competitors in

There's Work to be Done is a 25-minute film to provide ideas and encouragement for participants. It can be hired or purchased.
2. Good links must be cultivated with the media.
3. Super Valu will continue to promote it in whatever ways possible.
4. There needs to be a greater emphasis on specific tourism areas, as the main aim of the competition is to improve the countryside for the visiting tourist.

Tidy Towns has evolved from a simple cleaning-up operation to an entire programme of exterior design, concerned not only with physical appearance but also with the heritage of each area. Perhaps the 1990s will mark the more environmentally aware aspect of Tidy Towns !

FOOTNOTE

In 1994, the Government announced a new plan for Bord Fáilte which will allow it to concentrate on marketing Ireland abroad and withdraw from such domestic activities as hotel registrations and Tidy Towns. As this book was going to press, the announcement of a new organiser for the Competition was imminent.

Melanie A. O'Sullivan has a BSc Management Degree in Business & Marketing from DIT and the DIT Diploma in Public Relations.

GIVING A LIGHT TO THE COMMUNITY

The John Player Tops
by Jill Börnemann

BACKGROUND

The John Player Tops is a national competition for variety shows presented by non-professional performers drawn from business organisations and community groups. The aim is to develop team effort and informal networks. Personal accomplishments are put aside in favour of the overall effort. The success of the event is its ability to involve a large number of people, both directly and indirectly, from all over Ireland in a social activity which is both pleasurable and creative.

The basic concept of the John Player Tops is participation. People are encouraged and helped to develop their abilities in music, singing, acting, choreography, writing, design, lighting, organisation— in fact, every element of theatrical design and presentation.

Since it started in 1964, the Tops has provided a platform for local talent as well as a focus for social and community activity and it has grown into one of the most popular annual events in Ireland.

John Player & Sons, Dublin is a cigarette and tobacco company which employs 270 people. It has been at its South Circular Road location in Dublin since 1923. Its main brand, John Player Blue has been the most popular in Ireland for the past eight years. The parent company is Imperial Tobacco Ltd, part of Hanson plc.

John Player & Sons has provided the ongoing financial and management support for the Tops for more than 30 years, and the event is one of the longest running and most extensive arts sponsorships by any Irish company.

RESEARCH

John Player & Sons became involved in the Tops at a time when there were a number of local variety events in different parts of the country. For example, Dublin Dairies sponsored a variety competition in Waterford; there was a Parish Night in Dundalk run by Fr. Michael Dorman, as well as a Leinster Factories Talent Contest. John Player had participated successfully in some of these events, so when Niall O'Flynn, then public relations manager for the company, was approached to take over the Dublin Dairies sponsorship he was aware of the potential.

Impressed by the success of the Waterford Tops, the company set about developing and introducing the concept in other parts of the country. In 1969 a national dimension was introduced with the launching of a national final.

FROM JOHN PAUL TO SAINT JACK.......

In 1994, the John Player Tops won the Cothú—The Business Council for the Arts award for "The Best Arts Sponsorship in the Community". President Mary Robinson presented the award to Gerry Grogan, managing director, John Player & Sons.

The company was involved in a number of sponsorships around the country and a case was made for rationalising without losing valuable contacts or harming the reputation of the company. The idea of a national variety contest fitted the bill as it would integrate the company into local communities.

Over the years the event has undergone several name changes as a reflection of the changing structure and how the company itself was styled. Now it is known simply as The John Player Tops, a name which Gerry Grogan, chairman and managing director, says reflects the energy and vibrancy and forward-looking nature of the company.

The Tops summarises the aims and objectives of John Player & Sons which sees itself as a company for the people, lacking pretentiousness and producing brands which appeal to the ordinary citizen. The Tops remains an event for part-time performers who constantly strive for, and achieve, the highest standards of presentation. The concept is that organisations should attain success through their own resources and, in the process, develop apparent and latent talents in individuals..

In recent years tobacco companies have been under pressure from the Irish Government and the European Union. New legislation in 1989 put further restrictions on cigarette advertising. Companies can advertise the cigarette and its box against a plain, coloured background in print media, but all advertising on radio and television is banned. The government has placed an inflation-linked budget on advertising and marketing spend by tobacco companies and more recently this has come under review.

The Tops continues to provide John Player with an opportunity to keep its name before its 6,500 national retailers without abusing either the letter or the spirit of the Government regulations. The Tops has no direct commercial benefits for the company, research having shown that it does not increase the percentage of smokers, nor the company's share of the market. However, there is an enhancement of goodwill and reputation.

PLANNING AND IMPLEMENTATION

The Tops is divided into four stages; the local competitions, national quarter-finals, national semi-finals and national final. In local competitions, which are self-contained events in their own right, two different groups perform before an adjudicator and, when all have been seen, two are selected for the local final, which is adjudicated by a national adjudicator who adjudicates all local finals. He is the common denominator between all area finals and having viewed all such finals he nominates eight of the area finalists to go forward to national quarter finals.

The competition is intended primarily for groups drawn from business firms, public service organisations, small rural parishes and residents associations. There are no entry fees, but each group is responsible for financing its own show. Groups generally raise funds through collections, weekly draws, sponsorship, social functions, sales of work, etc as well as assistance from local communities and the sponsors.

The sponsors and the local organising committees are responsible for the running cost of the competition, theatre hire, prizes, programmes, adjudicators' fees, advertising, printing and receptions. Both John Player and the participating companies have opportunities for corporate hospitality at the various stages of Tops.

All participating groups receive cash prizes. These are on a scale for different stages of the competition. In addition groups receive cash grants from the sponsors and/or the local committees. Any profit made locally from the competition goes directly to a charity of the committees' choice.

The basic structure of the competition has remained constant for the past 30 years. The requirement is for a fast-moving 60-minute variety show, with a good mix of music, song, dance and comedy. However, each year the event is reviewed and various innovations are introduced. These include such developments as introduction of national quarter and semi-finals, changes in marking system, new award categories. The competition commences locally in March and the national stages conclude in early June. Participating groups start rehearsing as early as the previous September, though January is the most common start-up time, show planning having commenced some months earlier.

The competition is organised on behalf of the sponsors by a national organiser, Niall O'Flynn, now public relations consultant to the company. He works closely with local committees, who play a key role in the running of the area competitions. They also have an input into national sages but the administration of these is more centralised.

The Tops is a fine example of how a commercial sponsor and local committees can work together successfully. There is a high level of consultation and co-operation between the sponsors and the voluntary committees, and this has contributed greatly to the ongoing development of the event. The various stages of Tops enable John Player personnel to become actively involved at local level, as well as providing hosting opportunities.

Because the John Player Tops is about people it lends itself to human interest media coverage, in particular at local level. Such coverage in newspapers and on radio is generated locally and through the national structure. The competition is televised live annually by RTE, and the station has undertaken various other Tops-based television programmes over the years.

EVALUATION

The main objective of the Tops has been to keep the John Player name in front of retailers and consumers. This has been achieved. A survey of 360 leading Irish firms, carried out by Wilton Research & Marketing for John McMahon & Partners in 1986, showed that the John Player Tops was the second most recognised non-sport sponsorship after the Guinness Jazz Festival (which, incidentally, was initiated, and sponsored previously by John Player).

Some years ago Players commissioned its own research to compare the Tops with nine other top sponsorships in the country. The Carrolls' Irish Open golf came out ahead in terms of public appeal and awareness within the upper classes in the Dublin area but on a national basis the John Player Tops emerged as a much more popular sponsorship that people could identify with. However, it did not influence their buying decisions.

Between committees and teams, some 5,000 to 6,000 people participate directly in the Tops each year. Research indicates that over 350,000 people in the country have been involved one way or the other in the competition since its inception. The combined theatre audience figure exceeds 60,000 annually.

RTE have been televising the final in a three-hour live show since 1976. It is held on the June Bank Holiday weekend and attracts audiences in excess of 700,000 viewers. Indeed, the televised final is one of the most popular annual outside broadcast programmes on RTE. There is a repeat broadcast of the final at a later date, taking the two one-hour shows as individual programmes. Another show, *John Player Tip Tops*, comprising six half-hour shows, ran for a number of years, showing the best of those who did not make it to the final. Over the years the television presentation has been hosted by such people as Gay Byrne, Mike Murphy, Theresa Lowe, Fionnuala Sweeney and Marty Whelan.

More than £2 million has been raised for charity through the event, alleviating some the pressure on the company to comply with other requests for donations. The Tops generates an estimated £1 million of revenue each year for hotels, restaurants, equipment suppliers, transport suppliers, costume makers, musicians etc.

The competition has attracted a range of groups, from both commercial and community fields. National finalists have included St. Joseph's Youth Club, Strabane (1981), Digital Equipment International, Galway (1985), Cork Teachers and Students (1987), L & M Ericsson, Athlone (1988), Anglo-Irish Bankcorp, Dublin (1989), Aer Lingus, Dublin (1989), Analog Devices BV, Limerick (1991), Players' Anonymous, Tramore (1993), Waterford

Crystal (1994), Woodville Variety Group, Dublin (1994).

The John Player Tops brings benefits to the communities, through discovery of new theatrical talent, development of interest in the theatre, and the provision of many hours of entertainment for thousands of people. The creation of social activity within and between firms and community groups helps industrial and public relations and builds up community spirit.

DISCUSSION

The John Player Tops has been a public relations success because of the large number of people involved and the creation of community enthusiasm, as well as the extensive media coverage and subsequent recognition of the company name.

Initially, most of the participating groups in Tops were from companies but now some 90 per cent of the entries come from community-based groups. This is a reflection of a general social trend away from company-based recreational activities, which has seen a greater focus on community groups, which have become more assertive and active in many walks of life. Further, firms seem to have become hesitant about investing time and resources in social activities in a business environment which is placing increasing demands on cost structures and on manning levels. This trend from firms to community groups has in no way affected the standard of the competition, and it could be argued that it is advantageous to John Player as there is less competition for publicity. On the other hand, the involvement of high profile companies brings its own prestige and awareness to the event.

The John Player Tops has been an example of what many see as a golden rule: don't sponsor a competitor, sponsor the event. That way you will always be a winner, especially if you initiate the event or make it your own. Where the prize money is concerned the majority of this is fed back into the community and does not, as Gerry Grogan says, "end up in the hands of professional sports personalities from abroad".

The Tops is generally recognised as one of the most enlightened and successful sponsorships in the country, a fact which was endorsed by Cothú—The Business Council for the Arts in 1994 when it honoured the company with its award for "The Best Arts Sponsorship in the Community".

John Player does not reveal the exact cost of sponsorship, but it is minimal compared to the total advertising and marketing budget. Cigarette advertising is usually full colour and in newspapers and magazines. The total cost of the Tops for John Player would quickly vanish into a few glossy pages in a Sunday newspaper.

Jill Börnemann has a BA Degree in History of Art & Sociology from the University of Dublin, Trinity College, and the DIT Diploma in Public Relations.

HORSE CLASSIC GIVES BUD LONG REACH

The Budweiser Irish Derby
by Catherine Dolan

BACKGROUND

Anheuser Busch hold 44 per cent of the US beer market, more than twice as much as their nearest rival, Miller. In 1985, they were considering the introduction of their Budweiser brand into Ireland.

They had become involved with a sponsorship in Kerry, called the Shamrock Games, where the idea was to have American teams from many different sports come to Ireland for a mini-Olympics. The event was not a success but, because of their involvement, executives from Anheuser Busch were in Ireland in June 1985. Towards the end of their visit they went to the Curragh, 30 miles outside Dublin, for the Irish Derby, one of Europe's premier mile-and-a-half horse races for three-year olds. Since 1962 the event had been sponsored by the Irish Hospital Sweepstakes.

The Budweiser executives were entertained at the Curragh by Lord Hempel, senior steward of the Irish Turf Club. He told them that the Sweep were thinking of getting out and asked if they would be interested in being involved. They agreed, in principle, immediately.

The president of Anheuser Busch at the time was Denis P. Long. His grandparents came from Co. Kerry. Mike Roarty, executive vice president and head of marketing, also had a great affinity for Ireland, his mother being from Tourmakeady in Co. Mayo and his late father from Co. Donegal.

The decision to sponsor the Derby was taken for good marketing reasons. Anheuser Busch were heavily into sponsorship at home and were looking around for a prestigious sports event abroad because they were about to move into the European market of 320 million people.

The Derby fitted the profile that they wanted. It was a quality sporting event, giving an opportunity to extend the Budweiser name in Ireland and Europe, with live television transmission to Europe, USA, Canada, Hong Kong and elsewhere. They had considered sponsoring Wimbledon tennis, but it was unavailable to them. The Irish American connection was probably the clincher.

In June 1986 the Derby became the Budweiser Irish Derby. In the week of the race, Anheuser Busch signed a deal with Guinness to market, brew and distribute Budweiser in Ireland. The official launch was in November 1986.

HORSE CLASSIC GIVES BUD LONG REACH

PLANNING

Budweiser brought a new approach to sponsorship in that they did not just see it as sponsorship of the race. They thought it very important to be seen to back the organiser. Anheuser Busch have an annual marketing budget in excess of half a billion dollars in the US, a high proportion of which goes into sports sponsorship.

* they were an official sponsor of the 1994 World Cup, having been involved also in the 1986 and 1990 competitions.
* they own the St. Louis Cardinals baseball team.
* they are a major corporate sponsor of the US Olympic committee.

They sponsor, in one form or another, around 80 per cent of all American sports events, including such diverse sports as triathlons and pig-racing.

Fleishman-Hillard Saunders (F-HS) are the Irish public relations consultants to Anheuser Busch. Fleishman-Hillard in St. Louis, USA, have worked for the company for more than 40 years.

IMPLEMENTATION

When Anheuser Busch took on the Irish Derby it was clear that the Curragh Racecourse in Co. Kildare, where the race had always been held, needed a facelift. Road, rail and other communications networks were good but major expansion was needed to cater for a possible 20 to 30,000 spectators. The location had to be dressed for the occasion for both serious and social racegoers and a large number of national and international media and guests.

In the first year Anheuser Busch contributed around £70,000 just to paint the place; more than £100,000 to upgrade the television facilities on the roof of the stand, and around £250,000 to develop the in-field area at the track into a family zone. Now known as Budweiser Green, it has fast food facilities, TV monitors, car-parking and reception facilities with continuous side shows to provide further entertainment.

In the early years they brought from Busch Stadium their own experienced head of car-parking to assist at the Curragh. They also had their own design and sound people and a consultant from San Diego to look after the hostesses' uniforms.

From the start, in 1986, Budweiser set the tone and showed that they wanted the Derby to be seen as more than a racing event. They set up a large communications centre, under canvas, fully-equipped with telephones, facsimile and telex, typewriters, TV monitors.

Care was taken in the design of posters and signage. All Budweiser flags were five to six feet in length and two feet in width. Posters were a similar size. Both made impact with grace and style. The avenue of flags leading on to the racecourse made a very favourable and colourful impression. Each horse in the big race carried the Budweiser flag and logo on the saddle sheet, distinctive but not overpowering.

Entertainment boxes, at the top of the Main Stand, were sold to companies for client entertainment. The Members Lounge and Enclosure bars provided a varied selection of foods but only a single choice of beer ! VIP suites, located within the headquarters building, were made available by the racecourse management for the entertainment of the sponsors and their selected guests.

Managing the public relations for the Derby is still a sizeable job. Now, nearly ten years into the sponsorship, F-HS send out nearly 30 press releases in the lead up to the Derby. This means nearly one a day in the month leading up to the race and it achieves continuous coverage. The subject of the releases can range from personalities likely to attend to likely runners, horses that might be injured, thoughts of jockeys and trainers. There are always celebrities from the film and entertainment world who add to the social attraction of the event.

F-HS have about ten people on duty for this week-end every June. Anheuser Busch have been able to keep the same team in place since 1986, including John Saunders, Julian Davis, Jean Saunders, Rhona Blake and Suzanne Weldon. Individual executives look after the:

- Anheuser Busch executives and VIPs, who usually include the President of Ireland and the Taoiseach
- press tent, where there can be anything up to 500 journalists
- electronic media
- VIP tent
- parade ring
- representatives from Seaworld, the Anheuser Busch company which owns theme parks and sponsors one of the races.

F-HS are also heavily involved in other functions during Derby week. There is something significant every night.

Anheuser Busch initially sponsored the Derby for three years, but have renewed it periodically. It is probably the biggest sponsorship in Irish sport, believed to cost them approximately £1 million a year. In the early stages it was nearer £2 million.

In 1988 the race changed from its traditional Saturday to Sunday because of a clash with Ireland's game against England in the European Football Championships. Sunday has proved to be a better day. Also, the meeting has become a two-day festival. Initially, Budweiser sponsored races on both days but now they encourage other companies to get involved. They do not sponsor the Saturday races at all. Independent Newspapers and Dunnes Stores are among those involved. Budweiser see themselves as a catalyst to build up a big occasion. It has grown hugely since 1986 with many associated events—social events, dinners, blind date ball etc.

It has not all been trouble-free. In 1987 there was a bomb scare. Fortunately it was a hoax, but the race was delayed by 45 minutes. This was very embarrassing as it was going out live to the UK and then being shown back in the US.

F-HS learnt a lot that day. Ireland was the loser rather than Budweiser as the race was being televised all over the world. Adequate procedures had not been in place to cope with such a crisis. The security measures were immediately reviewed.

When Anheuser Busch took over sponsorship of the Irish Derby, Budweiser beer was not available in Ireland. It is now the best-selling lager in the Dublin area and its countrywide share is also increasing. Undoubtedly the sponsorship of the Derby has been a major factor in this success. The sponsorship gave Budweiser a good Irish base before it entered the market.

Budweiser gave the Derby a new glitz and glamour. By 1985 attendance had fallen to 14,000. The highest, in 1962, had been 18,000. When Budweiser took over, racing people felt the attendance would never improve as racing figures were down all over the country. In the first year the numbers jumped to 22,000 and have been consistently around 30,000 since then. The Budweiser Irish Derby is a major social and racing event.

The Derby has been very good for setting the tone for Budweiser in Ireland. The generous prize fund has helped to make it effectively the European Championship. Every year the winners of both the English and French Derby compete.

Appreciation for the sponsorship has been shown in recent years with the Lord Mayor of Dublin giving a civic reception for Anheuser Busch. Mike Roarty was asked in 1994 to be Grand Marshal at the St. Patrick's Day Parade in Dublin.

Media coverage

There is an enormous amount of press coverage of the Derby in both sports and social pages. F-HS target both news and feature writers, in addition to the racing correspondents. They look to regional press and to national and international fashion and social magazines and newsletters. UK newspapers also give extensive coverage. The race is now covered live on both ITV and BBC. In the first year it went out on ABC TV in the US and was on NBC for the next few years. Now it goes out on ESPN which is an all-sport network where Budweiser sponsor a one-hour special. More than 50 countries in all pick up the race on television. There is also live coverage on BBC Radio and the BBC World Service. Nearly 40 million people worldwide have heard it through the World Service.

Every press cutting is monitored down the smallest piece in a regional newspaper and sent to Anheuser Busch by F-HS. Coverage in the US is monitored by the US office.

"They are seeing Budweiser signage on the track, they are hearing Budweiser Irish Derby, they are appreciating the richest classic in Europe and all of those things work together majestically to make it a very strong marketing event, not only for Anheuser Busch but for Ireland", says Mike Roarty.

Corporate hospitality

The Derby gives Anheuser Busch an opportunity for corporate hospitality. In 1985, they offered a free Derby trip to the managing directors, and wives, of the top ten wholesalers for that year. There was an overwhelming response and in excess of 90 per cent of wholesalers took part. It surpassed the offer the company made of a free trip to the Olympics. The company offers similar incentives for other events but the Derby is rapidly becoming the favourite, with previous winners returning at their own expense. UK travel writers are also brought over because of the sponsorship by Seaworld Theme Park.

DISCUSSION

Anheuser Busch have a good attitude to sponsorship. This comes from their long involvement in sports sponsorship in the US. They can see its value and how it leads to enhanced reputation and increased sales. Surprisingly, the Derby is their only big horse-racing sponsorship.

Good sponsorship should be of mutual benefit to both parties. The Budweiser Irish Derby has achieved a lot for Anheuser Busch through association with an Irish event that has quality and a historical tradition. Anheuser Busch like to associate Budweiser with tradition and excellence. It is also good for Ireland, benefiting tourism and creating a highlight in the social calendar.

Catherine Dolan has an LLB Degree in Law from the University of Dublin, Trinity College, and the DIT Diploma in Public Relations.

OLÉ, OLÉ, OPEL —
DRIVING IRISH FOOTBALL INTO A NEW ERA

The Opel Sponsorship of the Football Association of Ireland
by Joseph Hanley

BACKGROUND

In November 1985, Denmark beat Ireland 4-1 at Lansdowne Road, Dublin, and the wits claimed that the Danish fans out-numbered the Irish ! This low ebb— even in those days the team did not get thrashed often at home—proved to be the catalyst for the Football Association of Ireland (FAI) to set about an investment programme to take it into the 21st century in a professional and businesslike manner.

Two problems immediately presented themselves—expertise and funding. However, two key appointments, in February 1986, addressed both of these areas head-on, and were eventually to transform the face of Irish football both on and off the pitch.

Donie Butler, with a background in newspaper marketing, joined the FAI as commercial manager. Butler had been nagging the FAI for some time to market soccer more actively and professionally. He had a lengthy pedigree in soccer administration in Kilkenny and had represented the Leinster Football Association on the FAI Senior Council for seven years prior to his appointment. Jack Charlton, England World Cup hero of 1966, took up his post two weeks later as Ireland's first full-time professional manager.

Butler immediately set to the task of raising funds to facilitate the progress he had envisaged. The initial idea was to hold an investment draw for 144 cars, for which people had to pay in £450. He needed the cars, so he made three telephone calls to motor companies. He did not even get to speak to the managing director's personal assistant at Ford; the Renault head, Bill Cullen, was out but he got straight through to Arnold O'Byrne, Opel's managing director for Ireland. O'Byrne showed immediate interest, met him within 24 hours and agreed broad terms of the deal in principle. It was signed on 19 March.

This sponsorship was to run hand-in-hand with the enormous growth in the sport's popularity in Ireland. Fuelled by Ireland's qualification for the European Championships in 1988, the Italy World Cup campaign in 1990, and USA '94, attitudes towards the sport would shift enormously in the space of a few years. The achievements of the Irish team, often the poor relations of international football, would galvanise national support and fervour. One of the constant features in this success story would be the name on the Irish shirt, the company that had shown faith when the others had scoffed: *Opel—Ireland's No. 1 Supporter.*

When Alan McLoughlin's equaliser against Northern Ireland hit the net at Windsor Park on a cold November night in 1993, the nation heaved a collective sigh of relief. It turned to ecstasy a few minutes later, when word came through that Spain had beaten

FROM JOHN PAUL TO SAINT JACK.......

Denmark and Ireland had definitely qualified for the USA. Arnold O'Byrne and Donie Butler had two of the broadest smiles in the country at that moment !

PLANNING

Opel had not been involved in any large-scale sponsorship in Ireland until Butler approached O'Byrne in 1986. They had supported some cultural and environmental projects, but that was all.

"The £400,000 for four years seemed an awful lot then, and our competitors thought we were mad", O'Byrne remembers. Various factors influenced his somewhat risky decision. He had recently returned to Ireland after many years working in England, and as a football follower he was aware of the high quality of Irish players performing in the English and Scottish leagues. He was impressed with the FAI's positive approach to the future and he was convinced that Opel was to be an integral part of it. Not only did O'Byrne want to sell 144 cars, but he also saw the broader picture. He saw the FAI being professionally re-structured; the situation, it seemed, could only get better.

From a purely business angle, the motor market was heavily dominated by Japanese models, and with Ford closing their Cork plant in 1985, O'Byrne believed that there was room for an 'Irish' biased product in the market place. But this was not to be a vacuous publicity exercise. Opel has a policy of purchasing car parts locally, thus helping to sustain badly needed employment in the automotive component sector. Irish Trade Board figures for 1994 placed Opel as the largest purchaser of components sourced in Ireland— acquiring some ten times the amount purchased by Japanese manufacturers. The slogan, *Opel - Ireland's No. 1 Supporter*, has meaning both on and off the pitch.

Another factor was that it was a 'clean' sponsorship. Opel's investment could be seen going straight to where it was needed; into the sport at all levels. Significantly too, the fans enjoyed an excellent reputation for goodwill and behaviour around the world, resulting in favourable rather than negative publicity.

IMPLEMENTATION

As well as this major deal, Butler also developed niche areas of sponsorship, where sponsors were called in for specific events. Harp Lager got involved with the Senior Cup; Bank of Ireland the Junior Cup; Mars, the Schools Cups and Soccer Skills programme, and Coca Cola, the Schoolboy Cups and coaching schemes.

When Ireland qualified for the European Championships in 1988, the public and corporate sector had still not fully switched onto soccer, but perceptions were gradually changing. Qualification for Italia '90 brought about a great awakening in the corporate sector. "There was a quantum leap compared to what we got in 1988", comments Butler. "But Italia '90 fades into insignificance with what we attracted for the USA tournament."

The new interest by other sponsors created problems for Opel in the run-up to Italia '90 when they were drawn into litigation with Drury Communications (the players' agent) and the Irish Permanent Building Society. Irish Permanent had paid more than £60,000 into the players' pool to use the squad in an advertising campaign, which Opel believed contravened their position as exclusive sponsors. Money resolved the issue with the FAI and Opel contributing sizeable sums into the players' pool, and the Irish Permanent scaling down its campaign. The episode highlighted the increasing demand for corporate involvement with the national team, and the excellent value Opel were getting for their annual fee of £100,000.

Opel signed another four-year contract during 1990, for a sponsorship that "exceeded all our wildest expectation". This time the contract was for £500,000 to the FAI. O'Byrne concedes the increase could have been much greater given the high profile that the Irish team had achieved. The latest four-year extension to 1998 is costing £750,000.

Other sponsors with the FAI on long-term arrangements up to 1998 include Umbro (who agreed major long-term textiles deals), Harp Lager, Mars, Coca Cola, Sportsworld, RTE, Ballygowan Spring Water and Quinnsworth supermarkets. Deals for USA '94 were negotiated with Bord Fáilte, Jacobs Biscuits, Dunnes Stores, Ballygowan, Oxford table-ware, *Irish Echo* newspaper, Grove Dale, Irish Shell, Castle Hosiery, Kellogg's, H.Flude, Bank of Ireland, Grant International, Telecom Eireann, Aer Lingus, Celtic Glass, Guinness, Jaguar Textiles, DHL and Penneys. Butler also took the endorsement package to the United States, striking a deal with Upper Deck, a Californian-based cards and stickers firm.

The players' own sponsorship efforts were co-ordinated by Drury Communications. The players' committee of Kevin Moran, Ray Houghton, Packie Bonner and David O'Leary, put together major deals with companies such as the Irish Permanent Building Society, Coca Cola, Opel and Rehab Lotteries. Their criteria for sponsorship was to deal with companies that were likely to maintain their commitment, and they limited their links to a few major firms rather than a large number of smaller ones, so that the demand on players' time was not too heavy.

Jack Charlton, Freeman of the City of Dublin and Honorary Doctor of Science of the University of Limerick, now popularly acclaimed as "Saint Jack", also benefited. Qualification for World Cup '94 greatly boosted the demand for his endorsement of products. He was able to fit in a considerable number of personal appearances—charging a reputed £2,000 a time. He carried out endorsements for Bank of Ireland, Shredded Wheat, Mitsubishi and Monaghan Champion Milk.

HB Ice Cream sponsored RTE coverage, while Bord Fáilte gave a 'visit Ireland' t-shirt to each fan who booked a package to the USA, along with a small information pack for potential visitors.

EVALUATION

The success for the team, the sponsorship and the sponsor have been remarkable.

While Jack Charlton has worked wonders with the team over the past eight years, the Opel sponsorship has enabled the FAI to transform the game at domestic level. At the end of 1993, they reported a 100 per cent increase in numbers playing soccer compared to 1986, when Charlton and Butler were appointed. Whereas just over 80,000 players were registered in 1986, the figure in 1993 stood at 161,357. This increase was mirrored in the number of teams, up from 4,124 to 8,802. The biggest area of growth has been in the schools. In 1986, only 100 schools were involved; but in 1993, there were 1,684 registered football-playing schools. There are 29 schoolboy league competitions and 42,240 players aged between nine and sixteen. The number of teachers taking FAI coaching courses has more than doubled.

Soccer is now the fastest growing sport in Ireland. Not only does it thrive in Dublin, Cork, Limerick, Waterford, Sligo, Louth and Galway, but there is significant expansion in places like Mayo, Roscommon, Donegal, Carlow, Kilkenny, Kildare, Meath, Clare, Kerry, Wexford and Tipperary.

Arnold O'Byrne believes that the sponsorship has benefited Opel in two major ways —marketing and sales.

There are obvious marketing and advertising advantages in having the company name featured prominently on programmes, tickets and perimeter advertising. There is product endorsement by the team and officials, who occasionally attend higher-level Opel functions and openings. The official mascot logo and all replicated clothing products feature the name. When other sponsors use Irish players in Irish kit, they have the name emblazoned across their chests. All of these factors strengthen the identity, visibility and awareness of Opel and if they do not actually convince a customer to buy the car, they at least help to put it on the short list.

Also, success breeds success. While the national team are doing well, people will perceive Opel as doing well, O'Byrne believes. Statistics would seem to bear this out, with Opel enjoying greater market share than ever. Their 10 per cent of the Irish market in 1990-91 had grown to 15.2 per cent three years later. If one adopts a hard-nosed approach to sponsorship being "all about selling more of a product", this is a very visible success.

The new income has permitted the FAI to invest extensively in the sport. Over the past four years they have distributed nearly £3.5 million to clubs and affiliated leagues around the country. They have helped clubs to purchase their grounds, and develop the facilities on them. They have increased the number of people playing the game, but these same people need assistance, thus creating a further demand on resources. Examples of development include a brand new stadium at Bishopstown in Cork, major improvements at Drogheda, Tolka Park, Monaghan and Waterford and virtually a new stadium for St. Patrick's Athletic in Inchicore, Dublin.

In June 1993, 33 recipients shared £500,000, sign of a shift in policy to fewer but bigger grants. The majority of the 1993 funds were directed towards more substantial projects.

DISCUSSION

Few sponsorships could claim to have been as successful as Opel's involvement with the FAI. This is due in part to the relationship being an ongoing, not just a 'sign and walk away' contract. "Good sponsorship is partnership based on respect and conducted professionally," states O'Byrne. Opel do not place unreasonable demands on the players and FAI, but instead they work closely for mutual gain. The fact that the present contract will take Opel's involvement into its twelfth year bears great testimony to the success of the alliance.

OLÉ, OLÉ, OPEL—DRIVING IRISH FOOTBALL INTO A NEW ERA

Opel executives believe that the sponsorship has had a remarkable impact on the company's reputation. They feel that much of the positive reaction is due to the timing of the initial involvement, when the team were held in generally low esteem.

Butler himself is reverential about the input of Opel, who "put its hands in its pocket when others would not dare." It is an accurate observation by one company spokesman that, "we would not get half the kudos if we did the same thing now."

Considering the plethora of companies that have since jumped on the bandwagon, following the team's success, there may be much in this statement. Opel has had to handle its position protectively in the face of competing 'marketing partners'. The hallmark of an outstanding sponsorship is when the sponsor becomes synonymous with the event or group, which the competing companies have failed to do. Market research carried out by Lansdowne would suggest that Opel have achieved this status. One now expects to see Opel emblazoned on the Ireland team shirts and, somehow, posters with players in Irish Permanent t-shirts do not look quite right.

Arnold O'Byrne reflects on this special position, "......it has been a dream sponsorship, and, if we were to pull out now, I think another company would have difficulty in killing the Opel name in Irish soccer."

Butler is unrepentant about involving such a large number of corporate sponsors. His attitude is that the FAI has the franchise to market 'the beautiful game' as a product, and they are merely maximising their opportunities when the national team are being successful. To fail to do so would be negligent. With a reserve fund of a previously unimagined £1.5 million, any accusation of negligence would be severely misplaced. To remain a respectable sponsorship prospect, Butler believes, the national team has to qualify for a major tournament every four years. With the enormous increase in involvement at school and club level, there should be no future shortage of home-grown players to select from.

FOOTNOTE

This experience was compiled before the summer hype and hysteria of USA '94. The whole nation was caught up in emotion as Ireland defeated the eventual finalists, Italy, by one goal to nil, came through the qualifying round and then fell to Holland. Even the players were amazed that defeat was treated as a national victory and the politicians and civic leaders demanded their presence for a fanfare homecoming in the Phoenix Park. What will happen if Ireland ever win the World Cup ?

Another measure of interest was the highest television viewing figures in Irish sporting history. The final match against Holland was watched by 47 per cent of private homes, an estimated 1,515,000, which does not include those watching in pubs, clubs and other venues. Viewing figures for the other games were Italy, 46 per cent; Mexico, 48 per cent and Norway, 53 per cent. AGM TAM, the company that carries out research for RTE, did a telephone survey which showed that 93 per cent of viewers, or over three million people, watched the Italian game.

When the fuss had died down and Ireland were well on their way to qualifying for the European Championships in England in 1996, it emerged that the World Cup finals had generated a record profit of £40 million, more than three times the projected figure of £13 million. This meant that Ireland could get a direct payout of more than £1.7 million, compared to £1.2 million for Italia '90 and £1.1 million for Germany in 1988.

Joseph Hanley has a BA Degree in Development Studies (English & Politics) from the University of East Anglia, Norwich; Postgraduate Certificate in Education, also from UEA and the DIT Diploma in Public Relations.

SOME FURTHER READING

I am frequently asked what are the best books about public relations. This is a very difficult question to answer because the emphasis within the profession is evolving rapidly and many new titles are being published. Some of these are appalling and one wonders how anyone ever issued them. Others are excellent but might not translate too easily from the United States to Ireland or the UK. I can be accused of bias because, like all lecturers since lecturing began, I found that none of the existing books were suitable for my students; so I wrote my own.

So, here are my dozen favourites:

Carty, Francis Xavier: *Farewell to Hype—The Emergence of Real Public Relations*, Able Press, Dublin, 1992. (£9 IR£ and stg). I wrote this book because many of the existing texts lacked a conceptual framework. They struck me as eclectic, with authors dwelling only upon topics that they favoured and leaving aside the others. This is the prescribed textbook for the DIT Diploma in Public Relations, but readings from all of the other good books are suggested to students for additional information. It is short in its first edition, a mere 236 pages, and a bargain at £9, but by the end of my life, a long time hence (I hope!) it will probably have gone through several further editions and may even be as long as Cutlip Center & Broom. It is still the first and only Irish textbook in public relations.

Black, Sam: *International Public Relations—Case Studies*, Kogan Page, London, 1993. (£22.50 stg). These 40 cases have been taken from the entries for the IPRA Golden Awards for Excellence and they demonstrate the rich variety of challenges and opportunities that confront public relations professionals in many different countries. Sam Black is a doyen of this business and has many other titles to his name. John M. Reed, in *IPR Review,* was grossly unfair when he said it was a "patchwork quilt" which relied on "the reportage of interested parties seeking recognition and not subject to impartial examination". Anybody who wants to attack *From John Paul to Saint Jack* can say the same, because Sam's book has been our model.

Bowman, Pat (editor): *Handbook of Financial Public Relations*, Heinemann, London, 1989. (unpriced—a publishing practice that I dislike). Still wears well and contains useful chapters on all aspects of financial public relations which was the growth sector of the profession in the 1980s. Includes case studies from the period when Margaret Thatcher determined that everybody in Britain would be a shareholder rather than a grocer.

Bruce, Brendan: *Images of Power—How the Image Makers Shape Our Leaders*, Kogan Page, London, 1992. (£16.95 stg). For anybody in political public relations, indeed for anybody at all, this is compelling reading. Margaret Thatcher appointed the author as director of communications for the Conservative Party and here he spills the beans. If you want to know how the news is managed, and what exactly are briefers, spin doctors, leakers, media lobbyists, parliamentary lobbyists and minders, you have the answers here.

Cutlip, Scott M., Center, Allen H., Broom, Glen M.: *Effective Public Relations*, Prentice-Hall Inc, Englewood Cliffs, New Jersey, 07632. (£25.50 stg). There have been seven editions of this book since it first appeared in 1952. It is the bible of public relations textbooks in the United States and it travels well with its basic concepts equally applicable in the UK and Ireland. Now with nearly 700 pages it is acclaimed as simply the best.

Dickinson, Sarah: *How to Take on the Media*, Weidenfeld and Nicolson, London, 1990. (unpriced). Excellent and essential for all public relations people, even though one Dublin bookshop got in a large supply and placed them under "advertising"! Dickinson says better what many of the other books say well, but unlike the others she gives a lot of attention to how to prepare one's client or boss for the print interview. A generation has been taught how to smile on television, but still the print journalist can more easily gut the unexpecting victim. Read Dickinson to learn how to be ready.

Haywood, Roger: *All About Public Relations*, McGraw-Hill Book Company (UK) Ltd, 2nd edition 1990. Now in a revised edition, with pictures, it was published originally as *All About PR* and slated for using the opprobrious nickname "PR" and being designed with a cover that made it look like a Maths textbook. Roger, a recent president of the Institute of Public Relations (UK) has written an excellent general text, but like most of the others, it is selective in the topics covered. Excellent for the checklists at the end of each chapter.

Lesly, Philip (editor): *The Handbook of Public Relations and Communications*, McGraw-Hill Book Company (UK) Ltd, 4th edition, 1991. (£28 stg). There is something on virtually everything to do with public relations here. The authors are all distinguished in their fields. With 874 pages it is heavy to hold but surprisingly easy to read.

Olins, Wally: *Corporate Identity — Making Business Strategy Visible Through Design*, Thames and Hudson, London, 1990. (unpriced). This is a beautiful book with 350 illustrations. It comes from the guru of corporate identity, a specialised but lucrative area of concern to public relations. Olins has captured many of the top assignments in corporate identity, including the two mentioned in *From John Paul to Saint Jack*, AIB and Irish Life.

Simon, Raymond and Wylie, Frank Winston: *Cases in Public Relations Management*, NTC Business Books, Lincolnwood, Illinois, USA, 1994. (£17.95 stg). This has been developed from earlier editions and is now sharply focused on its target. It combines longer descriptions of anonymous cases, reportage of special instances like the Hill & Knowlton debacle in the Gulf War and a few mini-cases where the scenery is arranged on the stage and the reader is told—now what would you do? If anyone doubted the position of public relations at the core of business management they would have to be converted by this 420 pages of compelling reading.

SOME FURTHER READING

White, Jon: *How to Understand and Manage Public Relations*, Business Books, London, 1991. (£7.99 stg). This is excellent (and also excellent value) and, with the spate of new titles in recent years, it has not received nearly enough attention. Jon tries to stand public relations upon its own two feet and away from the embrace and domineering influence of marketing. His emphasis upon public relations as a management function and not merely a set of communication techniques should be driven into every student.

Wragg, David W.: *The Public Relations Handbook*, Blackwell Business, Oxford, 1992. (unpriced but £45 stg for me and IR£55 for a library that I know). This book is excellent in parts and has a conceptual framework nearly similar to *Farewell to Hype*, but the price is appalling. With 350 pages and very good, but not extraordinary, can it really be worth three to four times the other texts.

And that is it, my special dozen. Apologies to the many authors whom I have left out, several of whom are my good friends.

A

A1 Waste 174
Abbey Theatre 114, 116, 163
ABC TV (USA) 184
Adam Foods 141
Aer Lingus 2, 7, 10, 13-4, 42, 150, 167, 179, 188
Aer Lingus Catering 150
Aer Rianta 14, 162-9
Aer Rianta Arts Festival 162-9
Aer Rianta International 162
AGM TAM 190
Ahern, Barry 59
AIB Group (Allied Irish Banks plc) 14, 126-9, 130, 193
Aisling, L.E. 13
All About Public Relations 193
Allihies 90
Altran Zodiac 143
Amateur Radio Society of Ireland 3, 7
American Shopping Centre award 101
Ammonite 166
Amsterdam 11, 29
Analog Devices, Limerick 179
Anglo-Irish Agreement 82, 83, 88
Anglo-Irish Bankcorp 179
Anheuser Busch 181-5
Ann Fox Public Relations 24, 26-7
Anna Livia Fountain 15
Aras an Uachtaráin (Residence of President of Ireland) 9, 88
Ark Life Assurance 130
Arks Advertising 60, 117
Armagh 5
Artane Boys Band 26, 167
Arts Council 114, 164
Arts Show, The (RTE) 164
Assurances Generales de France (AGF) 133
Athlone 39, 71, 179
Aungier St (DIT) (see Dublin Institute of Technology)
Australia 18, 20, 154

Automobile Association (AA) 25
Avonmore Co-op 140

B

B and I (now part of Irish Continental Group) 13
Baghdad 150, 152-4
Bahrain 162
Bailieboro Co-op 137, 139, 142
Baker, Don 76, 166
Balbriggan 165
Ballaghaderreen 25
Ballesteros, Seve 46
Ballsbridge 129
Ballymun Youth Theatre 163
Ballygowan Spring Water 25, 188
Ballylynch Stud 46
Bangkok 162
Bank of Ireland 14, 187-8
Bantry 143-9
Bantry Bay 143
Barry, Joe 19
Basle 103-4, 106-7
Beckett, Samuel 14
Behaviour & Attitudes Ltd 41, 81
Belfast 8, 166
Bell, Brian 133
Berlin 11
Betelgeuse 143-6
Bew, Paul 86
Bi-Bi Show (RTE) 100
Bill O'Herlihy Communications Group 151-2
Bishopstown, Cork 189
Black, Mary 166
Black, Sam 192
Black, Tony 8
Blake, Rhona 183
Blaney, Neil, TD 85
Bloody Sunday 55
Blueskies 42
Board of Works (Office of Public Works) 8
Boast, Melanie 26
Bolshoi 166

Bonner, Packie 188
Booksellers Association of Ireland (BAI) 109-10, 112, 114
Bord Fáilte—The Irish Tourist Board 1, 5, 13-4, 16, 20, 47, 51, 122-4, 170-5, 188
Bord Fáilte Tidy Towns Competition 170-5
Bord Iascaigh Mhara—The Irish Sea Fisheries Board 72, 81
Bord na Gaeilge (State-sponsored body to extend the use of the Irish language) 74
Bord Pleanála, An (Statutory board to deal with planning and development affairs) 106
Borris 49
Boston 1, 10
Bourke, Kevin J 130
Bowman, John 172
Bowman, Pat 192
Boyd, Brian 78
Brennan, Seamus, TD 48, 77, 81
Britain (see UK)
British Broadcasting Authority (BBC) 22, 23, 30, 40, 146, 152, 184
British Council of Shopping Centres 101-2
British National Lottery 40
British Open Golf Championship 47
British Rail 159
British Telecom 130-1
Broadcasting Act, The 54
Broderick's Grass Machinery 173
Brown, John 171
Browne, Noel 88-9
Bruce, Brendan 192
Brussels 11, 60, 67
Bruton, John, TD, Taoiseach (Prime Minister) 109
Buckley, Dan 141
Budweiser 181, 184-5
Budweiser Irish Derby 181-5
Building on Reality 35
Bulmers 74-5
Burger King 44
Burke, Helen Lucy 62
Burke, Ray, TD 96
Burson Marsteller 144
Bus Átha Cliath (Dublin Bus) 160

Bus Eireann (Irish Bus) 44, 160
Bushe, Andrew 145
Butler, Donie 186-8, 190
Butterly, John 98, 101-2
Byrne, Des 81
Byrne, Gay 38, 179
C
Cabra 3, 6, 9
Cases in Public Relations Management 193
Cathal Brugha St (DIT) (see Dublin Institute of Technology)
Callan 49
Canada 29, 154, 181
Cantwell, Jim 1-4
Cara Computers 150
Carlow 25, 49, 189
Carlow, County 170
Carman, Cathy 168
Carr, Joe 48
Carr Communications 81-2
Carrickmacross 34
Carroll, P.J. Holdings plc 50
Carroll's Irish Open Golf (see Irish Open Golf)
Carter, Jimmy 30
Carty, Francis Xavier 192
Castle Hosiery 188
Castlecomer 49
Catholic Press and Information Office 1
Cavan 25, 142
Cavan, County 137, 139-40
Ceann Comhairle (Speaker of Dáil Eireann) 85
Celtic Glass 188
Central Statistics Office (CSO) 65
Challenge of Champions 46
Channel Tunnel 97, 162
Chapters (Bookshop) 113
Charlton, Jack 186, 188
Chevron 149
Childers, Erskine 87
Christ, Jesus 59
Cider Industry Council 74-8
CIE Tours 20
City of Dublin Vocational Education Committee xii
Clare, County 189

Clarke, Darren 49
Clarke, Harold 109
Clarke, Yvonne 26
Clé—the Book Irish Publishers'
    Association 109, 112
Clerys 97, 100
Cloghran 168
Clondalkin Paper Mills 109
Clonmacnoise 3, 6, 10
Clonmel 74
Club Orange 44
Clune, Flan 163-4, 167
Coakley, John 86
Cobh 104
Coca Cola 187-8
Coffey, Des 118
Collins, Gerard, TD 152
Collins, Michael 31
Combined Action 76
Comiskey, Bishop Brendan 58
Common Agricultural Policy (CAP) 59,
    141
Common Market (see EU)
Confederation of Irish Industry 75
Connolly, John 146-8
Connolly Station, Dublin 157
Conroy O'Neill report 113
Conservative party (UK) 192
Cooke, John 63
Cooke's Café 63
Cooney, John 84
Cootehill 140
Coras Iompar Eireann (CIE) 4, 160
Corboy, Denis 54
Cork 11-2, 17-8, 25, 39, 72, 103-5, 107,
    143, 157, 166, 187, 189
Cork 89FM (Radio) 106
Cork Airport 145, 162, 166
Cork County Council 106
Cork Environmental Alliance (CEA) 106-7
Cork Evening Echo 158,
Cork Examiner, The 82, 106, 118
Cork Harbour 103-5
Cork Kerry Tourism 20
Cork Opera House 114
Cork Teachers and Students 179
Cork, University College (UCC) 107
Corporate Identity 193

Costello, Justice Declan 146-7
Costello Report 146
Cothú — Business Council for the Arts
    163, 165, 168-9, 177, 180
Cowen, Brian, TD 157
Cox, Dr. John 60
Council of Ministers (EU) 53
Crane, Patrick 109, 110, 112-3, 115-7, 173
Crazy Prices (see Quinnsworth)
Creedon, Donal 139-40
Creston, Stephen 8
Cuba 56
Cullen, Bill 186
Curragh, The 181-2
Currie, Austin 87-9, 91-2
Curzon Communications 16
Cutlip Center & Broom 192-3
D
Dáil Eireann (Lower House of the
    Oireachtas) 38, 52, 54, 82, 84-5, 87,
    93, 110-1, 115-6, 122-3
Daly, Cardinal Cahal 3
Dallas (Texas) 43
Daly, Bishop Edward 1-3, 6
Davey, Anne 41, 44
Davis, Julian 183
Dawson St, Dublin 25
Delaney, Niall 172
Democratic Left 85
Denmark 51, 55, 66, 67, 109, 186-7
Dennehy, Michael 1-6, 8
Dennehy, Tim 1, 6
Department of Agriculture 24, 139
Department of Education 165
Department of Finance 110
Department of Foreign Affairs 2, 8, 13,
    51, 55, 153, 165
Department of Health 150
Department of Posts & Telegraphs 1-2, 6,
    8, 51
Department of Transport 156-7
Derry 1, 55
Desmond, Barry 79
de Valera, Eamon 87-8
Dewe Rogerson 133
DHL 188
Dickinson, Sarah 193
Digital Equipment International 179

Dilger, David 140
Dollymount Strand 15
Donegal, County 72, 170, 181, 189
Donemark 147
Donnelly, Cllr. Michael, 26
Donnybrook 45
Dorman, Fr. Michael 176
Dowling, Anne 78
Drogheda 3, 6, 9, 25, 189
Drumcondra 76
Drury Communications 187-8
Dublin 3, 6, 12-6, 20, 22-3, 25, 31, 39, 42,
    44-5, 48-9, 60, 63, 76, 81, 84, 88, 92,
    95-7, 99-100, 104, 106, 113-4, 122,
    131, 134-5, 140, 145, 147, 150, 157,
    158, 160-1, 165-6, 168, 172, 176, 179-
    81, 184, 186, 189, 193
Dublin & Eastern Regional Tourism 11, 14
Dublin Airport 3, 9, 56, 162-3. 164-5, 167-
    8
Dublin Bay 15
Dublin Bus 97, 99
Dublin Castle 2, 4-6, 8, 23, 172
Dublin, County 76, 139, 165, 170
Dublin Corporation 11-2, 14, 88, 95-9
Dublin County Council 95-9, 101
Dublin Dairies 176
Dublin Earth Station Satellite (SBNI) 20
Dublin European City of Culture Year 165
Dublin Grand Opera Society 163
Dublin Institute of Technology (DIT) xii,
    62, 192
Dubln Promotions Organisation Ltd
    (DPOL) 11-3, 15-6
Dublin Millennium 11-6
Dublin Street Carnival 11, 15
Dublin, University College 93
Dublin Woollen Mills 15
Duffy, Jim 93
Duggan, Noel C. 18, 22
Dukes, Alan, TD 85, 115-7
Dun Laoghaire School of Art 13
Dundalk 39, 176
Dunnes Stores 97, 100, 183, 188
E
Earth Mother 166
Eason & Son 53, 109, 113
East Cork Environmental Group 105

Eastern Health Board 76
Eblana Theatre 114
Economic and Social Committee (EU) 53
Economic and Social Research Institute
    (ESRI) 75
EEC (see EU)
Effective Public Relations 193
Egyptians 59
Eipper, Chris 149
Elan Pharmaceuticals 71
Electricity Supply Board (ESB) 20
Elizabeth II, Queen 5
Emerald Star Line 174
Engineering Industry Association 101
England 81, 97, 183, 187, 190
Ennis 25
EOLAS (now part of Forbairt) 104
Ericsson, LM, Athlone 179
Ernst & Young 168
ESPN (Television) 184
Ethiopia 57
Evening Press 28
Europe 101, 103, 131, 135, 142-3, 181
European Broadcasting Union (EBU) 23
European Championships (Football) 183,
    186-7, 190
European Commission 53, 59-60, 67, 161
European Court of Justice 53
European Parliament 53
European Shopping Centre award 101
European Year of Safety, Health and
    Hygiene at Work 66-7, 70, 73
European Youth Campaign 51
European Union (EU) (ref. EEC, EC and
    Common Market) 49, 51-8, 62, 66-8,
    73, 101, 103, 105, 109-10. 115, 126,
    159-61, 177
Eurovision News 22
Eurovision Song Contest 17-21, 23
Eutelsat 20
F
Fanning, Gillian 59
2FM (Radio) 41, 42-5, 100, 102
96FM (Radio) 106
Farewell to Hype 192
Farquharson, Alan 21
Farrell, David M 81, 86
Faro (Lisbon) 166

FÁS—The Training & Employment Authority 11, 96, 99
Federal Bureau of Investigation (FBI) 4
Féile 78
Ferris, Cyril 4, 156-60
Fianna Fáil (political party) 56, 79-88, 90, 92-3, 124
Field, John 167
Finan, Mary 29, 30, 33, 36-7, 133
Financial Times 54
Fine Gael (political party) 55, 79-88, 92, 111
Finlay, Fergus 88-9, 91-2, 94
Finnigan, Bill 145
First Maryland Bancorp 126
First National Building Society 171-2
First Trust Bank 130
Fisher, Carolyn 76
Fishwick report 113
FitzGerald, Garret 79, 82-3, 85, 88, 92, 111, 115
Fitzpatrick, John 36, 38
Fleishman-Hillard (USA) 182
Fleishman-Hillard Saunders 182-4
Flood, Brian 152
Flynn, Padraig (EU Commissioner) 70, 93, 99
Fogarty, Robin 51-2, 54
Food and Agricultural Organisation of the UN (FAO) 24
Food Industries plc 137, 138, 139, 140
Football Association of Ireland (FAI) 186-90
Footsteps, The 15
Forman Dove Public Relations (now Grayling) 104, 142
Ford, Henry & Son Ltd 186-7
Foroige — National Youth Development Organisation (formerly Macra na Tuaithe) 51
Fossett's Circus 115
France 47, 59, 87
Fred Hanna Ltd 109
Friends of Cork Harbour 105
Friends Provident Life Assurance 13
Furlong, Eamonn 97
G
Gaelic Athletic Association (GAA) 171

Gaiety Theatre 114-5
Gallagher, Jackie 101
Gallagher, Michael 86
Gallagher, Patrick 165
Galway 3, 6, 9, 11-2, 15, 39, 76, 179, 189
Gandon Corporate Finance 138
Garda College Training Centre 77
Garda Síochána (Irish police force) 4, 21, 26-7
Garden of Gethsemane 59
Gardiner Street 15
Garrison House 174
Gate Theatre 114
Gay Byrne Show, The (RTE Radio) 39, 101
General Agreement on Trade and Tariffs (GATT) 141
General Election (1987) 79, 84, 90
General Electiion (1989) 85, 87
General Post Office (GPO) 13
Georgia 162
Germany 47, 191
Gill, Michael 109
Gill & Macmillan 109
Gilmore Communications 74, 78
Gleeson, Paul 2
Glengariff 143
Glenties 170
Glynn, Fr. Michael 4
Golden Vale Co-op 142
Golley Slater 41-2, 45
Good Morning America (Television) 48, 50
Goodman International 137-8, 140-1
Goodman, Larry 137
Gothenburg 166
Gorta — The Freedom from Hunger Council of Ireland 24-8
Government Information Bureau 51
Government Sales Office 53
Grace, Brendan 115
Grafton St, Dublin 29, 32-4
Graham, Professor Ian 60
Grant International 188
Grayling 59-61, 109, 114, 117, 137-9, 142, 173,
GRE Properties 96-8
Greece 59, 66-7

Green Glens arena 17-20, 22
Greencastle 72
Greene's Bookshop 109
Greenpeace 105-7
Gregory, Tony 85
Grogan, Gerry 177, 180
Grove Dale 188
Grube and Morgan 75
Guardian, The 8, 54
Guinness Book of Records, The 24, 26-8
Guinness Ireland 14, 181, 188
Guinness Jazz Festival 179
Gulf Oil 143-9
Gulf War 150, 154, 193
Gulliver 15
Gulliver Spectacle 15
H
H Flude 188
Hamilton, Peter 145
Handbook of Financial Public Relations 192
Handbook of Public Relations and Communications, The 193
Hanly, David 150, 152-4
Hanna, Fred 109
Hanson plc 176
Harney, Mary, TD 84
Harp Lager 187-8
Harris, Eoghan 91-3
Harte Designs 173
Harvey, Gerry 38
Haughey, Charles 39, 48, 81-5, 93, 101, 111-2, 124
Haywood, Roger 193
Hazelkorn, Ellen 86
HB Ice Cream 188
Health and Safety Authority (HSA) 66-7, 69, 71-3
Health Promotion Unit 76
Health, Safety and Welfare at Work Act, (1989) 68, 70
Heathrow Airport (London) 145, 166
Hederman, Ald. Carmencita 12, 172
Heffernan, Dave 76,
Heffron, Professor James 107
Hello ! 90
Hempel, Lord 181
Henchy, Deirdre 18, 20, 22-3

Heneghan, Pat 1
Heuston, Texas 145
HGW Paints 174
Hickson 72
Hill & Knowlton 193
Hillery, Dr. Patrick 9, 51-2, 54, 56-7, 87, 93, 109, 172
Hillier Parker 100
Hodges Figgis (Bookshop) 109
Hogan, Dick 106
Holland 47, 190
Hong Kong 181
Hosker, James 40
Hot Press 92-3
Houghton, Ray 188
How to Take on the Media 193
How to Understand and Manage Public Relations 194
Howth Head 45
Hunter's Yard, The 47, 50
Hyde, Douglas 87
I
Iarnród Eireann (Irish Rail) 20, 155-61
Ibn al Bitar Hospital 150
ICL Computers (Ireland) 12, 14
Images of Power 192
Imperial Tobacco Ltd 176
Inchicore, Dublin 189
Independent Broadcasting Authority 8
Independent Newspapers 183
Independent Television (ITV) 184
Industrial Development Authority (IDA) 103
Infopublique 67
Inistiogue 47
Institute of Public Relations (UK) xi, 193
International Financial Services Centre (Dublin) 16
International Public Relations — Case Studies 192
International Real Estate Federation 101
Interpol 4
IPRA Golden Awards for Excellence 192
IPR Review 192
Iran 151
Iran/Iraq War 150
Iraq 150-3
Ireland 51, 54-6, 66-7, 74, 81, 101, 103,

109, 114, 117, 126, 131, 133, 153, 162, 169, 181, 184-6, 190, 193

Irish Actors' Equity 31, 114, 117

Irish Books Marketing Group 112-3

Irish Business and Employers' Confederation (IBEC) 69

Irish Co-operative Organisation Society 140

Irish College of General Practitioners (ICGP) 64

Irish Congress of Trade Unions (ICTU) 69

Irish Council for the European Movement 52, 56

Irish Countrywomen's Association 56, 170-1

Irish Creamery Milk Suppliers Association 140

Irish Dairy Board 141

Irish Distillers 14

Irish Echo 188

Irish Farmers' Association 70-1, 140

Irish Farmers Journal 72

Irish Federation of Musicians and Allied Professions 117

Irish Glass Bottle Company 174

Irish Heart Foundation 63

Irish Hospital Sweepstakes 181

Irish Hotels Federation 20

Irish Independent 28, 70, 82, 109

Irish Life Assurance plc 14-5, 131-2, 134, 136, 193

Irish Life Dublin Theatre Festival 163

Irish Marketing Surveys 55, 86

Irish National Petroleum Corporation 149

Irish Open Golf Championship (ref. Carroll's and Murphy) 49, 50, 179

Irish Permanent Building Society 187-8, 190

Irish Press 70, 106, 145, 158

Irish Printers 81

Irish Rail (see Iarnród Eireann)

Irish Republican Army (IRA) 5

Irish Restaurant Owners Association (IROA) 118-25

Irish Shell 25, 188

Irish Theatre Club 116

Irish Theatre Managements' Association 114, 117

Irish Times, The 22, 58, 78, 80, 82, 84, 94, 101, 106, 146-7, 162, 166, 168

Irish Transport & General Workers Union (ITGWU—now SIPTU) 117

Irish Turf Club 181

Irish Wheelchair Association 101, 173

Island Wedding 167

Italy 47, 59, 62

Iveagh House 56

J

Jacob's Biscuits 188

Jaguar Textiles 188

Jefferson Smurfit Group 14

Jennings, Joe 1, 4

Jerusalem 59

John McMahon & Partners (now McMahonSheedy) 143, 179

John Paul 11, Pope, 1, 5-9, 124,

John Player & Sons, Dublin 176-80

John Player Tops 176-80

Johnson, Neil 76

Joint, Dick 166

Joyce, James 14

Joycean Trail, The 15

K

K Club 48

Kavanagh, Liam, TD, 79

Kavanagh, Paul 81

Keadue 172, 174

Keating, Pat 137, 140-2

Keating & Associates 142

Keenan, Peter 152-3

Kelloggs 188

Kelly, Andrew 152, 154

Kelly, Paul 41, 43-5

Kennedy Smith, Jean 169

Kenny, Shane 89

Kenny, Tony 115

Kenny's Advertising 117

Kent Public Relations Consultants (KPRC) 109-14, 116-7

Kentucky Fried Chicken 13

Kenwood 102

Keogh, Derek 162

Kerry, County 18, 155-7, 181, 189

Kerryman, The 159

Kiev 162

Kildare, County 48, 139, 182, 189

Kilfeather, Frank 35
Kilkenny 49, 186, 189
Kilkenny, County 46
Kilkenny Design Workshops 39, 53
Kilkenny Hunt 46
Kilkenny People 47
Killarney, 19-20
Killary, River 128
Killeen Investments 46, 50
Killeshandra Dairy Co-operative Society 137-42
Killybegs 72
Kilroy, Aisling 11, 13, 16, 116
King, Brenda 171-3
King's River 46
Kingston, David 136
Knock 3, 6, 9
Knox Johnston, Michael 50,
Korea 18, 20
Kredietbank 133,
Kremlin Gold Exhibition 165, 167
Kuwait 150, 151,
L
Labour party 53, 55, 79, 83-4, 86-91, 111
Laffan, Michael 81
Lakeland Dairies Co-operative Society Ltd 137-42
Lalor, Paddy 81
Lane, Bob 36
Lansdowne Market Research 76, 190
Lansdowne Road, 81, 186
Larkin, James 1
Larkin, Martin 81
Late Late Show (Television) 40, 105
Laver, Michael 79-80, 86
Leadbetter, David 50
Leckpatrick Co-op 142
Leeson Street, Dublin 22
Leinster Factories Talent Contest 176
Leinster Football Association 186
Leinster House 114-6
Leitrim, County 139
Lenihan, Brian 56, 87-9, 91, 93-4, 124
Lennon, Charlie 167
Lesly, Philip 193
Liffey, River 13, 15
Lilliput 15
Limerick 3, 6, 10, 25, 39, 166, 179, 188-9

Lisbon 166
London 100, 131, 153
London Stock Exchange 133, 135
London & Clydesdale Holdings 95, 98
Long, Denis P 181
Longford, County 139
Lopex plc 60, 117, 142
Lord, Miriam 28
Lough Egish Co-op 137-42
Louth, County 139, 189
Lowe, Theresa 179
Lynch, Jack 56-7, 81, 145
M
McCalmont, Major Victor 46
McCalmonts, The 47
McCourt, Winifred 137, 142
McCrohan, Jerry 130
MacCurtain, Eilish (see Pearce, Eilish MacCurtain)
McDonald, Ronald 31-3
McDonald's 29-34
McDowell, Sandra 59
McFarlan, Donald 27
McGinty, Tony 36
McGuigan, Barry 76
McGuinness, Brendan 75
McGuirk, Eileen 45
Mackeys Seeds 173
McMahon, John 145-6, 148-9
McMahonSheedy Communications 142, 145
McIntyre, Cyril 4
McKimm, Peter 77
McLoughlin, Alan 186
McMunn, Bill 99
Macnas 15
McNulty, Matt 11-2, 16
Macra na Tuaithe (now Foróige)
MacSharry, Ray 112
MacSweeney, John 152
Maguire, Colm 41, 44
Mahony, Tim 46, 48
Mair, Peter 86
Mandelson, Peter, MP 80
Malahide and Swords Young Musician Competition 163
Manchester 166
Mansion House 14, 25-7

Mara, P.J. 79, 81, 84
Marcinkus, Archbishop Paul 6
Market Research Bureau of Ireland (MRBI) 80, 86
Markpress 58
Mars 187, 188
Massachusetts State Lottery 40
Massey Ferguson 25
Maynooth 3, 6, 10
Mayo, County 181, 189
Mayo Clinic 150
Meath, County128, 189
Mediterranean 59
Mehigan, Mike 29-31, 34
Mercedes-Benz 126
Mercury Engineering 174
Merrell Dow 104, 107
Mexico 1, 190
Millar, Capt. Jack 2, 8
Millennium Radio 13
Miller Brewing Company 181
Miller, Liam 19
Millstreet 17-23
Minister for Finance 35, 37
Mitsubishi 188
Molloy, Colm 41-2, 45
Molloy, Robert, TD 84
Moloney, Michael 67
Monaghan 189
Monaghan, County 139
Monaghan Champion Milk 188
Monarch Properties 95, 98-102
Mooney, Jack 6
Moore, Honor 62
Moran, Kevin 188
Morning Ireland (Radio) 39
Morgan (see Grube and Morgan)
Morgan, Dr. Mark 76, 77
Morocco 18, 20
Morris, James 81
Morrissey, Sean 51
Morton, Isabel 41, 44,
Moscow 34, 162
Mount Ararat 59
Mount Juliet Hotel and Leisure Estate 46, 48-50
Mount Juliet House 47
Mountbatten, Lord Louis 5,

Moynihan, Malachy 36
Muintir na Tíre (Irish Community Development Movement) 171
Mullaghmore 5
Mullingar 25
Munster & Leinster Bank 126
Munster Express 47
Murphy Brewery 50
Murphy, Mike 179
Murphy's Irish Open Golf (see Irish Open Golf)
Murray, Noel 99
Musgrave, Donal 106
Myers, Kevin 162, 166
Myles Tierney & Associates (formerly PASS PR) 119

N
National Basketball Arena 101
National Children's Day Parade 33
National Children's Hospital, Harcourt St 32
National Lottery 35-40
National Parents Council Post Primary 78
National Ploughing Championships 72
National Rehabilitation Board 101, 174
National Song Contest 21
Nationalist and Leinster Times 47
Naval Service 13
NBC (USA Television) 184
Nealon, Ted, TD 86, 115-6
Neligan, Maurice 105
Network 2 (Television) 4, 129
New York 5
Newman, Bishop Jeremiah 6
Newman, John F 109
Nicklaus, Jack 46-50
Noah's Ark 59
Nore, River 46
North America 103
Northern Ireland 5, 40, 58, 82, 88, 123, 186
Norway 51, 55, 57, 190

O
O'Boyle, Seán 109
O'Brien, Joe 5
Observer, The 22
O'Byrne, Arnold 186-90
O'Casey, Sean 15

O'Connell Bridge, Dublin 15, 81
O'Connell Street , Dublin 34
O'Connor, Christy, Sr. 48-9
O'Connor, Jim 13
O'Conor, John 167
O'Curry, Anne 77
Ó Dálaigh, Cearbhall 87
O'Donovan, Bill 100
Ó Duinnín, Sinéad 67
O'Dwyer, Ursula 60, 64
Ó Fiaich, Cardinal Tomás 4
O'Flynn, Niall 176, 178
Offaly, County 139
O'Hanlon, Aidan 1, 4, 170
O'Hanlon, Brenda 36, 90-1
O'Hare, Frank 81
O'Herlihy, Bill 151-2
Oireachtas (Houses of Parliament) 52, 87
O'Kelly, Brendan 81
O'Kelly, Sean T 87
O'Leary, David 188
O'Leary, Michael 30
Olins, Wally 126, 193
Olive Oil Information Bureau 60-4
Olive Oil Information Campaign 59
Olympia Theatre 114, 117
Olympic Games 184
O'Mahony, Frank 109
O'Mahony, Peter Tynan 146
O'Mahony's Booksellers 109
O'Malley, Desmond, TD 84
Ó Murchú Diarmuid 159
O'Neill, Niall 166
Opel Ireland Ltd 186-90
O'Reilly. Emily 91, 94
O'Rourke, Mary, TD 69, 71-3
Oscar Theatre 114
O'Shannon, Cathal 6
O'Sullivan Public Relations 104
O'Sullivan, Michael 92, 94
O'Sullivan, Tadhg 77
O'Sullivan, Ted 125
O'Sullivan Ryan Advertising 125
O'Toole, Fintan 94
O'Toole, Paul 11, 16
Oxford (Tableware) 188
P
Pakistan 162

Palmer, Arnold 48
PAM 43
Panciroli, Fr. Romeo 5
Panel of Chefs in Ireland 62
Papal Nunciature 6, 9
PARC 150-4
Paris 153
Parker, Michael 139
Parnell, Charles Stewart 94
PASS PR (now Myles Tierney &
    Associates)
Patterson, Henry 86
Pearce, Brian 57
Pearce, Eilish MacCurtain 1, 51-8
Pedersen, Winfried 105
Pembrey, Vivian 109
Pembroke Communications 97-8
Penneys 188
Pepsi-Cola 44, 45
Peter Mark 44
Pettit, Stephen 168
Phelan Partnership, The 98, 100
Philips Electronics Ireland 14
Philpott File (Television) 30
Phoenicians 59
Phoenix Park 3, 6, 9, 88, 190
Pickens, T. Boone 149
Piggott, Lester 28
Players Anonymous 179
Plough and the Stars, The 15
Point Theatre, Dublin 22, 23
Poland 1, 2 , 4, 162
Portugal 59, 66, 67
Post, An 35, 37, 39, 116, 173
Potter Maureen 32, 115
Premier Dairies 13
Prime Time (Television) 159
Programme for National Recovery 82
Progressive Democrats (political party)
    79-87, 93, 139
Prone, Terry 81
Proportional Representation (PR) 80, 91
Provincial Bank 126
Public Relations Handbook, The 194
Public Relations Institute of Ireland xi,
    xii, 1, 4-5, 8
Public Relations of Ireland (now Bill
    O'Herlihy Communications) 152-4

FROM JOHN PAUL TO SAINT JACK.......

Q

Quinn, Senator Feargal 116
Quinn, Ruairi, TD, 79, 91
Quinn, Vincent 67
Quinn McDonnell Pattison 97-8
Quinnsworth 96-7, 100, 188

R

Radio 1 (RTE) 44
Radio Kerry 157-9
Radio Telefis Eireann (RTE) 2, 17-23, 26, 37, 41-2, 44, 48, 54, 72, 83, 89, 100, 129, 146, 152-3, 157, 164, 168, 171, 179, 188, 190
Rathmines xii
Reck, Ald. Padge 76
Reed, John M 192
Rehab Lotteries 188
Reilly, Philip 99
Renault Distributors186
Reuters 7-8
Regester, Michael 145
Reynolds, Albert, TD 135
Rhine, River 104
RICH (Responsible Industry for Cork Harbour) 105
Ring, Christy 166
Ringaskiddy 103-4, 107
Ringaskiddy Residents Association (RRA) 105-7
Ringsend 15
Roarty, Mike 181, 184
Roberts, Alison 168
Robinson, Nick 91-2, 94
Robinson, President Mary 24, 87-94, 168, 172, 177
Roche, Dick 109-10
Roche, Stephen 12
Roches Stores 97, 100
Rock, Dickie 166
Rogers, John 88, 89, 91
Roscommon, County 172, 189
Rosney, Bride 91
Ross, Senator Shane 58
Rotary Club of Ireland, The 123
Rowe, Jim 59,
Royal and Ancient St. Andrew's 48
Royal Bank 126
Royal Dublin Golf Club 46

Royal Dublin Society (RDS) 21-2
Royal Hibernian Hotel 31
Royal Hibernian Way 13
Royal Hospital Kilmainham 38-40, 69
RTE Commercial Enterprises 18
Rusk, David 11, 16
Russia 20
Ryan, Gerry 44-5
Ryan, Tim 86
Ryder Cup 49

S

San Diego 182
Sandoz Pharma 103-8
Sandymount, Dublin 172
Sandymount Strand 15
Saatchi & Saatchi Advertising (Ireland) 81
St. Audeons' Church 15
St. Joseph's Youth Club, Strabane 179
St. Louis, USA 182
St. Louis Cardinals 182
St. Patrick's Athletic 189
St. Patrick's Cathedral, Dublin, 15
St. Patrick's College, Drumcondra 76
St. Patrick's College, Maynooth 10
St. Patrick's Day 11-2, 166
St. Patrick's Day Parade 38, 184
St. Petersburg 162
St. Peter's Square 5, 124
St. Stephen's Green 15, 32
St. Vincent's Hospital 150
Saunders, Jean 183
Saunders, John 183
Savage, Tom 81
Scandinavia 47
Scanlan, Gerry 127
Sculptors' Society of Ireland 15
Seager, Pat 11, 16
Sean McDermott St. 6
Seanad Eireann (Upper House of Oireachtas) 52, 54, 87, 115-6, 123
Seaworld 183
Seaworld Theme Park 184
Services Industrial Professional Technical Union (SIPTU) 71
Setanta Communications 67, 69, 71-2
Shamrock Games 181
Shandwicks 67
Shannon Airport 162, 166

Shannon 1, 3, 7-8. 10
Sheehan, John 76
Shelbourne Hotel 32, 48
Shields, Brush 76
Shoppers, The 15
Shredded Wheat 188
Showerings 74-5
Simon & Wylie 193
Sinn Féin (Political party) 82
Sinnott, Gerry 117
Sinnott, Richard 86
Six One News (Television) 154
Sky Sports (Television) 48
Slane Castle 16
Slattery, Padraig 46-7, 49
Slattery Public Relations 46-50
Sligo 25, 71, 160-1, 165, 189
Sligo, County 5, 170
Smiley, Ronny 24-8
Smith, John 8
Smith, Peter 4
Smurfit family 15
Smurfit, Jefferson 15
Social Democratic and Labour Party
    (SDLP) 88
Society of Irish Playwrights 117
South Circular Road, Dublin 176
Spain 2, 59, 116, 186
Sportsworld 188
Spraoi Atha Cliath (Spirit of Dublin) 12
Spring, Dick, TD, Tánaiste (Deputy Prime
    Minister) 79, 87-9, 91, 94
Square, The (Tallaght) 95-102
Startrek (Television) 18
Stephen's Green Centre, Dublin 97
Stevenson, Leonie 26
Stokes Kennedy Crowley 14
Strabane 179
Straffan House 48
Sun, The 4
Sunday Business Post 168-9
Sunday Independent 14, 39, 58
Sunday News, The 8
Sunday People 8
Sunday Press 39
Sunday Times, The 22, 30, 98
Sunday Tribune 39, 130, 168
Sunday World, The 22, 39

Superphone 25
Superquinn 14
Super Valu Supermarkets 171-2, 174
Sweeney, Fionnuala 22, 179
Sweetman Peter 1
Swift, Jonathan 15
Switzerland 103
Symonds Cider Company 75
T
Taggart, Paschal 141
Taisce, An — The National Trust for
    Ireland 171
Talbot, Matt 6
Tallaght 95-9, 101
Tallaght Community Council 95, 99
Tallaght Hospital 101
Tallaght Regional Technical College 101
Tallaght Strategy 85
Tanzania 24-5
Taunton Cider Company 75
Telecom Eireann 20, 188
Temple Bar (Dublin) 16, 168
Templemore 77
Tetrarch, The 46
Texas 145
Thatcher, Margaret 192
Thomastown 46-7
Thorn EMI 81
Thurles 78
Tierney, Myles 118-21, 124
Tidy Towns (see Bord Fáilte Tidy Towns
    Competition)
Time 30
Times, The 54, 168
Tipperary, County 77, 189
Tobin, John 129
Today Tonight (Television) 93
Tolka Park 189
Tostal, An 170-1
Total 144, 146-7
Tour de France 12
Tourmakeady 181
Town of Monaghan Co-op 137, 142
Toyota Ireland 46
Tramore 179
Tralee 155-6, 159-60
Treacy, Seán 85
Treaty of Rome 53

Trinity College, Dublin 42, 88
Tullamore 76
U
U2 12
Ulysses 15
Umbro 188
United Kingdom (UK) 22, 29, 34, 51, 54-5, 60, 74, 87, 101, 109-10, 126, 131, 133, 141, 145, 183-4, 192-3
United Nations 150-1, 153-4
United Nations General Assembly 5
Universe Leader 143
University Concert Hall (Limerick) 166
University of Limerick 188
Upper Deck 188
US Food & Drugs Administration 103
USA 2, 18, 20, 29, 36, 40, 87, 126, 131-2, 135, 144, 169, 181, 184-5, 187-8, 190, 192-3
US Olympic Committee 182
V
Vatican 4, 8,
Vatican Press Office 4
Veritas Publications 109
Vietnam 162
Vikings 12, 15
Viking Festival 15
Vintners Federation of Ireland 77, 120
Virgin Megastore 92
Virginia Milk Products 140
Visual Communications Group 129
W
Wales 97
Walsh, Fiona 59
Walsh, Tom 72
Wasserman, Ray 41
Waterford 39, 176, 189
Waterford, County 189
Waterford Airport 47
Waterford Crystal 179
Waters, David 161
Waterstones 113
Wayne, John 28
Weldon, Suzanne 183
West Lodge Hotel, Bantry 146
Westmeath, County 139, 170
Westmeath Co-op 137
Wexford 76

Wexford, County 189
Wexford Community Action Programme 76
Whelan, Marty 179
Whiddy Island 143-6, 148-9
White, Jon 194
Willis Books 109
Wilson Hartnell Advertising 36
Wilson Hartnell Public Relations 29-34, 36-7, 90, 133
Wilton Research & Marketing 179
Wimbledon 181
Windmill Lane 81
Windsor Park 186
Wolff Olins 127, 129-30, 136,
Woodville Variety Group 180
Woodworth, Paddy 168
Workers Party 84-5, 91
World Cup (Football) 182, 186-8, 190
Wm. Gaymer & Son 75
Woman's Heart 164
Wortmann, Martin 86
Wragg, David 194
Y
Yeats, Síle 106
Youngs Advertising 117
Z
Zambia 150
Zig and Zag 15, 42